D0940556

OpenView Network Node Manager

Designing and Implementing an
Enterprise Solution

ISBN 0-13-019849-8

9 780130 198495   90000

Hewlett-Packard® Professional Books

OPERATING SYSTEMS

Fernandez	Configuring CDE: The Common Desktop Environment
Lund	Integrating UNIX® and PC Network Operating Systems
Madell	Disk and File Management Tasks on HP-UX
Poniatowski	HP-UX 11.x System Administration Handbook and Toolkit
Poniatowski	HP-UX 11.x System Administration "How To" Book, Second Edition
Poniatowski	HP-UX System Administration Handbook and Toolkit
Poniatowski	Learning the HP-UX Operating System
Poniatowski	UNIX® User's Handbook
Rehman	HP Certified, HP-UX System Administration
Sauers, Weygant	HP-UX Tuning and Performance
Stone, Symons	UNIX® Fault Management
Weygant	Clusters for High Availability: A Primer of HP-UX Solutions

ONLINE/INTERNET

Amor	The E-business (R)evolution
Greenberg, Lakeland	A Methodology for Developing and Deploying Internet and Intranet Solutions
Greenberg, Lakeland	Building Professional Web Sites with the Right Tools
Ketkar	Working with Netscape Server on HP-UX
Klein	Building Enhanced HTML Help with DHTML and CSS

NETWORKING/COMMUNICATIONS

Blommers	OpenView Network Node Manager: Designing and Implementing an Enterprise Solution
Blommers	Practical Planning for Network Growth
Lee	The ISDN Consultant
Lucke	Designing and Implementing Computer Workgroups

ENTERPRISE

Blommers	Architecting Enterprise Solutions with UNIX® Networking
Cook	Building Enterprise Information Architectures
Pipkin	Halting the Hacker: A Practical Guide to Computer Security
Pipkin	Information Security: Protecting the Global Enterprise
Sperley	Enterprise Data Warehouse, Volume 1: Planning, Building, and Implementation
Thornburgh	Fibre Channel for Mass Storage
Thornburgh, Schoenborn	Storage Area Networks: Designing and Implementing a Mass Storage System

PROGRAMMING

Blinn	Portable Shell Programming
Caruso	Power Programming in HP OpenView
Chaudri, Loomis	Object Databases in Practice
Chew	The Java™/C++ Cross-Reference Handbook
Grady	Practical Software Metrics for Project Management and Process Improvement
Grady	Successful Software Process Improvement
Lewis	The Art & Science of Smalltalk
Lichtenbelt, Crane, Naqvi	Introduction to Volume Rendering
Mellquist	SNMP++
Mikkelsen, Pherigo	Practical Software Configuration Management
Norton, DiPasquale	Thread Time: The Multithreaded Programming Guide
Wadleigh, Crawford	Software Optimization for High Performance Computing

IMAGE PROCESSING

Crane	A Simplified Approach to Image Processing
Day	The Color Scanning Handbook
Gann	Desktop Scanners: Image Quality

OTHER TITLES OF INTEREST

Kane	PA-RISC 2.0 Architecture
Markstein	IA-64 and Elementary Functions

OpenView Network Node Manager

Designing and Implementing an Enterprise Solution

John Blommers

Hewlett-Packard Company

www.hp.com/go/retailbooks

Prentice Hall PTR
Upper Saddle River, New Jersey 07458
www.phptr.com

Library of Congress Cataloging-in-Publication Data

Blommers, John.
    OpenView network node manager: designing and implementing an enterprise solution /
      p. cm.
    Includes bibliographical references and index.
    ISBN 0-13-019849-8
    1. Computer networks—Management. 2. OpenView. 3. Client/server computing. I. Title.

    TK5105.5.B5686 2000
    005.7'13—dc21

                              00-060697

Editorial/production supervision: *Nicholas Radhuber*
Cover design director: *Jerry Votta*
Cover design: *Talar Agasyan*
Manufacturing manager: *Maura Zaldivar*
Acquisitions editor: *Jill Pisoni*
Editorial assistant: *Justin Somma*
Marketing manager: *Julie Tiso*

Manager, Hewlett-Packard Retail Book Publishing: *Patricia Pekary*
Editor, Hewlett-Packard Professional Books: *Susan Wright*

Published by Prentice Hall PTR
Prentice-Hall, Inc.
Upper Saddle River, New Jersey 07458

Prentice Hall books are widely used by corporations and government agencies for training, marketing, and resale.
The publisher offers discounts on this book when ordered in bulk quantities. For more information, contact Corporate Sales Department, Phone: 800-382-3419; FAX: 201-236-7141;
E-mail: corpsales@prenhall.com
Or write: Prentice Hall PTR, Corporate Sales Dept., One Lake Street, Upper Saddle River, NJ 07458.

Other product or company names mentioned herein are the trademarks or registered trademarks of their respective owners.

Printed in the United States of America
10 9 8 7 6 5 4 3 2 1

ISBN 0-13-019849-8

Prentice-Hall International (UK) Limited, *London*
Prentice-Hall of Australia Pty. Limited, *Sydney*
Prentice-Hall Canada Inc., *Toronto*
Prentice-Hall Hispanoamericana, S.A., *Mexico*
Prentice-Hall of India Private Limited, *New Delhi*
Prentice-Hall of Japan, Inc., *Tokyo*
Pearson Education Asia Pte. Ltd.
Editora Prentice-Hall do Brasil, Ltda., *Rio de Janeiro*

Contents

10   Managing Firewall Environments With NNM . 177

11   Periodic Maintenance Tasks for NNM 191

12   A Day With NNM 207

13   Troubleshooting NNM 219

Preface

This book is about planning, implementing, and maintaining Hewlett-Packard OpenView Network Node Manager (NNM) for the corporate network.

The book isn't a rehash of the excellent NNM manuals or training workbooks. It is recommended that the reader attend an NNM training class before using this book and deploying NNM.

Most importantly, this text is not a marketing document. The author has been with NNM since the 1.0 days when the product wasn't based on the developer's kit, and the main application was called *xnm*. The material between the covers is based on the fairly unique perspective of an HP consultant.

This book focuses on the UNIX version of NNM and attempts to remain version-agnostic. Where certain features are version-specific, this is noted.

Finally, the book is written for people with some experience in network operation, management, planning, and configuration.

A comprehensive glossary of network and system terminology is provided for reference.

Acknowledgments

Acknowledgments

I want to first thank my wife, Teresa, for her support during the short writing cycle I had available in which to write this book.

Next, I need to thank Roxie Strackbein, my manager at HP, who, at the time I proposed writing this book, provided the encouragement and support I needed to press forward with this writing effort.

Thanks go to the hard-working analysts, administrators, developers, and managers at my favorite customer site for their willingness to hire me for two years to assist in the rollout of NNM across their company. My hat is off to Majed Barbar, Duane Harkness, Kevin Wenk, Walt Anderson, Ken Chinn, Grant Bohnet, Jerry Snyder, Dennis Huss, Paul Carlson, Dave Troje, John O'Meara, Scott Borow, and Ken Yang.

Let me extend great thanks to my stable of the most faithful and loyal technical reviewers I could have asked for — Duane Harkness, Dave Brink, Wendy Studinski, Tim Antonsen, Harry Lynch, Eric Pulsipher, and Paul Rice.

In the consulting arena HP depends on principal consultants to find, qualify, book, and monitor business. Therefore I must also thank Ralph Frid for his successful efforts in linking me to so many interesting NNM networking engagements.

Finally, let me mention my Norwegian forest cat, Mister Newton, for his efforts at keeping my lap warm during the writing process. He is totally *puzzled* about the black box with the play buttons I spent hours with while he slept.

Mister Newton

List of Figures

List of Figures

List of Tables

Author Biography

John Blommers is a 16-year veteran with Hewlett–Packard Consulting who has had the pleasure of recommending, developing, and implementing HP OpenView Network Node Manager (NNM) as a network management solution for HP customers. He began working with NNM in the version 1.0 days when the application was called *xnm*. He's installed it at dozens of HP customer sites and taught the HP customer training.

The author's background is strong in the networking and UNIX arenas. As a network consultant, he designs, audits, and troubleshoots customer networks. For new networks or application upgrades, he develops network capacity plans with the aid of simulation technology, with over a dozen to his credit in the past few years.

Mr. Blommers has a Bachelors of Applied Science degree in Electrical Engineering from the University of British Columbia, and a Master of Science degree in Applied Mathematics from the University of Victoria, Canada.

The author teaches at the University of Washington, Outreach Department, in the Data Communications Certificate Program. He currently teaches LAN/WAN Design and Management and Advanced Network Management.

## CHAPTER 1

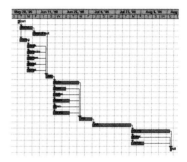

The NNM Project
Deployment Plan

Introduction

For small networks a single Network Node Manager (NNM) system may suffice, but large, multisite worldwide networks will need many NNM systems. A formal project plan is needed for larger implementations to ensure a successful deployment. This plan must cover the following aspects of network management:

- A *requirements analysis* is best performed early in the project because of the obvious downstream impact that occurs should the rate of change of the requirements exceed the rate of engineering. The requirements analysis explores the number of NNM systems to be deployed, how many active users are expected, what transaction response times are acceptable, the number and kinds of maps users will need, what reports are needed, what devices should be managed, the security implications, and reliability and uptime issues.

- The NNM *deployment project plan* should be alive and shared with the user community. A web site is ideally suited for sharing documents, including the project plan, operations agreements, configuration guides, best practices, and product manuals. PDF format is the ideal format for shared documents.

- The *operations agreement* documents what features and capabilities the NNM deployment is supposed to provide to the user community. It represents the requirements as seen from the user perspective and includes roles and responsibilities. This agreement is developed early in the project cycle.

- An absolutely critical step in the project plan is choosing *a scalable computer platform* that ensures users get good NNM performance for many years. This means the system has expansion capabilities for CPU, disk, RAM, and network connectivity.

- A *pilot test* is crucial to ensure the success of a large NNM deployment. Lessons learned here help to build confidence, and sites participating in the pilot test become allies and advocates for the new capabilities NNM brings. You will also discover information about the network infrastructure that is valuable in steering the impending deployment around difficult network devices and configurations.

- The project plan also provides a *training schedule* for the user community. Depending on their role, users may require the shorter operator training or the full operator and administration class. Timing and budget constraints will determine if on-site training is appropriate.

- Most large corporate networks are geographically dispersed and serve multiple logical business entities. The IT group will therefore deploy multiple NNM systems and each will operate in its *management domain*. Experience during the pilot test will help determine the best way to configure each NNM system so that the actual network topology it manages corresponds very closely with the desired model.

- Planning for ongoing *problem resolution* in support of the NNM deployment means formalizing a support plan, recruiting a support staff, defining a problem escalation plan, and publishing procedures. This includes a formal support staff list, a list server for general technical discussions, and an NNM test lab for problem duplication, testing, and development.

- A *backup strategy* is needed in the event that data is lost due to a hardware failure, or if a database is corrupted, a user deletes a file or map inadvertently, there is a change in requirements, or a patch or upgrade must be rolled out. The strategy should minimize scheduled downtime.

- For large NNM deployments, there is good reason to consider *HP's IT Operations product* for system administration of the NNM systems. This allows a central site to monitor the critical resources of each NNM system, upload patches, perform backups, manage the print spooler, execute periodic health checks, and perform general system administration.

- There is incredible value in recruiting one or more *experienced consultants*, system administrators, and project managers into the NNM deployment team. These people can provide the necessary personnel resources and expertise that may not be easily drawn from the existing IT group. This helps ensure that project's success and timely completion.

- A *victory celebration* is recommended upon the successful completion of the NNM deployment project.

- *Support* for the NNM systems has to be planned after they are deployed across the corporate network. A schedule to apply patches should be created that minimizes downtime and risk. Minor and major NNM releases may require wholesale software upgrades. You may also find that more users are taking advantage of the NNM systems which may require some of them to be upgraded to maintain satisfactory performance levels.

Determining the Requirements that NNM Must Satisfy

This section provides some sample questions and answers to help you, the IT group, define the requirements that the user community will impose on their NNM network management solution. An analyst will most likely interview that community to complete the requirements analysis.

What types of maps are needed? NNM provides an autolayout feature that creates a hierarchical map based on the discovered topology. This complete map shows IP connectivity between subnets and routers and may be quite dense for large networks. While it's terrific for technical staff troubleshooting, it may not be appropriate for other users. The customization features include partitioning, hiding icons, and map filtering.

What devices should be discovered and managed? By default, NNM will discover IP devices whether they support the Simple Network Management Protocol or not. Is it necessary to discover every device on the network, or is the goal to manage the network infrastructure alone? Should servers and network printers be managed? You can write a discovery filter to control what types of devices NNM discovers.

How responsive should the NNM system be for the users? Is a 30-second response time acceptable at a busy hour, or is 5 seconds more reasonable? What is the maximum number of concurrent users for which this response time goal is desired? When even more users are active, is a degradation in the response time acceptable? Most users prefer response times to be less than 2 seconds.

What kinds of users will be operating the NNM tool? Will these be help desk staff, troubleshooters, ad-hoc users, map builders, developers or administrators? Some of these users have quite different needs and may not need the same NNM features enabled. Be sure to identify all your user types early.

What kinds of reports are needed? NNM makes some built-in tools available from the NNM graphical user interface (GUI) while others are available from the shell prompt (or from the MS-DOS prompt in Windows). Will users need to create large 24-bit color screen shots and print them or will they capture them on a personal computer? Will event histories be needed to document problems? Are performance graphs needed online? How long do event histories need to be maintained? In most cases you will need to provide basic screen capture and print capabilities and offer performance charts.

Will the user community have a variety of platforms from which they access NNM, such as Windows, Linux, UNIX, X-terminal, and Macintosh? Will they be able and willing to run the necessary X-Window emulators to gain such access? Is a web browser interface sufficient? Is command line access also needed from these platforms? If users don't have the appropriate software you will need to obtain it, test it, and provide support for it.

How much security is needed for the normal operation of NNM? Will the normal UNIX login/password scheme suffice? Do user accounts need to be consistent on all the systems that run NNM? The answer is yes in most cases.

How available should the NNM tool be? Should it be 99% or higher? Are scheduled maintenance outages not part of this figure? Should the NNM application be available all day, every day? Note that the need to back up the database, map customizations, and other data requires at least a degraded mode of operation whereby the NNM daemons are paused (for NNM 6). Is backup polling an acceptable solution to achieve high availability of the NNM tool overall? The usual answer is that it is necessary to have the network management tool always available, 99% is not considered highly available, and backup polling is a requirement.

How large is the network to be managed? For sufficiently large networks, it becomes impractical to provision a large enough box in a central enough location to host the NNM application. The single computer becomes large and expensive to support the user base; the processor capacity and network bandwidth become excessive as well. A distributed management solution is called for so that NNM systems, called collection stations, can be located within the geography of their management domains, close to their users. To retain a single view of the network, a management station imports device and topology data from the collection stations and creates a new network map representing the entire enterprise.

Sharing Project Plans and Information on a Web Site

To best serve the users, developers, and managers of the NNM project, it is in everybody's best interest to share information on a web server. The pages must be served up fresh, however, so it is important to keep documents and other information up to date. Nobody goes back to a stale web site. Any time that someone requires information about the NNM project, they visit the web site and view or download the information they need.

Documents made available on the web site should be converted to Adobe's Portable Document Format (PDF) so that any user, irrespective of their computer platform, can read and print them. This also prevents document alteration. At this writing, version 4.0.5 of the Acrobat Reader provides the new page rotation feature. There is also a web browser plug-in so PDF documents can be viewed directly on the web. This is an important mechanism for delivering vector drawings to the user because such drawings are scalable, whereas bitmapped images are generally not. The PDF approach frees the user from having to purchase, install, load, and learn the authoring tool. It also avoids the common problem of different document versions.

The kind of information appropriate for sharing on this web site include HP NNM PDF manuals (downloadable from HP's OpenView web site), project plans, operations agreements, service level agreements (SLAs), organization charts, configuration guides, custom procedures, best practices, tips and techniques, network drawings, and sample NNM maps.

Drafting, Defining, and Finalizing an Operations Agreement

The operations agreement is between the users of the NNM tool and the Information Technology (IT) department. The operations agreement spells out what the NNM tool is expected to do, how support is provided by IT, what problem escalation procedures are in place, the uptime goals, the content of the maps, the definitions for the performance thresholds, and the type of performance data collected. This agreement may swell to a 50-page document and see many revisions and heated arguments before it is accepted by all parties.

The users and supporting parties for the NNM tool are enumerated in the operations agreement. The supporting parties are usually the IT department and the system administration group. The system administration group not only supports the system running the NNM tool, but also the Windows, Linux, UNIX, and Macintosh systems from which users access NNM via X-windows or web browsers. These users typically include the NNM map builders, the help desk, ad-hoc researchers, and the 'wires and pliers" troubleshooters that use NNM to chase network problems. In smaller organizations, a few individuals may wear the hats of the system administrators, map builders, researchers, and users.

The operations agreement also lists the exact locations where the NNM systems will be installed, the conditioning of the AC power, the type of racking, and the type of LAN connection needed. The geography each NNM system will manage is also defined. While the operations agreement may contain these and other requirements, the requirements document may, of course, be separate.

After the NNM systems are operational, users will doubtless want more features and greater functionality. Rather than taking these change requests directly to the IT department, the operations agreement may identify a change board or steering committee. In larger companies, this board brokers enhancement requests and balances them against budgetary and developer resources.

Choosing Scalable Hardware at Each NNM Site

Selecting a hardware configuration that turns out to be too small after a few months is an embarrassment worth avoiding. The resulting response time degradation will be remembered as a bad user experience that may limit the acceptance of the NNM system throughout the user community. Whatever the initial sizing estimates for each NNM system, it is important to choose a scalable system.

A scalable system is one that can be upgraded in the field so that the impact on the operation of the NNM tool is minimized to just a few minutes of downtime. A non-scalable system is maximally configured in some way. Scalable means that hardware components can be upgraded to increase performance and reduce transaction response time.

A scalable system has room for additional CPU cards, or the existing CPU cards can at least be upgraded with perhaps larger cache sizes. Additional CPUs won't increase the performance of a single-threaded process, but multiple processes can use the additional CPUs to alleviate the pressure caused by multiple concurrent users.

There should also be spare memory slots available, or the existing memory should at least be upgradable with larger capacity RAM "sticks." When the operating system isn't able to provide the necessary memory to all running applications, the virtual memory (VM) system accesses the disk to page out memory. As the rate of VM activity increases, disk I/O can become a performance bottleneck.

Additional drive bays should be available to add disk storage (or to stripe additional disks) and additional disk I/O channels (such as a SCSI bus) should be available to expand the disk I/O bandwidth. At the very least, it should be possible to swap out an existing hard drive for a larger one, but this requires a data backup and recovery step, necessitating greater downtime. Since a large NNM database can become a performance bottleneck, striping the volume it resides on with two to four disk stripes can dramatically improve response time.

On rare occasions the system's standard Ethernet LAN adapter may become a performance bottleneck, especially when NNM is managing a large number of LAN-attached devices with an aggressive polling strategy. It is prudent to reserve the option of upgrading the LAN adapter to fast Ethernet (100BASE-T) to reduce network latency. Fast Ethernet is particularly important if you do network backups, since a standard Ethernet link drastically increases backup time. Naturally, the NNM system should be attached to a dedicated Ethernet switch port to avoid contention with shared media LAN traffic. Ideally, the port is configured for full duplex (FDX) operation to avoid collisions and to potentially double the throughput. Be careful to monitor this port—autonegotiation back to 10mpbs and half duplex (HDX) operation is a common problem.

The reader might ask "why not size the NNM system properly in the first place?" The answer is that HP provides sizing guidelines in the PDF document entitled *Network Node Manager 6.0 Performance and Configuration Guide*. This guide requires that the NNM administrator be able to estimate such parameters as the number of active users, the number of managed devices, the number of interfaces (objects in the database), the arrival rate of network events, and the amount of historical SNMP data to be collected. The estimates for these parameters will have an unavoidable uncertainty.

Even the definition of "properly" in the reader's question is subject to interpretation. The parameters may change over time. Once the NNM tool is accepted by the user community, the number of active users can easily be double that of the initial estimates. As users make demands on the system, their expectations of response time will change, and it will become necessary to scale up the system to maintain high user satisfaction. Additional maps may be requested to satisfy new requirements. Additional NNM features may be used that weren't anticipated, further consuming system resources. Additional third-party applications may be added later as NNM becomes the accepted platform for network management. The network will very likely grow in size and scope faster than anticipated and sooner than expected. Finally, as HP releases new versions of NNM, the sizing guidelines will change too.

In practice, you will probably want to use the sizing guidelines for an initial sizing estimate, then apply a factor to allow for growth. Next, conduct a pilot test on the largest management domain to gain experience and modify the sizing formula accordingly. Finally, deploy scalable systems.

Setting the Scope and Conducting a Pilot Test

Before deploying NNM across the enterprise network it is important to build up confidence in the product's implementation. A pilot test is an excellent and recommended way to build that confidence. Several sites should participate in the pilot test. The pilot users become effective evangelists, or champions, for the NNM tool. They also help bring good success stories and best practices to the table. A successful pilot test should be considered a prerequisite to an enterprise-wide NNM deployment.

The pilot test is a project in itself. The duration of the pilot should be fixed to, say, a few months. Rules for using the NNM systems should be agreed to and followed. For example, all participants in the pilot must be fully NNM trained. User feedback is encouraged (all kinds). Success stories should be shared with the same enthusiasm as children trading Pokemon cards. Lessons will be learned. Weekly conference calls among the pilot participants should be used to keep the project on track and to administer appropriate kudos to outstanding contributors.

During the pilot, you discover what is really attached to the network. You may find to your total amazement that community strings are not always configured consistently in network devices. You may find equipment that has been forgotten or recently installed. You will learn the impact of the SNMP traffic on router CPUs. "Bad" SNMP agents turn up as well. You will also deal with autodiscovery and autolayout challenges.

At the early stages of the pilot test, the discovery filter will be wide open. This is convenient because it corresponds to the NNM default of "no filter at all." For the purpose of obtaining an inventory of network devices, this is a good first step. You will then configure the discovery filter to limit NNM to discovering just the kinds of devices you are interested in managing, such as routers, switches, bridges, hubs, network printers, servers, and terminal servers. The size of the NNM database will be relatively enormous without the discovery filter, and the system will perform much faster after the filter is applied.

During the pilot the various users will have an opportunity to learn how to best build maps suited to their needs. SNMP data collection and threshold settings can be perfected. Finally, the amount of disk space needed to support the required functionality can be estimated. It will become apparent at this time what system sizing is needed to achieve good response time.

The remote support model can be tested during the pilot to ensure that it can be implemented across the enterprise. Hiccups in remote installs can be ironed out. User convenience scripts may be developed. You can evaluate how long a backup takes, how quickly a map synchronizes, and how responsive the SNMP grapher is for long data collections.

At the end of the pilot test, you will have confidence that victory is at hand.

Identifying, Developing, or Buying NNM Training

For a large, enterprise-wide rollout of NNM, a great many users will require training. A 20-site rollout with 10 users per site means 200 training units have to be purchased. Not all users have the same training needs. Training needs can be loosely grouped into three categories: full, dual, and basic.

The IT staff probably builds, configures, updates, and patches the NNM systems remotely, so these administrators are already trained simply because they are the same people responsible for the pilot test. These people need the full NNM training. The remote user community falls loosely into the two remaining categories. The users that need to configure the NNM tool (such as the map builders) or conduct ad-hoc data collections (such as the capacity planners) should take dual training that covers both administration and use of NNM. Users that take advantage of predefined functionality need only basic user training.

HP provides NNM customer training all over the world, and customers travel to conveniently located training centers to take basic or advanced classes. Equipment is generally limited to a simple classroom lab environment. HP also provides on-site classes at customer locations. When the economies of scale apply, customers with many students find this approach economical, with the additional benefit that students can train directly on their corporate network.

Ideally, the training that users receive is delivered at their own facilities using the corporate network and working on their customized version of NNM as delivered by the IT group. This conflicts with vendor-supplied training that is uniformly delivered and dependent on repeatable labs and exercises. Consequently, the IT group in large companies may recruit their corporate training group to develop in-house, customized NNM training. Alternately, the IT group may contract their favorite NNM training supplier to deliver a customized on-site course.

Defining Management Domains

You normally want to manage the network along management domains by dividing the network based on geography, business communities of interest, functionality, or network architecture. Geography is a common divider, and a map of the country (or continent or world) is often customized to reflect management domains. The pilot test provides a good proving ground for defining and implementing management domains.

There is a risk of missing pieces of the network within the intended management domain. This means portions of the network remain unmanaged. For single-station NNM implementations there is only one management domain, and the discovery process is manually directed into all corners of the network until no new subnets are discovered. For multistation NNM implementations, there is a risk that the domains may not fit snugly against each other, leaving gaps. For example, management domains A and B may discover a router and its subnets, leaving these subnets initially unmanaged. Which domain should set which subnet icons to the managed state? This illustrates why a considerable amount of bookkeeping is needed to ensure that the management domain pieces fit snugly into the overall network puzzle.

So is it better to allow gaps between the management domains or to allow overlaps? Most will agree that it's far worse to leave a section of the network unmanaged than to have overlapping management domains. What are the consequences of having network devices managed by more than one NNM system? Managed devices will receive twice the number of SNMP queries and they will be pinged twice as often. When a device goes down, two groups will be working on the problem instead of one, unless, of course, network management is centralized. When a network device sends an SNMP trap, where is it sent? It's sent to the NNM management stations(s) in the local SNMP agent software's TrapForwarding list.

Network administrators may configure access control lists (ACLs) on their routers. These can limit access to specified services such as SNMP to specific devices or subnets. For example, to secure the SNMP service on a router, only the local NNM system is allowed access to it. This is a far more robust security mechanism than an unpublished SNMP community string. It has the side effect of limiting the opportunity for overlapping management domains to occur.

Given a strategy for determining the management domains, configuring the NNM system appropriately is more straightforward. By default, the initial management domain is the subnet the NNM system finds itself on. This can be expanded using the *netmon* daemon's *seedfile* parameter. The *seedfile* is a list of devices in the management domain, typically routers, which have rich ARP caches and excellent network connectivity to help drive NNM's autodiscovery. Manually directed autodiscovery is appropriate initially, whereby the map builder manually manages appropriate subnets as they are discovered until the desired section of the network is discovered.

Since defining the management domain is initially an iterative process, it's nice to be able to repeat it. Manual methods are not easily repeated, so once everybody is satisfied that the management domain is correctly defined, a list of routers for the *seedfile* should be created and maintained. It is recommended that a master list of all *seedfiles* (for each collection and management station) be centrally maintained. If it is ever necessary to rebuild an NNM system from scratch, knowing the appropriate *seedfile* information is essential.

Planning for Ongoing Problem Resolution

Let's begin with defining the term customer. HP sees people who buy and use NNM products as customers. But the IT group in a company considers its NNM users as customers too. Consequently, the corporate NNM users call their own IT department for support with NNM problems, and the IT department calls the HP support group with their NNM problems.

To support its NNM customers, the IT group develops a list of staff members such as the project lead, the local site champions, the on-site consultant, the NNM staff, and the system administrators. The list includes names, roles, telephone numbers, and pager numbers. Since most corporate networks require around the clock support, appropriate coverage hours become part of the support requirement.

For general information exchange, the IT group may set up a list server such as *listserv* or *majordomo* to which customers subscribe.

Anyone with a question or a useful tip can send an e-mail message to the list. All list subscribers receive a copy of it, and anybody can post a response or news. The list is archived and searchable via a web interface.

Problems that need attention may be users with account access difficulties, operating system anomalies, network outages, NNM misconfiguration, poor performance, training shortcomings, security violations, user X-term freezes, and DNS configuration errors.

The IT group should have a small lab environment with one or more licensed test NNM systems and representative network equipment. Some tough NNM problems found in the field are better reproduced in a lab environment where downtime is not a problem. A test system can be reconfigured and brought down as needed to work a problem.

This lab can be made more useful if the NNM systems in it belong to a "golden subnet," which is configured into the corporate network equipment ACLs. This allows a lab NNM system to discover and troubleshoot problems with network equipment in the field. The lab system can then be used as an emergency backup collection station also. This may become part of the disaster recovery plan.

Planning for System, Database, and Map Backup and Recovery

A reliable NNM system takes advantage of mirrored disks. Downtime is minimized by adopting the following procedure. First, pause or shut down the NNM subsystem. Next, break the disk mirror, then restart NNM, which is now running without active mirroring. Back up the volumes on the inactive mirror disk, and when it's done, establish the mirror again, which automatically silvers the active disk onto the one just backed up. Since hard drive storage is so economical, some system administrators create triple mirrors for added reliability. This leaves the NNM system running on a mirror pair while the third mirror is backed up. The common term for striping is RAID 0 and for mirroring it is RAID 1; the combination is called RAID 1+0.

Note that NNM provides *ovbackup.ovpl*, which automates an orderly synchronization of all databases. It creates a database snapshot in a staging area and is meant to be invoked by the operating system backup process. If you use this feature, you won't need to be concerned about the location of the operational database as described below.

The preferred backup mechanism transfers the data from each compressed disk volume image onto a dedicated backup system across the network. Here, the benefit of a fast Ethernet adapter on both the NNM and the backup system becomes apparent, as it is important to keep the backup interval small. The task of automating and managing the backups is usually left to the system administrators, who are skilled in the technologies of mirroring, backups, and disk management.

The largest amount of data to be backed up resides in the database (everything under *$OV_DB*). However, it's prudent to capture everything on the NNM installation and working volumes. This ensures that NNM configuration files (stored under *$OV_CONF*) are backed up too.

Static configuration files and software in general can always be reinstalled rather than restored from backup. For example, registration files (ARF) (stored under *$OV_REGISTRATION*) don't change operationally unless users are allowed to create ad-hoc MIB applications. DNS configuration files (such as */etc/named.conf* and files under */var/named*) are static and need to be backed up just once.

Map builders learn early to save their Root and Internet submap customizations (the default location is */var/opt/OV/tmp/ipmap.out*). That's because they invest a fair amount of time in their labors. For large maps, these text files exceed one megabyte in size. Rather than use the default file name to save the map customization file, map builders (who may manage multiple NNM system maps) typically include a data stamp and possibly a site stamp in the file name. Paranoid map builders will save copies of these files on their personal workstations, but the daily NNM system backup should include them as well.

Be prepared to rebuild an NNM system remotely from scratch. This may become necessary when the disk drives are corrupt or crash. A skilled system administrator is able to build a bootable CD-ROM containing the operating system and the NNM installer. This is sufficient to allow an NNM system to be booted from the CD-ROM and rebuilt from the NNM image remotely. The remote installation process is completed by using an NFS mount from the NNM system back to the installation server.

The reconstruction of a remote NNM system is completed by NFS mounting the backup server backup volume, copying the compressed volume image across the network to another volume on the NNM system, and restoring the archive back to the target volume. The system administrator directs this interactively in a telnet window.

It may come to pass that the backup data is a faithful backup of corrupt data. For example, suppose that for a number of weeks the NNM database grows more corrupt until it becomes unusable. The backups are therefore also useless; it may take a long time to find a good backup, and if such a backup is found, it may be too old to be useful. In that case, after the operating system and NNM application are installed (or simply validated as being good), the NNM database has to be rebuilt via autodiscovery. Using a good copy of the *seedfile* and discovery filter, allow autodiscovery to rebuild the object and topology databases. When autodiscovery has converged (new object discovery has ceased), create new maps with the appropriate names and import the customization files.

The Benefit of Using ITO for NNM System Management

HP's IT Operations (ITO) product (now Vantage Point Operations or VPO) is a network and system management platform built on top of the NNM runtime components. The basic autodiscovery engine, the database, and the user interface elements are the same as NNM uses. This makes ITO an ideal solution for managing a large number (20+) of NNM systems distributed across the enterprise network.

In a pure HP environment, ITO can be used along with additional bolt-on products for a complete system administration solution. For automatic backup and interactive restore operations, use the OmniBack product. For system software configuration control, use SoftWare Distributor. To manage the printing subsystem, use OpenSpool. To monitor system performance, use PerfView and MeasureWare. For general system monitoring, use ITO's customizable agents (not to be confused with SNMP agents or MeasureWare agents). The ITO software should run on a separate system controlled by the IT group.

The pilot project is an ideal time to gain initial experience with ITO for managing the NNM systems. Occasionally, one of the NNM daemons will terminate or the *syslogd* daemon may cease operation. ITO can detect this, restart the daemon, and log the event. Sometimes an *ovw* process becomes disconnected from its X-display and loops, consuming CPU time and reducing response time for the other users. ITO can be customized to detect a spinning detached process, send it a SIGHUP signal to terminate it, and log the event. ITO can monitor the health of the connection between each NNM collection station and the management station and log an event when the management station cannot communicate.

ITO can be configured to monitor the size of log files and warn users when they grow beyond acceptable limits. Even the free space on critical disk volumes can be monitored. Using the MeasureWare agent, ITO can detect excessive utilization of a wide range of system resources. Since NNM systems require a writable map to be open at all times, ITO can verify that this is the case.

As the IT staff becomes more experienced with solving NNM problems, more and more functionality can be rolled into the ITO system to improve problem detection, automate many of the trivial fixes, and automate e-mail or paging to the on-call staff for critical problems. Or, you can do these directly in NNM locally.

The Value of Consultants, System Admins, and Project Managers

For a large (20+) NNM system project there is just too much work for only one or two people to complete the activities in a reasonable time frame. A great deal of skill in many areas is required and this is hard to find in a single person.

For large NNM deployments, skill in basic networking technologies is a must. Knowledge of hubs, repeaters, bridges, switches, routing switches, routers, and application gateways is needed. So is an understanding of DNS, X-windows, TCP/IP, routing, and LAN/WAN infrastructures. A network consultant can help with this.

Since NNM runs on an operating system, skill is needed in building and configuring the O/S, creating install scripts, automating processes, troubleshooting, account management, disk volume management, backup and recovery, and configuration of the networking subsystems. A dedicated system administrator can provide this service.

Skill with NNM installation, configuration, customization, maintenance, updating, training, and mentoring is also needed. Consultants are key people here.

Since the project is large, skill is needed in coordinating the various players, tracking project milestones, scheduling meetings, identifying critical paths in the project plan, locating resources, and interfacing with the steering committee. Therefore, a project manager is needed.

For special requirements that NNM does not satisfy, custom code has to be developed to deal with customized maps, configuration file management, data display routines, and SNMP database truncation scripts. This requires skill in Perl, C/C++, and shell scripting, plus training in the NNM developer kit. This kind of work is best done by a software developer.

The Victory Celebration

A successful project meets all of its objectives by a given date, and a declaration of victory is appropriate. This is necessary in order to recognize the accomplishments of the IT group and its associates. One way to recognize accomplishment is through a formal letter signed by the IT managers and framed in wood commending the participants and expounding on their accomplishments. Perhaps each person could also get a gift certificate. Finally, a victory lunch with brief and funny speeches may be appropriate.

Planning for Operational Patching and Upgrading

With a fully operational NNM deployment, there comes the task of maintenance. Some or all of the NNM systems may require a patch or an update. The underlying operating system or one of its subsystems (such as DNS) may require patching. A parameter may require tuning. Performance may be poor at some sites, requiring additional disk striping and memory. The IP address of an NNM system may have to be changed because the system must be moved to another location. A third-party package such as CiscoView, Optivity, or NetCool may require a patch. These are routine matters.

Less routine is the annual or biannual upgrade cycle. The operating system may be due for an update, a third-party product update with desirable features may become available, or better yet, a compelling NNM upgrade is now available.

The benefit of the NNM test lab is that all of the above can be tested as much as necessary until the patch, update, or change is demonstrated as safe, functional, and doesn't break existing functionality. It is inadvisable to test patches on operational NNM systems. To minimize the number of outages, try to batch changes into one outage.

After validating the change, schedule an outage for each NNM system. Perform the required work during this time and verify full functionality. If something goes wrong, either back out of the patch or revert to a backup. Always have a backout plan. Finally, declare the outage over.

For NNM upgrades, additional concerns present themselves. Some file formats (such as *snmpCol.conf*) may change, requiring conversion. There may be new daemons that ITO should be configured to monitor. Changes in the menu structure is a foregone conclusion, and there will be additional functionality. The NNM upgrade release notes (*Help:What's New in the GUI*) is a must-read for learning about new features and changes, and the HP Education Center's Delta Training class is a valuable resource. Users should be advised of the changes they'll see after the upgrade and learn how to take advantage of new features. In-house training materials must also be upgraded.

Occasionally, a single site will have a unique problem. For example, a new subnet may be discovered by an NNM system where one of the devices has a badly behaving SNMP agent which returns data that causes *netmon* to terminate or loop. If a patch is available, it may be appropriate to directly patch that system. In this example, you would turn on full logging for the *netmon* daemon and wait for the problem to occur. Review the *netmon.trace* log file for the offending device and put its IP address in the *netmon.noDiscover* file.

## CHAPTER 2

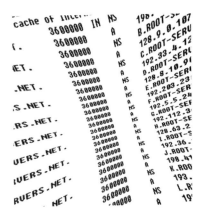

Planning a Robust Domain Name System

Introduction

Network Node Manager may do hundreds of forward and reverse lookups at a busy time as it goes about the business of discovery, configuration management, and status checking. This requires a reliable, accurate, high-performance Domain Name System (DNS). This chapter reviews the operation and configuration for DNS as it is assumed the reader is already familiar with it.

DNS is a critical, heavily-used resource for NNM. DNS efficiently provides name-to-address (forward) lookups as well as address-to-name (reverse) lookups that are critical to NNM's configuration management.

Before DNS there was */etc/hosts*, a simple linear file containing the names and IP addresses of networked systems. The size and distribution problems associated with this file proved a serious limit to scalability.

DNS provides explicit support for multihomed devices such as routers and servers with multiple network adapters. An address lookup for a multihomed device returns all the IP addresses associated with it, which in the case of a router, can be considerable.

DNS offers a number of reliability features to ensure the service is always available to client systems (such as NNM). These include multiple name servers at the client, caching, primary and secondary servers, and a hierarchy of name servers to delegate authority.

Delegation in DNS allows local authoritative name servers to be maintained by local network administrators all over the enterprise network, yet, from the client perspective, the information seems to come from the local name server. For large corporations with multiple independent business locations, DNS fits well.

Sample configuration files for the DNS client as well as the DNS server (for UNIX) are given in this chapter. BIND version 8 is assumed, and the sample files are real, having been tested on the author's own Red Hat Linux system.

Given that DNS is mission-critical, name servers must not become overloaded. Happily, the implementation is very efficient, but it's highly recommended that an NNM system run a caching-only name server to avoid needless network traffic.

To ensure that DNS servers are available at all times with accurate information, secondary name servers can be set up to copy domain data from the primary name servers. This helps keep down the loading on the primary name servers as well.

At the end of this chapter there is a comprehensive diagram that shows the architecture of a large DNS implementation. It shows the root name servers that glue the primary name servers together, the secondary name servers that feed from them, and the DNS client systems that use these servers.

For a complete guide to DNS, refer to *DNS and BIND*, Third Edition, by Abitz and Liu, O'Reilly & Associates Inc., ISBN 1-56592-010-4.

Why DNS Is So Important to NNM

NNM discovers devices via the IP address found in ARP caches, seed files, routing tables, and ICMP echoes. In IP networks, devices are given names, and in large networks this name space is divided into a hierarchy of subdomains. This eliminates name collisions on large networks where there is a high degree of configuration checking done, generating a high rate of DNS forward and reverse lookups. This lookup mechanism can be a performance bottleneck.

A common problem is NNM combining two routers into a single node. This is usually caused by bad DNS data.

DNS is an efficient mechanism for looking up IP addresses and names because it was designed for that purpose. Caching is one of the mechanisms DNS servers use to create efficiency.

All large companies with large networks depend on their DNS implementations to distribute the authority of names and IP addresses to smaller, more manageable authoritative subdomains. Note that the web-based services on the Internet would not function at all without DNS. Imagine constructing HTML with hard-coded IP addresses. DNS scales very well to the largest networks.

A large part of network management involves routers with multiple interfaces, each with one or more IP addresses. High availability servers usually have multiple IP addresses and interfaces. Devices with multiple interfaces are said to be multihomed. DNS is specifically designed with multihoming devices in mind. In addition, the NNM manual recommends DNS.

You can use NNM's *ovtopodump* command to ferret out devices that don't have DNS entries:

> *ovtopodump -Lr > report_name*

By doing so, you get a very useful one-line summary for each device in the NNM database. On a UNIX system you can pipe the output of the *ovtopodump* command into one or more filters (such as *sort*) for some specific purpose. For example, suppose you want to find out which devices in the management domain don't have DNS entries. Simply do the following:

> *ovtopodump -Lr | sort > report_name*

and examine the entries near the top of the sorted list. The numeric selection names percolate to the top of the list, neatly identifying the devices without DNS entries.

The History of /etc/hosts

Historically, systems on the Internet used the file HOSTS.TXT to propagate host IP addresses and name information. This is a plain text file that is searched from beginning to end for each forward lookup (a name is provided and an IP address is returned) or an inverse lookup (an IP address is provided and a name is returned). The file format for HOSTS.TXT and *etc/hosts* is given in Figure 2-1.

```
ip_address     name     alias_names # comment
15.24.44.65    yoda     hubvwa      # hp840 box
15.24.47.253   router   router_if_1 # local side
15.24.53.253   router   router_if_2 # remote side
```

Figure 2-1   The format of *etc/hosts*.
The fields are delimited by white space. Field 1 is the IP address. Field 2 is the formal name of the system. Additional fields (up to the comment character #) are alias names for this device. An optional comment is allowed after the # sign.

HOSTS.TXT had to be kept up to date, so a single site updated it with information provided by the Internet's many hostmasters, and it was downloaded on a daily basis by all systems that used it. This is how the HOSTS.TXT file was kept consistent across the Internet. The HOSTS.TXT file grew to several megabytes and the amount of download traffic it generated became problematic. In short, HOSTS.TXT proved not to be a scalable solution.

Creativity became stifled because every host name on the Internet had to be uniquely named.

If a few sites did not faithfully update HOSTS.TXT, they would often suffer connectivity problems with sites that had recently updated or changed some of their IP addresses. Even a single error could render some systems or entire subnets unreachable.

The HOSTS.TXT mechanism provided little else in the way of information. For example, to send e-mail to a system not connected directly to the Internet, the sender needed to know the mail systems in the path and make them part of the e-mail address.

To sum up, the Internet needed a name service that would:

- Reduce network traffic

- Delegate authority of information

- Improve update propagation time

- Be a true standard

- Provide additional fields such as mail exchange records

- Offer high reliability

- Scale very well

Enter DNS/BIND (Domain Name Service/Berkeley Internet Nameserver Daemon). It meets every one of the above requirements, especially the scaling requirement, very well. DNS scales to the size of the Internet and is absolutely necessary for web applications to work.

Router Interfaces and DNS

A router is a multihomed device because it has multiple network adapters. A file server with two fast Ethernet adapters is another example of a multihomed device. Each network adapter is typically assigned an IP address on a different subnet. You can reach a multihomed device using any one of the network adapters by specifying the IP address. For example, suppose the router named *myrouter* has two network adapters with the IP addresses 15.24.44.65

and 192.6.173.101. You can log in to *myrouter* using any of these commands:

> *telnet 15.24.44.65*
> *telnet 192.6.173.101*
> *telnet myrouter*

You normally don't want to bother specifying the IP address of one of the adapters. If adapter 15.24.44.65 is down, then the *telnet* command to that address will fail to reach the router.

DNS is designed to handle multihomed devices. *nslookup* is a command line interface for testing DNS. If you type in the command

> *nslookup myrouter*

then *nslookup* will return a list of IP addresses. All interfaces should have the same name as the router.

Note that it is not uncommon for web servers to have DNS records for addresses related to logical nodes. NNM tends to provide a confusing representation in such cases.

Some router interfaces such as HSSI (high-speed serial interface) are configured with subinterfaces that have IP addresses assigned to them. Sometimes a single router adapter is assigned one or more secondary IP addresses. Routers are sometimes given a unique low-numbered internal loopback IP address. All these logical interfaces should have the same name as the router. This is just good practice for the proper operation of NNM. Many sites do not adhere to this practice and name each interface uniquely.

One name for all router interfaces is a wonderful innovation. But how do you know which IP address you're going to use when you try to *telnet* to *myrouter*? Depending on which version you are running,

DNS returns its list of IP addresses according to one of the following rules:

- Return the "nearest" IP address first

- Return the same fixed IP address list

- Return a round-robin list of IP addresses

NNM works properly when DNS returns the same fixed list of IP addresses. Note that some DNS implementations truncate very long lists of IP addresses (which require more than 512 bytes in the packet). This is problematic with more current versions of DNS that must verify that the forward and reverse lookups are consistent before returning a result.

A network manager often needs to access a router because one or more interfaces are down. If the *telnet* command is used how do you know which interface you're going to reach? The answer is that *telnet* and *ftp* are DNS-aware. This means that they understand when a list of IP addresses is returned for a name lookup. Thus, these commands will try each interface in the list until contact with the router is made.

DNS is well-suited for multihomed devices.

Reliability Designs for DNS

DNS is a mission-critical service. Networked applications depend on it and NNM is no exception. The architecture of DNS provides several mechanisms to ensure reliability of the service:

- client access to multiple name servers

- caching at the name server

- primary and secondary name servers

To understand how these architectural elements provide reliability, consider the client-server DNS model first. An application (such as *telnet*, *ftp*, NNM, Navigator, and *sendmail*) that needs to connect to another system by name is a DNS client. This client code is known as the resolver and it is guided by an editable configuration file called *resolv.conf* (that's resolve without the last letter) in UNIX. *resolv.conf* defines the following parameters:

- the default domain of the client system

- an optional search list of additional domains

- up to three name server IP addresses

Windows client systems provide a GUI for configuring the DNS resolver (as shown in Figure 2-3 on page 37).

The purpose of listing three name servers is to increase the statistical probability that at least one name server can be reached. On real networks, a name server may crash or the network path to it may go down. For example, suppose that each of our three name servers has a reliability of 99% and that they are independent of each other (different AC power, different subnet, different building, different router, different administrator, different software). The statistical reliability of our example name service is therefore $1-(1-0.99)^3 =$ 0.999999 = 99.9999%, which is remarkable given the 99% reliability given for each name server.

NNM makes such heavy use of DNS that it seems logical to install a name server on the same system. This reduces DNS-related network traffic. This also reduces the latency of the DNS service by eliminating network latency between the NNM system and the name server system. Therefore, the first name server listed in the file *resolv.conf* is 127.0.0.1, the standard IP address for *localhost*, which is the standard local IP loopback address.

How should this local name server be configured? It's perfectly acceptable to install DNS configuration files on the NNM system. This may not be consistent with the existing architecture and implementation of the corporate name servers. Therefore, it is common practice to configure DNS as a caching-only name server on the NNM system. Every time NNM makes a DNS query, the result is cached in local memory until the time-to-live for the entry expires.

This means that updates to the name servers are automatically propagated to the NNM system name server within the time-to-live interval. The caching feature improves the performance of forward and reverse lookups. If the authoritative name servers should go down during the time-to-live interval, this event is hidden since the local cache still holds the necessary information.

Another reliability element in the DNS architecture is the secondary name server. The primary name server is authoritative because its configuration files are local. These database files are configured by the local hostmaster. Other name servers may be configured as secondary name servers by referring to the primary name server. The secondary name server copies (using a zone transfer) the primary name server database to its local disk. The zone transfer is repeated when the time-to-live expires.

Note that the major difference between a caching-only name server and a secondary name server is that the caching-only server caches entries one at a time as they are looked up, while the secondary name server transfers the entire DNS zone at startup time.

The Purpose and Use of Delegation

Large corporate networks, and the Internet itself, consist of a large collection of IP networks and subnetworks distributed across a great many geographic sites. Each geography or business entity rules over its management domain. IP addresses are allocated within subnets, devices are allocated names, and these names are assigned to a subdomain. Each management domain administers its own name servers and retains total authority and control over the database entries. Every conceivable device with an IP address should be represented by the DNS servers. The local hostmasters update their name server database as necessary to reflect devices that are new, renamed, or renumbered.

Within a very large corporate network there could be hundreds of authoritative name servers for hundreds of subdomains. For example, a few subdomains within the domain acme.com could be east.acme.com, west.acme.com, north.acme.com, south.acme.com, and corp.acme.com. Each of these domains belong to sites that are independent business units. Their computer and network equipment are assigned IP addresses, names, and even subdomains by the local network administrators. This responsibility is delegated to them. Local network administrators also administer the local name servers, thus mirroring this delegation.

The acme.com corporate name servers at each site are generally used by all local systems. Systems located at east.acme.com use the local name servers, even if they need access to an off-site system. This works because at corp.acme.com there are root name servers that are configured with the IP addresses of all authoritative name servers for all the acme.com subdomains. Every name server at the five sites is configured to direct requests it can't satisfy to the root name server for resolution. Such an architecture scales to the largest imaginable corporation. Clearly, the hostmasters within acme.com must work together to glue their name servers into a fully functional DNS.

Note that each of the five sites in acme.com are at liberty to assign duplicate names to their equipment. For example, each site might maintain a mail gateway named email. But there isn't a naming conflict because the mail gateway names, when fully qualified, are unique: email.corp.acme.com, email.east.acme.com, email.west.acme.com, email.north.acme.com, and email.south.acme.com.

In practice, when the local network administrators need to change the IP address of email.west.acme.com, they update the local authoritative name servers with the new data at the same time. When the mail server email.acme.corp.com needs to forward messages to email.west.corp.com, it will use the IP address it gets from DNS, which will be the new one.

Sample DNS Configuration Files

The DNS resolver uses */etc/resolv.conf* to determine the local subdomain, up to three name servers, and a search path (see Figure 2-2). The name server daemon *named* reads its configuration file */etc/ named.conf* (or */etc/named.boot*) to locate the directory (such as */var/ named*) for the database files, as shown in Figure 2-4. Database files such as *db.cache* point to other name servers, as shown in Figure 2-5. The two main database record types are address and pointer. Address records contain the IP addresses of names in a subdomain (see Figure 2-6). Pointer records contain the names corresponding to IP addresses (see Figure 2-7).

```
search north.acme.com south.acme.com acme.com
nameserver 127.0.0.1
namersever 10.121.119.60
nameserver 10.121.120.60
```

Figure 2-2   /etc/resolv.conf.
The UNIX operating systems use the text file */etc/resolv.conf* to store the DNS resolver configuration entries. BIND version 8 resolver will append each of the search domains to the query name in an attempt to find a match.

In the interest of completeness, the equivalent to */etc/resolv.conf* in the Windows world is a GUI buried in the Network Control Panel. See Figure 2-3 for an example.

At this point it is important to emphasize that the period at the end of domain names is absolutely critical when configuring your own name server database files. To troubleshoot name server configurations, use *nslookup, dig,* or *named* itself (by sending it a SIGINT signal to dump its database to a file for inspection). To build an initial set of database

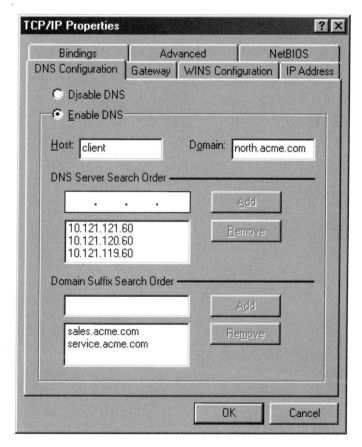

Figure 2-3   DNS Network Control Panel.
The Windows equivalent of */etc/resolv.conf* is the Network Control
Panel. The GUI enforces the (standard) maximum number of DNS
servers to three.

files from */etc/hosts,* your system may have a utility such as
hosts2named or *h2d*.

When a client attempts to resolve a name, a period at the end of that
name implies a fully specified domain, otherwise the SEARCH
domains are tried along with domain name pruning until the name
server succeeds or the SEARCH and pruning process is exhausted.

```
options {
directory "/var/named";
};
// named.local defines localhost
zone "0.0.127.in-addr.arpa" {
type master;
file "named.local";
};
// db.10.121.119 defines  pointer records for north.acme.com
zone "119.121.10.in-addr.arpa" {
type master;
file "db.10.121.119";
};
// db.10.121.120 defines  pointer records for north.acme.com
zone "120.121.10.in-addr.arpa" {
type master;
file "db.10.121.120";
};
// db.10.121.121 defines  pointer records for north.acme.com
zone "121.121.10.in-addr.arpa" {
type master;
file "db.10.121.121";
};
// db.15.24.44 defines pointer records for blommers.org
zone "44.24.15.in-addr.arpa" {
type master;
file "db.15.24.44";
};
// named.north defines address records for north.acme.com
zone "north.acme.com" {
type master;
file "named.north";
};
// named.blommers defines address records for blommers.org
zone "blommers.org" {
type master;
file "named.blommers";
};
// db.15.24.42 defines address records for blommers.org
zone "42.24.15.in-addr.arpa" {
type master;
file "db.15.24.42";
};
```

Figure 2-4   /etc/named.conf,
The DNS name server daemon, *named*, reads its default configuration
file */etc/named.conf* every time it starts or restarts. Therefore, when
the database files change, *named* must be restarted to make the
database changes effective.

```
;         This file holds the information on root name servers needed to
;         initialize cache of Internet domain name servers
.                         3600000   IN  NS    A.ROOT-SERVERS.NET.
A.ROOT-SERVERS.NET.       3600000       A     198.41.0.4
.                         3600000       NS    B.ROOT-SERVERS.NET.
B.ROOT-SERVERS.NET.       3600000       A     128.9.0.107
.                         3600000       NS    C.ROOT-SERVERS.NET.
C.ROOT-SERVERS.NET.       3600000       A     192.33.4.12
.                         3600000       NS    D.ROOT-SERVERS.NET.
D.ROOT-SERVERS.NET.       3600000       A     128.8.10.90
.                         3600000       NS    E.ROOT-SERVERS.NET.
E.ROOT-SERVERS.NET.       3600000       A     192.203.230.10
.                         3600000       NS    F.ROOT-SERVERS.NET.
F.ROOT-SERVERS.NET.       3600000       A     192.5.5.241
.                         3600000       NS    G.ROOT-SERVERS.NET.
G.ROOT-SERVERS.NET.       3600000       A     192.112.36.4
.                         3600000       NS    H.ROOT-SERVERS.NET.
H.ROOT-SERVERS.NET.       3600000       A     128.63.2.53
.                         3600000       NS    I.ROOT-SERVERS.NET.
I.ROOT-SERVERS.NET.       3600000       A     192.36.148.17
.                         3600000       NS    J.ROOT-SERVERS.NET.
J.ROOT-SERVERS.NET.       3600000       A     198.41.0.10
.                         3600000       NS    K.ROOT-SERVERS.NET.
K.ROOT-SERVERS.NET.       3600000       A     193.0.14.129
.                         3600000       NS    L.ROOT-SERVERS.NET.
L.ROOT-SERVERS.NET.       3600000       A     198.32.64.12
.                         3600000       NS    M.ROOT-SERVERS.NET.
M.ROOT-SERVERS.NET.       3600000       A     202.12.27.33
; End of File
```

Figure 2-5 */etc/named.cache.*
The name server uses this file to locate the root name servers. This
example cites the Internet's root name servers at the time of this
writing. For name servers inside a firewalled intranet, the private root
name servers will be specified here.

Loading Factors for DNS Systems

Administrators of DNS are very considerate of the mission-critical
nature of these systems. A high CPU load factor on a name server
would be cause for concern. So, naturally, the administrators frown
upon an NNM system sending bursts of DNS requests in the
hundreds-per-second range all day long. Fortunately, DNS is very
efficiently implemented. All network queries arrive inside lightweight

```
        north.acme.com.  IN    SOA   mylinux.blommers.org.  root.mylinux.blommers.org.
(
                                          1997022700 ; Serial
                                          28800      ; Refresh
                                          14400      ; Retry
                                          3600000    ; Expire
                                          86400 )    ; Minimum
        ;
        ; Name servers
        ;
        north.acme.com.                   IN      NS    mylinux.blommers.org.


        ;
        ; Addresses for the canonical names
        ;
        localhost.blommers.org.           IN      A     127.0.0.1

        router.north.acme.com.            IN      A     10.121.119.64
        router.north.acme.com.            IN      A     10.121.120.64
        router.north.acme.com.            IN      A     10.121.121.64

        email.north.acme.com.             IN      A     10.121.121.60
        fileserver.north.acme.com.        IN      A     10.121.121.61
        imacdv.north.acme.com.            IN      A     10.121.121.62
        printer.north.acme.com.           IN      A     10.121.121.63
        same.north.acme.com.              IN      A     10.121.121.200
```

Figure 2-6   /var/adm/named.north.
This name server configuration file contains the names and
corresponding IP addresses of all systems in the domain
north.acme.com.

UDP packets and all replies are satisfied either from RAM cache or
from another name server. Only simple operations are performed, and
just a little data is transmitted. Disk I/O is created only when *named*
must refresh a domain, restart, dump its database, swap, or write a
syslog message. You definitely want to provision enough RAM to
always keep *named* in memory.

To address the perception that the DNS server might be overloaded, it
is prudent to run a caching-only name server on the NNM system. A
caching-only name server has no authoritative database files, refers
unknown lookups to the name servers listed in its *db.cache* file, and
returns lookups from its RAM cache.

```
     121.121.10.in-addr.arpa.  IN  SOA  mylinux.blommers.org.  root.mylinux.blom-
mers.org.  (
                                        1997022700 ; Serial
                                        28800      ; Refresh
                                        14400      ; Retry
                                        3600000    ; Expire
                                        86400 )    ; Minimum
     ;
     ; Name servers
     ;
     44.24.15.in-addr.arpa.IN NS mylinux.blommers.org.


     ;
     ; Addresses point to canonical names
     ;
     60.121.121.10.in-addr.arpa. IN PTR    email.north.acme.com.
     61.121.121.10.in-addr.arpa. IN PTR    fileserver.north.acme.com.
     62.121.121.10.in-addr.arpa. IN PTR    imacdv.north.acme.com.
     63.121.121.10.in-addr.arpa. IN PTR    printer.north.acme.com.
     64.121.121.10.in-addr.arpa. IN PTR    router.north.acme.com.
     200.121.121.10.in-addr.arpa. IN PTR   same.north.acme.com.
```

Figure 2-7   /var/adm/db.121.121.10.
This name server configuration file contains the IP addresses and
corresponding names of all systems in the 10.121.121 range.

NNM Caching

NNM caching is not the same as DNS caching, but the topic is raised
here so the reader will appreciate that two kinds of caching are at
work.

NNM performs a great many repetitive operations on the same
devices. To avoid potentially expensive lookups of information from
other services, it caches this information to improve overall
performance. This information is written to disk, and survives an
ovstop, *ovstart*, or reboot sequence. The downside of this data
persistence is that external network configuration changes can cause
NNM to lose contact with those devices that changed. The solution is
to issue an *xnmsnmpconf - clearCache* command to clear the SNMP
configuration cache. This should be done when the names and IP
addresses of SNMP-managed devices change and NNM does not

track the change. It may be necessary to delete the offending device from all maps before clearing the SNMP configuration cache. When the NNM database is deleted in preparation for a "starting over" discovery, it is also prudent to clear the SNMP configuration cache.

Primary, Secondary, and Other Mysteries

With the emergence of BIND (Berkeley Internet Name Daemon) version 8, terms like primary server and secondary server are replaced by master server and slave server, respectively. The name of the configuration file */etc/named.boot* is now */etc/named.conf* and the syntax of the file is improved to be more flexible and more readable. There's even a Perl script (*named-bootconf.pl*) to upgrade the configuration file syntax.

BIND version 8 is very desirable because of its many new and important features. It can check that names in the database or in replies conform with RFC 953. There is full control over message logging. An access list of allowed slave servers limits opportunities for crackers/hackers to attempt zone transfers. This also means you need to coordinate with the DNS support group if you want to run NNM as a secondary/slave DNS server. There is a synchronization feature to allow a master server to notify its slave servers of a database update. Dynamic updates are supported by allowing an authorized system to send an update message to the master server. This is especially useful in DHCP (Dynamic Host Configuration Protocol) environments.

The Bigger Picture of a DNS Implementation

This section sums up the relationship among the various architectural elements of a DNS implementation.

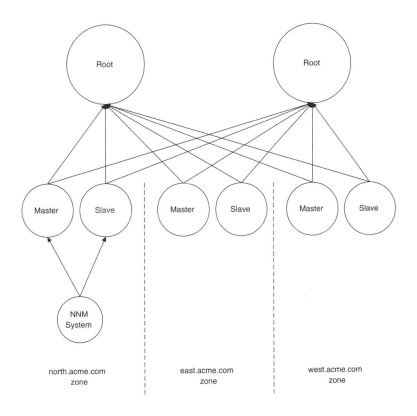

Figure 2-8   The big picture of DNS.
An NNM system is configured with a caching-only name server and refers to the two master servers in the *north.acme.com* zone. These in turn refer to the two root name servers that are configured with the authority records that point to the six name servers.

## CHAPTER 3

Defining the Management Domain

Introduction

The management domain is the set of subnets that NNM manages. Within these subnets NNM will flex its considerable autodiscovery muscles and attempt to manage every device that passes through the discovery filter. NNM ignores subnets that are not in the management domain. That means a remote network device won't be discovered even when the NNM system is otherwise aware of it, which it might be if a network administrator *telnets* to it.

Defining the management domain begins with an understanding of the communities of interest in the network. Users and the equipment they use are located in IP subnets somewhere on the network, so these subnets need to be identified. This helps determine which subnets should be included in the management domain and what parameters should be included in the discovery filter.

Geographies often align with business entities, so simply listing all the subnets in the geography defines the management domain. This is by far the most common arrangement. Listing all the routers in the geography in the *seedfile* is usually an excellent first approximation to defining the management domain.

Estimating the size of a management domain means determining how many managed devices are in it. This is a critical estimate because the NNM system must be adequately sized for this number of managed devices. Several methods for making this estimate are reviewed in this chapter.

When the initial management domain is defined, you need a strategy for defining and discovering it in anticipation of first discovery. This means gathering community strings, SNMP SysObjectID, a.k.a. system object identifiers (OID), and obtaining icons for managed devices. It also means being prepared for a wide range of discovery difficulties, including bad SNMP agents and crashing NNM daemons.

Armed with this strategy, you can prepare your configuration files for first discovery. These files include the *netmon seedfile*, the discovery filter, the DHCP filter, the *xnmsnmpconf* command line input file of community strings, the polling parameters for *xnmpolling*, and the *netmon.noDiscover* file.

Determining the Communities of Interest in a Network

A community of interest may be defined by the end-to-end systems used by a given business unit. For example, site network managers are interested in their community of hubs, bridges, switches, brouters, and routers. A WAN manager in a given country is interested in the community of domestic carriers, service providers, and the effected distribution routers. Web site managers are interested in their community of servers, storage attached network (SAN) disk drives, and printers. e-mail administrators live in their community of e-mail and gateway servers, and keep an eye on DNS because it serves up Mail Exchange (MX) records. Managers of file and print servers work within their community of interest. An engineering group's community of interest is their workstations, servers, and network printers.

Some business units may be geographically dispersed. They have a presence at multiple sites within a corporation. For example, multiple research labs are a community of interest, as are marketing groups and consulting groups.

Some organizations that use the corporate network don't want their equipment to be managed. This may stem from distrust, concern over configuration control and stability of the equipment, or security issues. There may be "unauthorized" or "nonstandard" equipment in use on the network and they don't want it discovered. After all, when it's easier to apologize than to ask for permission, it's prudent to avoid disclosure as well. Simple paranoia may be at work.

For example, as a routine part of configuration management, NNM attempts to download the default page of a web server. The web server logs each page access, which can fill the log file on small local servers in a few weeks. The server administrator does not want NNM to manage their web service, just their equipment.

For another example, consider the network staff that manages the Internet access routers. They monitor the CPU utilization for these routers, which may have huge routing tables. Each SNMP request for a routing table entry is CPU intense. Needless NNM queries of the routing table (a standard aspect of autodiscovery) can raise a router CPU to nearly 100% utilization. It can be difficult to downplay this by noting that the SNMP process in a router has low priority. Short bursts of high CPU utilization due to SNMP operations are acceptable, but continuously high utilization is a bad thing because it can mask real high-CPU problems such as those caused by route flapping.

The IT group providing the NNM tool to the user community must consider the community of interest and use it to help define the NNM management domain.

Discovering communities of interest may be labor-intensive. You need to talk to a lot of people in a lot of departments to understand the organizational network needs. Factoring in the periodic organizational changes and the addition of new network services, it could become a full-time task merely to keep the community of interest profile updated. Centralized versus distributed support structures can have a big impact on the community of interest.

Enter Remote Monitoring (RMON2) technology. Network devices with embedded RMON2 SNMP agents are capable of sampling network packets and identifying the application (via the TCP or UDP port number). External probes can be installed when there aren't any embedded agents available. Tools such as Agilent/HP NetMetrix are able to consolidate the output from many RMON2 probes and display a diagram depicting the network source-destination traffic pairs by application type. This makes identifying communities of interest an automated affair and avoids the pitfall of collecting inaccurate data from interviews.

Geographic Regions and Business Relationships

Geography is the most common and obvious definer for communities of interest. Campus buildings define LAN boundaries and the WAN is the point of demarcation between geographies. The community of interest is often mirrored by the organization that supports it. Multiple small remote sites may be relatively dependent, but for the purposes of defining an NNM management domain, these may be added into a larger geographic domain.

Some corporations have many, nearly autonomous sites with their own independent network staff and support organizations. Some point-to-point WAN links may exist between them as needed, and each may have an Internet connection for their own purposes. Here, the communities of interest closely parallel the autonomous business units.

Another common management domain model defines sites by geography, leaving all network matters within the geography to be managed locally. The local equipment at the site may be used by many independent business subunits within the corporation, but the network itself is managed by a local entity. A central corporate support organization then deals with the WAN links between all these geographies. This includes the routers, DSU/CSUs, and other elements that belong in the corporate IP network backbone.

This model does not force each geographic management domain to locate its staff at the site. Naturally, there is a need for at least one IT employee's presence at all but the smallest of locations. Given the relative ease with which network electronics can be remotely managed, both the staff assigned to manage the site and the NNM system can be located elsewhere. However, the NNM system is generally placed centrally within the physical network it is managing so that it can continue to operate even if the WAN into the site is out of order.

Finally, there is the matter of the IT test and R&D labs. Where are they best situated? The IT group's domain of interest is the entire corporation. The equipment in the labs needs to be "close," in the network sense, to the heart of the corporate network. This is so that new NNM configurations can be tested across selected geographies from a central location with minimum impact on operational NNM systems.

Estimating the Size of a Management Domain

You desperately need to have a handle on the size of the management domain in order to properly size a new NNM system. There is nothing more embarrassing than to deploy an NNM system, go through the autodiscovery and map building process, create user accounts, and then have nothing but complaints about performance from these same users.

Motivated to limit embarrassment, you begin estimating the management domain. How many devices and interfaces will be in it? There are several approaches available to us, so let's review them one at a time.

One estimate for the number of devices is to take the number of subnets in the management domain times the maximum theoretical number of IP addresses available in each subnet. This represents an upper bound on the estimate.

Another estimate (one based on operational metrics) is to visit each DHCP server in the management domain and add up the number of temporary and permanent leases. If the temporary leases are good for several days, and the DHCP servers are sampled late in the week, this should give a pretty accurate high watermark for the number of active devices in the management domain.

A third way to estimate the number of devices is to visit each router and server in the management domain, harvest the ARP caches, and remove duplicate entries from the list. The best time to do the harvesting is during the busiest hour, since ARP cache entries age out of the table. A typical aging value for servers is 20 minutes. A typical aging value for routers is four hours. The ARP cache aging parameter is often tuned by the network managers to suit local needs, since ARP caches are a rich source of information about the network. Allowing their entries to age and drain from the tables represents a loss of valuable data.

Another way to count the number of active devices in the management domain is to ping the IP broadcast address locally inside each subnet and count the number of unique replies. The router can be manually instructed to produce the ping. This works on local LANs. Once again, this misses devices that are not active at the time. Not all systems are capable of pinging the IP broadcast address. Nor do all systems reply to it. This method will underestimate the actual number of active devices.

You can estimate the maximum number of devices in the management domain if you know the number of switch, router, and hub ports available. Since not all ports will be in actual use, this number represents a practical upper limit based on the existing network topology.

Yet another estimate for the number of active devices is to simply count the number of users on the network itself. Assuming that individual workstations are to be managed, this method may be the simplest of all. Almost everyone in an office environment has at least one workstation connected to the network; the ratio will likely be far less in a factory manufacturing environment. Find out how many employees and contractors are located within a management domain, and you have your estimate.

Given that you have all these estimates for the number of devices in the management domain, there is every chance they are all different. You don't know how accurate some of them are. All the more reason to delay the sizing exercise until the successful end of the NNM pilot project. The pilot will yield precise numbers against which our estimation methods can be validated for accuracy.

Depending on the goals of the network managers, the actual number of active devices may deliberately exclude Macintosh, Wintel machines, X-terminals, and Linux workstations. Some hard-core network managers are mainly interested in the network infrastructure itself, and consider DHCP, WINS, DNS, file and print, and web servers to be application systems best managed by an application management platform such as ITO. Non-SNMP devices are not to be discovered or managed under this philosophy.

Whatever the actual size of the management domain turns out to be, it would be foolish to assume that all conditions remain stable. The estimates should be scaled to account for growth that may come from additional systems, new employees, new sites, and corporate mergers. Since our estimates still have uncertainty, it's also prudent to pad them with your favorite fudge factor.

Strategies for Defining and Discovering the Management Domain

You need to develop a plan for first discovery of the management domain. This involves the *seedfile*, community strings, SNMP OIDs for wildcard groups of managed devices, device icons, and cooperation from the management of the managed sites.

You need a list of all the routers that interconnect the LAN segments at each site and the WAN links between the sites. This will form the basis for our first *seedfile*. It's expected that the list will include routers outside the desired area and will miss some inside it. Your strategy is to develop this *seedfile* so that you can start a discovery from scratch if necessary to rebuild any NNM database. If you don't have a clear idea of which routers to include, then NNM can begin with the local router and you can coax the autodiscovery process outwards into the network.

Since network management is based on SNMP, you must be certain that you know all the access (read) community strings for these routers. Hopefully, this community string is "public" and you can leave the NNM defaults alone. Routers may still be discovered, even if their community string isn't known, but they won't be recognized as routers and they'll show on the map as generic IP devices with a generic, faceless icon.

Most network equipment vendors provide icons for their products that usually ship as a component of their element managers and are installed into the NNM icon database automatically. If you want each network device to have a unique and appropriate icon, you'll have to install the element manager.

If no satisfactory icon is available for a particular device on your network, it's time to get comfortable with a bitmap editor. For NNM 6.x and later, standard GIF images are supported. If you prefer to use the Macintosh for icon creation, use the GraphicConverter program or Adobe Photoshop. The software HiJaak Pro or Paint Shop Pro are good bitmap editors for Windows systems when creating GIF files. Be sure to review appendix D of the manual *Managing Your Network with HP OpenView Network Node Manager* for the requirements on these icons. For NNM 5.x the standard UNIX *bitmap* editor is used to create your icons. Note that *bitmap* creates only monochrome bitmaps. See Figure 3-1 for a sample icon creation session.

All network devices with SNMP also provide a sysObjectID (OID) which uniquely identifies it. For in-depth information, you can refer to the section called "Unique Properties of the SNMP MIB Object" in Chapter 11 of the HP manual *Managing Your Network with HP OpenView Network Node Manager*. NNM uses this OID to locate an icon for the device and to determine how it should be displayed. For

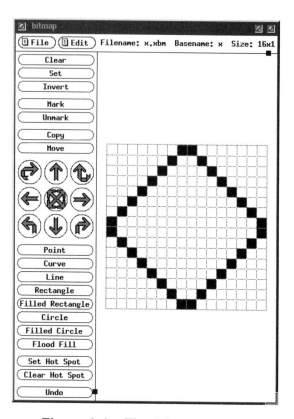

Figure 3-1   The *bitmap* editor.
This X-Windows client application creates and edits monochrome X bit
maps (XBM) and saves them in an ASCII format with the *xbm*
extension. NNM displays these bitmaps inside the device icons on the
map. This makes it easy to identify device types uniquely. For NNM 6.x
and later, GIF bitmap files are supported.

example, routers should be displayed on the Internet submap and
below, while an Ethernet switch should be shown only in and below
the subnet map.

Part of your strategy is to determine the OID of the devices to be
discovered. As with icons, equipment vendors ship their OID
mappings with their element managers and they are installed in the

right directories automatically. If you don't have this OID, and it's not already in HP's *oid_to_sym* and *oid_to_type* files, you'll have to keep track of them and maintain the files as part of the ongoing strategy.

Despite your best efforts at strategy during first discovery, many things will go very wrong. Among them:

- unexpected devices will be discovered
- faceless icons will appear
- local network managers will say you're overloading equipment
- devices will be undiscovered
- subnets will be dangling and unconnected to anything
- overlap with other domains
- rampant discovery of undesired devices
- bad subnet masks will turn up
- routing problems will present themselves
- the *netmon* daemon may spin or core dump
- X-sessions and GUIs will lock up

Each of these mistakes, problems, and issues can be dealt with during the pilot project. Valuable lessons will be learned. Be stout of heart. If you make no mistakes and nothing goes wrong, then you'll have learned nothing.

Configuration Files for Controlling the Management Domain

This section consolidates information about the configuration files NNM uses to define and control the management domain.

The *seedfile* is a simple list of devices that support SNMP. As an indirect result, the *netmon* daemon will use this list at startup time to define the subnets in the initial management domain. Well-connected devices such as routers are recommended, but sometimes other devices with rich ARP caches (such as servers) may be used. To inform netmon about the *seedfile*, insert the command line string "*-s / path/seedfile*" into the *$OV_LRF/netmon.lrf* file, execute *$OV_BIN/ ovaddobj $OV_LRF/netmon.lrf* to register the change, stop *netmon* with *$OV_BIN/ovstop netmon*, and restart it again with *$OV_BIN/ ovstart netmon*. A sample *seedfile* is given in Figure 3-2.

```
routera.domain.com
routerb.domain.com
routerc.domain.com
routerx.domain.com
```

Figure 3-2   A sample *seedfile*.
This is a list of devices meant to define the initial management domain subnets. Well-connected devices such as routers with rich ARP caches make good *seedfile* entries. Server systems may also be entered since their ARP caches will be rich with the IP addresses of their client systems.

The *filters* file provides rules for the *ovtopmd* daemon to include or exclude devices based on their attributes. This is the core tool for controlling what devices are discovered and subsequently placed on the map. The filters listed inside this file are named, and one of these names is given to *ovtopmd* in the *$OV_LRF/ovtopmd.lrf* registration file by adding the parameter "*-f filter_name*", registering the change using *$OV_BIN/ovaddobj $OV_LRF/ovtopmd.lrf*, and stopping and starting the ovtopmd daemon to effect the change. The *filters* file may be used to ensure certain devices are included, such as a list of servers, along with network devices such as routers, switches, and the like. The *filters* file is located in the directory *$OV_CONF/C/*. A sample file is given in Figure 3-3. Note that HP provides a template *filters* file, so back it up in case of human error. The precise filter definition syntax and object attributes available may be found in Appendix A of

```
Filters {
OurSelves "This Node Manager" {
isNode && ("IP Address" == "10.24.5.201")
}
Hosts "The Hosts" {
isNode && (
("IP Hostname" == "box1.acme.com") ||
("IP Hostname" == "box2.acme.com")
)
}
ServerRoomNodes "Devices in local Server Room(s)" {
isNode && (
("IP Address" ~ 10.22.9.*) ||
("IP Address" ~ 10.11.5.*)
)
}
Networks "Any network" { isNetwork }
Segments "Any segment" { isSegment }
Nodes "Any node" { isNode }
Routers "Any Router" { isRouter }
Bridges "Any bridge" { isBridge }
Hubs "Any multi-port repeater" { isHub }
CiscoNodes "All Cisco devices"
{ isNode && ( "SNMP sysObjectID" ~ .1.3.6.1.4.1.9.* ) }
        CiscoAdapterCards "Non-Cisco device with Cisco Workgroup Adapter
Cards"
                { isNode && ( "SNMP sysObjectID" ~ .1.3.6.1.4.1.9.5.2 ) } }
XyplexNodes "Xyplex Terminal Servers"
{ isNode && ( "SNMP sysObjectID" ~ .1.3.6.1.4.1.33.* ) }
        IntermecWirelessNodes "Intermec 2100 Wireless Access Point Nodes"
                { isNode && ( "SNMP sysObjectID" ~ .1.3.6.1.4.1.469.1000.1.6
) }
DatumNTPNodes "Datum Time Server"
{ isNode && ( "SNMP sysObjectID" ~ .1.3.6.1.4.1.601.99.1.1 ) }
IBMHostNodes "IBM Hosts running TCP/IP"
{ isNode && ( "SNMP sysObjectID" ~ .1.3.6.1.4.1.2.2.1.2.4 ) }
        NetworkGeneralSnifferNodes "Distributed Sniffer Server"
                        { isNode && ( "SNMP sysObjectID" ~
.1.3.6.1.4.1.110.3.1.1.2.1 )}
NetsNSegs "All networks & segments" { isNetwork || isSegment }
}
FilterExpressions {
LocalDiscoveryFilter "Discovery filter for local management domain"
{ (CiscoNodes && !CiscoAdapterCards) ||
        XyplexNodes || IntermecWirelessNodes ||
    DatumNTPNodes || IBMHostNodes ||
                NetworkGeneralSnifferNodes ||
        ServerRoomNodes || Hosts || OurSelves }
NetInfrastructure "Any network connecting device and what they connect"
{ Routers || Bridges || Hubs || NetsNSegs }
NetBackbone "Networks and gateways/routers"
{ Routers || Networks }
}
```

Figure 3-3   A sample *filters* file.
This hand-edited *filters* file contains a collection of named filter expressions. The *ovtopmd* daemon can be configured to use one of them for a topology filter. You can specify a discovery filter defined in *filters* using the *$OV_BIN/xnmpolling* GUI directly at the command line or from the *ovw* menu.

the document *A Guide to Scalability and Distribution for HP OpenView Network Node Manager.*

It is important to note that NNM uses filters in four different ways. All are defined in the file *$OV_CONF/C/filters* and all have the same syntax. These filters are called the Discovery Filter, Map Filter, Persistence Filter, and Topology Filter.

A **Discovery Filter** controls what NNM discovers. The filter is applied in a pulldown menu called *Options:Network Polling Configuration:Discovery Filter Option*. The precise location of the menu depends on the version of NNM and on any local menu customization.

A **Map Filter** determines what objects are displayed on the *ovw* map. It is applied using the pulldown menu *Options:Map Configuration*. Again, the location of the menu depends on the version of NNM and on any local menu customization.

A **Persistence Filter** places filtered objects into memory and immediately places discovered objects on the map if they pass the filter. This supports tightly integrated third-party applications that depend on objects being in memory. It is applied from the pulldown menu *Options:Map Configuration:IP Map*, and the exact menu location is NNM-version dependent.

A **Topology Filter** operates at the collection station to control what objects will be passed to the management station. The filter name is defined in the *$OV_LRF/ovtopmd.lrf* file.

SNMP community strings are stored with a host of other SNMP configuration information. This information is controlled with the *$OV_BIN/xnmsnmpconf* GUI. When a device is found to have a non-default read community string and no amount of arm twisting will convince the device administrator to change it (to "public"), then *xnmsnmpconf* is the tool for informing NNM. Otherwise, it won't be possible for NNM to manage the device. A screenshot of *xnmsnmpconf* is given is Figure 3-4. Refer to the *xnmsnmpconf* online manpage for details.

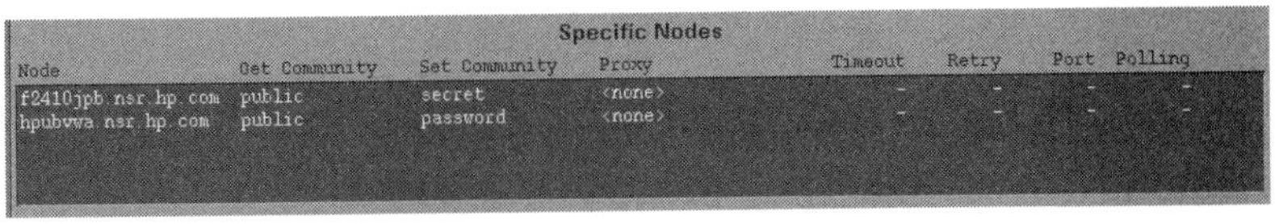

Specific Nodes							
Node	Get Community	Set Community	Proxy	Timeout	Retry	Port	Polling
f2410jpb.nsr.hp.com	public	secret	<none>	-	-	-	-
hpubwva.nsr.hp.com	public	password	<none>	-	-	-	-

Figure 3-4   A sample SNMP configuration screenshot.
This graphical user interface to NNM lets the network manager define SNMP community strings, several SNMP time-out values, and the status polling interval. Incorrect community strings will result in poor autodiscovery performance. For example, a router may be discovered as a simple non-SNMP device if the correct community string is not defined here.

Note that for large networks with many non-default SNMP community strings, it isn't practical to use the GUI because it's just too labor-intensive. Instead, use the command line interface for *xnmsnmpconf*, which allows configuration data to be read from a plain text file.

Imperfect SNMP agents are found in real networks. Occasionally, a badly behaving SNMP agent will confuse *netmon*, causing it to core dump, spin in an infinite loop, or simply waste a thread by polling the same device endlessly. If sufficient logging and tracing is enabled for *netmon* (*netmon -M 63* is fully verbose), then the *$OV_LOG/netmon.trace* file will show the offending device. To prevent *netmon* from continually "stumbling" across these offending devices, place their IP addresses, one line each, in the *$OV_CONF/netmon.noDiscover* file.

NNM's polling parameters are stored in the *$OV_CONF/polling* file. They're intended to be configured using the *xnmpolling* GUI (or appropriate command line options), as shown in Figure 3-5.

During initial discovery, it may be prudent to turn off the auto adjusting polling feature and instead adopt a fixed interval (of 5 to 15 minutes) to ensure NNM retains its aggressive discovery behavior. This may save considerable time during the initial discovery for the pilot, but it's not necessary operationally after initial discovery of the

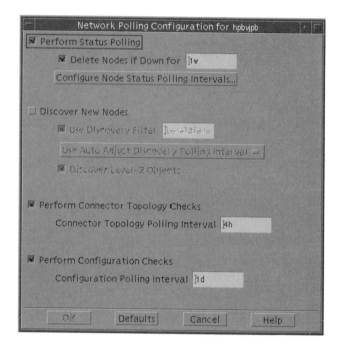

Figure 3-5   The polling GUI.
This is the graphical interface to all NNM polling functions. It is used to turn off polling, turn off autodiscovery, control autodiscovery's aggressiveness, and define the interval for topology and configuration checking.

production NNM systems. Note that it's possible to turn discovery off with this GUI. Don't do that unintentionally.

?!

## CHAPTER 4

The Excitement of First Discovery

Introduction

First discovery of your network is the best of times. It's like the first telling of a great story, a vacation to a new and wonderful land, or a new career full of promise. Cherish the experience, oh network manager, for hard work follows as surely as night follows day.

First discovery is often done without a *seedfile* in place. The default management domain is the set of subnets connected to the NNM system and where only full discovery can occur. This environment is often a test lab. The purpose of discovery is to verify correct cooperation of the network infrastructure with NNM. Any obvious problems will be found early in the game.

With no *seedfile*, the management domain expands as layer after layer of newly discovered subnets are manually managed. This carefully and controllably directs NNM into those areas you desire it to go. Newly discovered problem devices are easy to locate and deal with when you discover them slowly and carefully. NNM develops an inventory of network and system equipment, and uncovers all types of configuration problems.

In a large network you don't have the luxury of manually directing autodiscovery at every collection station because it takes too long. Instead, craft a *seedfile*, which is often a list of routers inside the management domain. Taking advantage of our earlier discovery, you can install a discovery filter to ensure that only the desired equipment is discovered. The *seedfile* often misses a few routers and sometimes lists a few that are not in the management domain, so the discovery process is usually augmented with some manual stopping and starting as the *seedfile* is corrected and the database is purged of unwanted devices.

Discovery sometimes seems to fall asleep and new devices don't appear as rapidly as usual. The fix is to instruct NNM to poll nearby routers and switches. This forces *netmon* to harvest their ARP caches immediately, hopefully identifying the IP addresses of shy devices. Sometimes a simple *ping* does the trick.

Non-uniform SNMP community strings are a curse upon the network and a curse upon the administrator who has to configure them into NNM. NNM discovery will not work with incorrect community strings. It's better to standardize "public" on the community string and use access control lists to implement device security. This is mainly an issue in a large network. In a small network it's much easier to use non-uniform community strings.

The performance of discovery is directly tied to the *netmon* daemon. The *netmon.lrf* file provides a place to install *-q* and *-Q* options to control the size of the *ping* and SNMP queues. The performance of *netmon* can be tracked graphically using the pulldown menu *Performance:Network Polling Statistics*. You can also monitor the ICMP polling queue with the command:

> *snmpget localhost nnmICMPSecsUntilNextPoll*

and the SNMP polling queue can be monitored with the command:

> *snmpget localhost nnmSNMPSecsUntilNextPoll*

As discovery stabilizes, the NNM Internet submap (a.k.a. the Internet Submap) often becomes very crowded as the icons shrink to mere specks on the LANscape. Containerizing the Internet submap and adjusting level 2 discovery parameters are ways to control the map clutter.

Containerizing the Internet submap requires a strategy to ensure that the map remains consistent across multiple, redundant management stations. Otherwise, users will be faced with different maps under fail-over conditions.

Map customizations represent a considerable investment in time and energy. Maps should be saved and backed up as often as changes are made to the Internet submap.

Map builders across a large company should share their best practices with each other in the interest of efficiency and cooperation. Given the interdependence of management stations and collection stations, changes made in one place affect at least the management stations.

Discovery Without a *seedfile*

What? You don't want to define a *seedfile* at all? You want to start up NNM and let it start discovery without one? What is the management domain in this case? It's the local subnet on which the NNM system is located. Discovery will use the routing table, interface table, and ARP cache of the NNM system. The routing table will suggest local routers. The interface table will suggest local subnets, so there may in fact be multiple subnets in the initial management domain. The ARP cache will provide a list of IP addresses as candidates for autodiscovery.

When the shouting is over, the default Internet submap will show the managed local subnets connected to the NNM system, the managed routers present on each subnet, and all the unmanaged (wheat color) subnets (actual and secondary) present on other interfaces on these routers. Autodiscovery will stop at this point and focus only on the managed subnets. If there's no discovery filter defined, then every IP addressable device will eventually be discovered, assuming their IP address is found in the ARP cache of some local SNMP-enabled device that has been discovered. Routers and server ARP caches are generally rich sources of local IP addressable devices.

Autodiscovery also knows how to take advantage of the MAU (media access unit), repeater, and bridge MIBs (management information bases) in intelligent hubs, bridges, and switches. Any such conforming devices will allow NNM to find which physical port devices are connected to what port, even if those devices don't have an IP address. The result can be a very accurate representation of the physical topology.

Why limit discovery to just the local subnets? Perhaps you want to check out the basic NNM installation, verify that autodiscovery works, and do it on a local subnet without impacting the rest of the corporate mission-critical network. You want to verify that the Ethernet switches are working properly and that NNM laid out the physical topology accurately.

Manually Guided Discovery

Given that you have now discovered the initial management domain, our next step might well be to cautiously manage (using the pulldown menu *Edit:Manage Objects*) a few subnets connected to the local routers. This expands the management domain accordingly, which will trigger NNM to autodiscover within these new subnets. Assuming the SNMP community strings are already defined in NNM, new routers will undoubtedly be discovered in the newly managed subnets, and the Internet submap will sprout new routers with new unmanaged subnets attached. By proceeding carefully while allowing the autodiscovery process to converge, it is possible to manually guide NNM through the desired management domain. This process may add a few hours to the discovery process, but it is a controlled friendly process that can be reversed at any point by unmanaging (using the pulldown menu *Edit:Unmanage Objects*) unwanted portions of the network map.

Another advantage of a manually directed discovery is that any troublesome SNMP agents will be easier to identify. For example, if you just managed a subnet, and a minute later (after discovery has stabilized) the *netmon* daemon core dumps, then it's immediately clear where the problem device is located.

If you want to study the impact of autodiscovery on a Cisco router CPU, you can monitor the *busyPer* MIB variable and observe how it rises and falls as NNM harvests its ARP cache, routing table, and interface table. You can use the MIB browser for this purpose

(*Tools:SNMP MIB Browser*) and press the graph button to automatically poll and graph this data.This type of data is helpful in educating network managers about the impact NNM will have on their routers, and reassure them that it won't hurt their normal operation one bit.

Another advantage of manually directed discovery is that you will find all kinds of errors along the way, one at a time. An icon may be missing, a community string may be incorrect, a switch may have old firmware that limits NNM's autolayout capabilities, or a device may incorrectly pass the discovery filter because of a typo.

A final advantage of a manually guided discovery is that devices that are hard to discover are characterized. For example, devices that don't communicate with other devices on remote subnets won't have ARP cache entries in the local routers. In such cases, just manually *pinging* these devices on the NNM system will let NNM discover them. This is because the *netmon* daemon listens on a raw ICMP (internet control message protocol) socket, picks up the *pinging* activity, and harvests the responding device's IP address.

Initially, as new subnets and routers are discovered and managed, you will want to allow NNM to redraw the Internet submap. At some point, however, as this map becomes cluttered, you should turn autolayout off for the Internet submap and drag icons into appropriate positions. This is fairly painless because you're in total control of the discovery process.

Discovery Guided by a *seedfile*

After performing a few manual discoveries, you will develop the necessary confidence and data to automate the process. Armed with a list of routers in the management domain, you can create the *seedfile*, delete the object, topology, and map database, and restart the NNM daemons. Since this process is intended to be repeatable, it's common to delete the database multiple times until all the configuration files, including the *seedfile*, are just right and discovery proceeds the way you intend.

Remember to place the *seedfile* in a safe and stable location independent of the NNM installation tree, such as */opt/config/seedfile*. Assign ownership and permissions to the *seedfile* as appropriate to your local management processes.

To delete the NNM object, topology, and map database (this assumes the flat file database of NNM 6.x and later), there are two options. To keep the old database around, perform these steps:

• stop the daemons with *$OV_BIN/ovstop*

• rename the *openview* directory with *mv openview openview.old.* Pre-NNM 6.1. delete old event log files with *rm $OV_LOG/xnmevents.**. for NNM 6.1 *cd $OV_DB/eventdb ; rm -rf $OV_DB/eventdb/*/**

• clear the SNMP cache with *$OV_BIN/xnmsnmpconf -clearCache*

• start *ovwdb* with *$OV_BIN/ovstart ovwdb*

• execute the command *$OV_BIN/ovw -fields*

• start the daemons with *$OV_BIN/ovstart*

To remove the database instead of saving it, just delete the entire subdirectory (*rm openview/*/**) instead of renaming it in the above steps. Note that alarms may be deleted.

The process of deleting the database and starting over again may be necessary because the *seedfile* is usually incomplete at first. It may contain routers outside the intended management domain or be missing routers in the intended management domain. As you test the new *seedfile*, new problems will emerge, necessitating another round of discovery. A final database scrub and rediscovery is needed to validate the final *seedfile*.

Note that if you merely want to add a router to the *seedfile*, there's no need to scratch the database. Just stop and start *netmon* to force it to read the *seedfile* again. If you want to delete a router from the *seedfile*, and if it's easy to delete the unintentionally discovered topology by hand, then do so, and stop and start *netmon* again.

What do you do if the *seedfile* is accidentally erased and there is no backup? You may go back to your notes and retype the file. After all, the file is probably only 50-100 lines long. Is there an automatic way, however, to regenerate the list from the NNM database? Why not use *ovtopodump -f filtername* to print out all the routers, where *filtername* is a filter defined in the *$OV_CONF/C/filters* file that correctly matches routers? This list will include routers that have unmanaged subnets attached. Using such routers in the *seedfile* will expand the management domain one layer of subnets and routers outside the current one. Use the Internet submap for guidance and trim the extraneous routers from the *seedfile*.

Note that subnets that are initially discovered from *seedfile* routers are managed by default. Subnets later added to these routers will be unmanaged by default. For a non-*seedfile* router that is autodiscovered afterwards, NNM leaves all subnets initially unmanaged except for the already-managed subnet(s) on which the router has interfaces.

Discovery driven by a *seedfile* is very fast most of the time. An exception is during quiet periods on the network when ARP caches have drained and many workstations are turned off. Under such conditions, autodiscovery can be painfully slow. Sometimes it's helpful to include the jump start parameter "-J" in *netmon.lrf*. This allows *netmon* to instruct a remote system with an HP SNMP agent to transmit an ICMP echo request to its IP broadcast address, forcing all active machines on the subnet to answer with an ICMP echo reply. This fills the ARP cache of the remote system, which *netmon* then harvests.

Note that if the NNM system acts as a management station which is not intended to do autodiscovery on its own, the *seedfile* should contain only the names of the associated NNM collection stations.

Demand Poll to Coax Along Discovery

When NNM isn't discovering devices fast enough to suit your needs, you need to intervene. NNM may have backed off its discovery aggressiveness, or the *netmon* configuration checks may be scheduled for a time later than you care to wait. Usually, you have a good idea which device has the necessary information and can direct NNM to poll the node at once. The "Poll Node" menu item, formerly called "Demand Poll," brings up a GUI that is equivalent to the command line *nmdemandpoll*. It forces *netmon* to immediately interrogate the device for its basic configuration, interface table, routing table, and ARP cache. This information usually allows NNM to discover additional devices and topology. However, there are wrinkles to this approach.

Perhaps *netmon* is already busy harvesting a large ARP cache on a slow router, in which case it will be pointless to poll it. The *netmon* SNMP queues may be nearly full, again rendering intervention moot. If local SNMP community strings are wrong, the only helpful intervention is to correct them. The NNM system itself may be temporarily overloaded, robbing *netmon* and the database daemons of needed CPU cycles.

Polling a node is more potent than *pinging* it. Recall that *netmon* listens on a raw ICMP socket for new IP addresses in the management domain, and schedules a poll anyway. A manual poll simply changes when *netmon* polls the node. Once a device is experiencing a poll, the device CPU utilization will rise dramatically, accompanied by a spike in network traffic.

Network maintenance is often scheduled over a weekend. New switches may be installed and old ones removed. Network traffic is low during the off hours—ARP caches may be drained and autodiscovery may have backed off. It may be prudent to write a UNIX *cron* job to sweep the network electronics with an *nmdemandpoll* script.

Note that NNM is very stubborn about removing information from its database. NNM may retain old interfaces for a reconfigured or replaced switch even while newly discovered interfaces are added. Polling the switch won't help. Deleting the switch and pinging it is often the quickest way to fix this because the switch will be rediscovered in its current configuration.

The Curse of Multiple SNMP Community Strings

NNM starts with a single global default community string, which is initially set to "public." You can also inform NNM about specific community strings based on a range of IP addresses (wildcard), or community strings for specific devices. Security conscious network managers often use a variety of community strings to prevent hackers/ crackers from obtaining information about the network from SNMP agents. It is the author's experience that tremendous grief results from this approach to security, and so, wherever practical, access lists (such as those used in the Cisco IOS to limit access to a service via a list of allowed clients) should be used instead.

You may receive push-back from system and network administrators if you approach them to change SNMP community strings to make your life as an NNM administrator easier. Explain that a uniform SNMP community string policy reduces administrative overhead for all concerned. Point out that a standardized default community string improves autodiscovery and NNM's effectiveness. For cases where a non-default community string is important, let your colleagues know that you can inform NNM of any non-default community strings for the systems and network devices NNM manages.

DNS Problems

One area of grief is DNS, badly implemented name servers, and security features in DNS. For example, consider a router with a large number of primary and secondary IP addresses. Suppose that a client such as NNM requests the name for 1.1.1.1 (using the standard resolver). As a security precaution, the resolver insists that the resulting name should map back to the same IP address. But some DNS name servers truncate long lists of IP addresses (because they don't revert to TCP for replies longer than 512 bytes), then the original lookup request returns no name. This will confound NNM because it can't map the IP address to a name, and thus can't use the proper community string to communicate with it.

Another example of DNS grief is simply a change in the name and IP mappings. If a device's IP address is changed, and if DNS properly reflects it, the community string isn't going to be correct if NNM is still configured with the old IP address, and NNM will therefore fail to communicate with the device SNMP agent.

Obviously, if the DNS is configured and implemented properly, and if you can use names instead of IP addresses to associate custom SNMP community strings, and if you keep NNM's SNMP configurations up to date, you can avoid these problems. In a large, distributed, dynamic corporate network that's a lot of ifs.

Fine-Tuning the Discovery Filter

First discovery is quite a thrill. Watching the Internet submap as NNM discovers a new network is always a fresh experience. Once that discovery is complete, it's time to assess what's in the database. The discovery filter is often initially left open to identify every IP addressable device. This bloats the NNM database. So now it's time to inventory all the OIDs on the network. Many familiar OIDs will be present, but some unexpected ones are found that have to be tracked down. NNM ships with a large, helpful list of well-known vendor OIDs, but your network may host some mystery vendors.

Armed with fresh insight into the network components, you will probably have to modify the *filters* file to include additional sysObjectIDs and reject others. Using the sysObjectID in the discovery filter is a good idea because it offers a simple, elegant method to define devices independently of other difficult-to-define and hard-to-manage attributes such as IP addresses, which are subject to change in a real network. You have to decide what devices you want to discover and place on the map. Recall from Chapter 3 that a map filter determines what devices are shown on a given map, while a discovery filter determines what devices *netmon* admits into the database.

Note that it's not necessary to scrub the database and rediscover the network merely to remove devices that you've decided not to include in the *filters* file. Executing *ovtopofix -f filtername* will subject the current database to the revised discovery filter *filtername* and remove devices that don't pass the filter.

One strategy for developing a discovery filter is to define all network equipment by OID. A note of caution: Some vendors include the O/S version as part of their sysObjectID. If you upgrade the O/S on one of these systems, then your filter may no longer work. Use wildcards to get around this, i.e., wildcard the O/S part of the OID. This technique works well for network managers who want to manage only their infrastructure. Administrators of file and print servers will usually want to see only their file servers, network printers, and network scanners on the map, so their NNM system will have a different discovery filter. If both users share the same NNM system, then the discovery filter will have to pass both sets of devices, and a map filter can be defined to give each user the view of the devices they want to manage.

Tuning and Observing *netmon* Queues

During first discovery you may notice that *netmon*'s CPU utilization is remarkably lower than expected, the rate of discovery is correspondingly depressingly low, or device status changes are displayed late by NNM. Yet, the overall system utilization is quite low. You want to know why *netmon* isn't discovering devices faster and what you can do to improve the situation.

Enter the *netmon* optional *-q ICMP-queue-length* and *-Q SNMP-queue-length* parameters in the *netmon.lrf* file. Both default to 20 on UNIX systems and 3 on Windows NT systems. These values may be increased according to the following guidelines:

The *ICMP-queue-length* parameter should be increased only if *netmon* is getting behind (as indicated by the queue always being at its maximum) because the operating system buffer for holding incoming ICMP replies may overflow, resulting in random false status changes. The SNMP-queue-length parameters should be increased only if *netmon* is getting behind, because the operating system limits the number of open file descriptors per processes. This is a kernel tunable parameter and the default is often set to 64. (As an aside, note that the *snmpCollect* daemon is similarly constrained.) Remember to record the changes in the *netmon.lrf* file with *ovaddobj* before you stop and restart *netmon*.

The theory behind increasing these maximum queue lengths is that it lets *netmon* issue more outstanding requests. This increases throughput and helps *netmon* keep up with its polling schedule. For example, using the default queue length of 20, you can expect *netmon* to keep up as long as the average response time to SNMP requests is 50 milliseconds or less.

Increasing the maximum SNMP queue length also increases *netmon*'s resistance to slow and unresponsive SNMP agents. For example, on a bad day, *netmon* may be polling 15 slow devices on the network (or perhaps they are located on a remote LAN via a congested WAN link). This limits *netmon* to polling only five other devices at a time for the duration.

How large may these queue limits be? A rule of thumb is 200. After you increase the queue values, check *netmon*'s queue behavior often. Be alert for anomalous behavior in discovery and polling, and check the log files for potential problems caused by too high a queue value.

Check *netmon*'s polling activity using the NNM menu *Performance:Network Polling Statistics*, then wait a minute or so for the 10-second polling samples to demonstrate a graphical trend. A command line method for checking *netmon*'s activity is *netmon -a 5*. This signals the running instance of the *netmon* daemon to dump the size of the *ping* (ICMP) and SNMP lists to *$OV_LOG/netmon.trace*. An effective way to use this feature is to open two shells in separate windows. In the first window type in *tail -f $OV_LOG/netmon.trace* and in the second window type in *netmon -a 5*. Every time you type *netmon -a 5,* the output appears in the other window.

The effectiveness of *netmon* tuning is predicated on the assumption that there are no other inhibitors to its performance. If the NNM disk I/O system is heavily utilized (check this with HP Glance/Plus Motif, the *top* command, or the *iostat* command), tuning *netmon* to increase its throughput will yield no benefits. If the DNS servers are terribly slow, or if a low-bandwidth, highly-utilized WAN link separates the NNM system and its management domain, then tuning *netmon* won't improve performance much.

The *netmon* workhorse is frequently patched, updated, and revised as HP evolves the NNM product. New features and command line arguments come along and some old ones go away. Keep the online manpage handy. Windows NT users should look in the online help for the *netmon* Reference Page. It is usually the most current documentation available because the HP patches often update manpages along with code changes. In this way, new ways to tune *netmon* will come to your attention.

My Window Is Full of Icons

When first discovery is finished, the Internet submap may be filled with a nest of wagon wheels. This is to be expected in corporate networks containing hundreds of routers and thousands of subnets. This large IP-centric display accurately portrays the network's connectivity and is very useful for troubleshooting network problems once you get past first impressions. Still, there is a compelling reason to partition this large map into a few dozen containers. Ease of use is one reason, and response time is a second. The partitions usually represent management domains or geographic regions.

Even inside a subnet icon there may be hundreds of switches, bridges, routers, and segment icons. The panning tool is your friend here, since the task of partitioning each subnet is too labor-intense to be worth the effort.

In a subnet with many switches and hundreds of switch ports, the number of segment icons can be daunting. It's possible to avoid displaying much of the layer 2 clutter using NNM 6.1's *-k segRedux=TRUE* parameter in *netmon.lrf.* It eliminates segments with only two devices and connects them directly. If layer 2 layout isn't of interest, you can use the *-k bridgeMIB=FALSE* option in *netmon.lrf* and no additional segments will be created for switch and bridge ports.

Note that *segRedux* is "on" by default for a clean install of NNM 6.1. It is "off" by default for upgrade situations.

Strategies for Containerizing the Internet Submap

To address the objection that there are too many subnets, routers, and multihomed hosts on the Internet submap, a map builder will add containers (location icons) to the map and label them according to their geography or purpose. Then judicious select, drag, and drop operations will place most of the icons into their appropriate "home" containers. The steps are simple:

- *export MAP_CUSTOMIZATION=true* (NNM 5.x only)

- start *ovw* and create a new map

- open the Internet submap

- turn autolayout off for this submap

- turn overlay off

- create containers by adding and labeling location symbols

- leave routers that connect sites in the Internet submap

- drag site routers into their appropriate site icons

- arrange locations and routers geographically

- export the customization

See Chapter 8, "Map Customization," of the manual *Managing Your Network with HP OpenView Network Node Manager* for reference.

Saving Map Customizations

The environment variable $MAP_CUSTOMIZATION (needed for pre-NNM 6.x only, standard menu item in NNM 6.x) allows *ipmap* to inform *ovw* that two new menu items should be available under the *File* menu to import and export an ASCII customization file. This file records standard information for all the icons in the Internet submap. It does not save customized objects such as manually added connections. The customization file is oh-so-welcome in reconstructing a map. This may be necessary because the map builder ruined the map beyond repair, a collection station had a database crash and had to rediscover its management domain, or the local database consistency was so bad that *ovtopofix* did not have the power to repair it.

A few minor wrinkles may present themselves after importing a map customization. The customization may contain icons not yet discovered, so a warning is issued. A device selection name may have changed, so it's not put into its "home" container but left in the Internet submap. Devices may be discovered that aren't in the customization, and they too are left in the Internet submap. The net result is that the Internet submap is not yet "pretty" due to the orphan icons that have no "home."

Rather than despair over this misfortune, use a simple trick to restore the map to its original state. Follow these steps:

- add a helper[1] container icon to the Internet submap

- drag the helper container to a clear location

- use a selection rectangle to select orphan icons

- drag these orphans into the helper container

- repeat until all orphans are in the helper container

- drag the helper container near the cluster of other containers

- resize the Internet submap window slightly; *ovw* will redraw the map with the original icon sizes

- open the helper container

- drag the orphans into their proper "homes"

- save the customization again

A big benefit of the helper container is that it quickly circumvents the incorrect scaling on the reconstructed map caused by orphans being placed far from the original symbols.

---

1. The term "helper" container is not an official NNM term.

Leveraging Lessons Learned With Other Map Builders

In a large company there will be a need for multiple management stations to ensure high availability of the NNM platform. To achieve full redundancy, each management station takes advantage of the same collection stations. There is every reason to locate management stations in physically independent locations, so they may be managed by different map builders. Yet the maps should look the same if the collection stations are to be useful backups for each other.

To keep the management station maps consistent, the map builders obviously need to agree who will modify the map any given day, so the others can import it without losing local map changes. The map customization file is in plain ASCII text format, but it may be over a megabyte in size, so it should be compressed before e-mailing it. Another way to share the file is to simply FTP it (UNIX way) or share the folder (Windows way) among the NNM systems. A third way to share map customization files is to install a web server on the NNM system and provide a simple web interface to the map customization directory.

Cooperating map builders should share their best practices to minimize the amount of time they spend with their Internet submaps. For example, if one map builder is also a developer skilled at writing OpenView applications with the developer toolkit, and if she wrote a handy utility for aligning columns and rows of map icons, she should share it with her peers.

CHAPTER 5

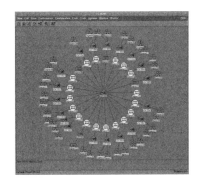

Map Management Strategies

Introduction

Map management includes consideration for where the read/write maps will be displayed so that read-only map users benefit from an up-to-date topology. Possible choices include a dedicated monitor and a virtual network console (VNC).

It's rare to find default NNM maps that are sufficient to meet user needs, so designated map builders will periodically make initial changes and additional minor changes as needed. For large networks with multiple management stations, it's critical to share map changes and back up these customizations periodically.

A common home map is the Internet submap, which is the first map the users see when launching *ovw*. Autolayout is almost always turned off for the Internet submap to retain the icon layout. The map overlay feature is often turned off for the Internet submap so that it remains displayed when users open other submaps.

NNM uses the Bridge-MIB (RFC 1493), MIB II (RFC 1213), the IF MIB (RFC 2233), and the Repeater MIB (RFC 2108) to ferret out how switches, bridges, and repeaters conforming to these standards are connected together.

Onion Peel sells a third-party map management tool capable of enhancing map customization and map appearance.

There is sometimes a need to capture an *ovw* map when troubleshooting a problem, documenting a process, or sharing information. UNIX, Windows, and Macintosh systems acting as X-terminals for NNM are able to take screenshots and process them with native graphics applications. To capture a map, an NNM map snapshot (pulldown menu *Map:Snapshot*) can be taken. This creates a named read-only navigable map, rather than a screen capture.

Modern networks increasingly contain special devices such as routers with secondary and software loopback addresses, multihomed hosts, devices with transient IP addresses obtained from DHCP, virtual LANs (VLAN), adapters (such as HSSI) with numerous subinterfaces, and frame relay links. Map customization will maximize NNM's usefulness to display them.

Where The Read/Write Map Is Displayed

When no one is looking at the network map, is NNM still monitoring the network? Of course! The NNM daemons are always running in the background. The *netmon* daemon in particular continues to poll all managed devices for status and configuration. The *snmpCollect* daemon continues to collect SNMP data. The event subsystem continues to collect events, traps, and to react to configured actions. The database is continually updated as *netmon* discovers new objects and as nodes that are down too long are deleted. The maps are another matter.

You've noticed that every time you launch *ovw*, a map synchronization occurs. Look closer and you will see *ovw* remove icons, add new ones, and change the status of others. Map synchronization takes only a few seconds if the map was recently closed, but it can take a great deal of time if the map hasn't been open for days. The synchronization process lets *ovw* update the map database with the aid of *ipmap*. All events that occurred since the last time the map was open must be processed to ensure the map is up to date. Note that as long as a read/write copy of a map is open, it is updated dynamically as network events take place. Therefore, a read/write copy of all operational maps should be kept open to keep them current.

Now a read/write map is an editable map, too. Clearly, only the map builders should have read/write access to operational maps, and all other users should open read-only copies of maps. The map builders are the owners of their maps, so by default operational users can only open them in read-only mode. So far, so good. But if the read/write map is not open, then the read-only maps won't get topology updates. One disadvantage of read-only maps is that their users can't take a map snapshot, for which read-write access is required. Read-only maps do get status updates because status can be changed without a map being writable. OK, so this means you need to keep a copy of all writable operational maps open all the time, in a safe place. The map builder still makes any necessary changes at one time or another, possibly on an ad-hoc basis or at scheduled times.

This discussion assumes that NNM is running in a multiuser environment with remote X-Windows or the web as the primary access to the map. It's not necessarily applicable to a small Network Operations Control Center (NOCC) with a single dedicated management workstation and on-site-only access requirements.

Where is a safe place to keep read/write operational maps open? A safe place is important because you don't want a read/write map *ovw* session locking up or terminating for any reason, whether caused by equipment failure or interference from carbon-based units. Here's a list of some possible display locations:

- the map builder's workstation

- a dedicated network X-terminal that nobody accesses

- the NNM console located in a secure location

- the virtual network computing (VNC) console

Given that network management is a 24x7x365.23[1] operation, it's clear that the map builder's workstation is not an appropriate location to display the read/write operational maps. Map builders don't spend the day focusing on just maps, their workstations will be used for other activities; an occasional workstation reboot might be necessary, and even map builders have been known to take vacations.

---

1. This is why we have leap years, remember?

An X-terminal (for the UNIX version of NNM) dedicated to display the read/write maps would be acceptable. This X-terminal could be any of the following:

- a Windows machine running an X-terminal emulator such as Exceed from Hummingbird or Reflection/X from Walker-Richer-Quinn (WRQ)

- a real X-terminal

- a UNIX workstation (for which X-Windows is the standard GUI) such as a RISC HP-UX computer or an Intel-based computer running Red Hat Linux

- a Macintosh running an X-terminal emulator such as MacX from Apple

- any other computer capable of running X-Windows

The dedicated X-terminal can be located in a network operations and control center (NOCC) in plain sight with the screen locked but not covered. The actual submap displayed would be the one showing the management domain for which the NOCC is responsible.

Another alternative is to display the read/write maps on the console of the NNM system which also runs X-Windows. The display should be locked, but not covered, to prevent interference with the *ovw* sessions. Since the NNM system is available 24x7x365.23, it's an excellent choice. The downside is that the display and keyboard cannot be used operationally, which wastes this resource.

Displaying the read/write maps on the virtual network computing (VNC) console may be the best solution. A VNC can simulate an X-terminal on the UNIX system, so it's always running. To gain access to it, use the *vncview* command, supply a password, and a copy of the VNC display is sent to a large window on your X-terminal display. It's fully interactive. This allows the map builder to attach to the VNC and make map changes at any time of the day or night. The user updates the affected read-only map using the *Map:Refresh* pulldown menu.

VNC was developed by AT&T laboratories. To learn more about this free, unsupported, cross-platform software see the FAQ at:

> http://www.uk.research.att.com/vnc/Faq.html

The NNM system administrator will have to write a small shell script that runs at boot time to bring up the VNC environment and launch *ovw* sessions with read/write maps. ITO or a similar tool should monitor these *ovw* sessions to ensure they are always running.

The map builder might need to terminate a remote read/write *ovw* session in order to open a read/write map for editing purposes. The appropriate steps for doing this as safely as possible using NNM 5.x are:

- use *ovwlistsessions* to get the session ID for the read/write map

- use *ovsession -k ID* to gracefully terminate the session

- if *ovw* won't terminate, determine its process ID (PID) and issue a graceful *kill -15 PID* or a brutal *kill -9 PID* as necessary

- issue *$OV_BIN/ovw -rw -map map_name* to edit the map

For NNM 6.x, HP recommends *ovuismpd* be used. Use *ovstatus -v ovuispmd* to list the active *ovw* sessions and *ovstop -c ovuispmd* to gracefully terminate all of them at once. Use *ovstart ovuispmd* to allow users to invoke *ovw* again. Note that *ovpause* causes *ovspmd* to pause *ovuispmd*, suspending the active *ovw* sessions. Finally, *ovresume* causes *ovspmd* to start *ovuispmd*, resuming suspended *ovw* sessions.

Managing Map Customizations

Rule number one for managing map customizations is that they are intended to preserve the location of icons only in the Internet submap. Don't customize the contents of subnets because this information is not saved. Nor are manually added connectors. Don't assume that other customizations will be preserved. All that happens when you import a map customization file is that *ovw* moves icons on the Internet view to their previous locations. Any objects inside icons on the Internet submap are simply placed inside them according to the current database. Since objects are identified by their selection names, changing selection names isn't a good idea, either.

Rule number two is to export map customizations whenever you make a change to a production map. Then back it up to a safe place. Don't assume the nightly backup script will run in time to save your work.

Rule number three is to keep the number of maps to an absolute minimum. Discourage the notion that users can create their own custom maps even if they are not meant for production use. The ideal number of maps is one. Of course, if the user community needs distinctly unique maps, you have to provide them. The more open read/write maps, the more system overhead.

Rule number four is to automatically schedule (use *cron*) at least a weekly database consistency check and repair:

> • terminate all *ovw* sessions
>
> • stop the *netmon* process
>
> • *ovw -mapcount -vuDR*
>
> • *ovtopofix -csh*

Rather than rephrase it, let's read from the *ovw* man page: "*ovw -mapcount* is a troubleshooting command that checks the consistency between the map database maintained by *ovw* and the object database maintained by *ovwdb*. It checks the values of map reference counts stored in the object database and corrects these values, if necessary." No other *ovw* sessions should be running at this time.

Again from the man page: "The *ovtopofix* command is used to detect and correct inconsistencies that may have developed between the IP topology database maintained by *ovtopmd* and the database maintained by *ovwdb* for the *ovw* command." The *netmon* daemon must be stopped while *ovtopofix* runs.

Using Autolayout and Overlay Features

A few minor but very user-friendly features available in NNM are the autolayout and the overlay features.

The Internet submap is usually customized. A great deal of sweat equity is built into this one map, and a single indiscretion can wipe out the work. Therefore, the very first step in map customization is to turn "autolayout off for this submap." Be very cautious not to turn "autolayout off for all submaps" because you'll find a lot of icons on top of each other inside the subnets and segment submaps later on.

Map overlay is a very handy, time-saving feature. Turn it off for the Internet submap. Make the Internet submap the home map. When a user opens the map, it displays the Internet submap as intended. As the user double-clicks on subnets and containers, they open in a separate window, leaving the Internet submap open and available. It's difficult to convey how incredibly convenient this little feature can be.

How NNM Uses the Repeater and Bridge MIBs

Let's follow the sequence of events as NNM goes about autodiscovery. The *netmon* daemon reads a router name from its *seedfile,* polls it, and finds a new interface. The appropriate subnet is added to the topology database. Since the router is in the management domain, so are all its subnets, and the new subnet is put in the managed state. A segment with the unique name *Segment1* is created and a router icon is placed inside, representing the interface on that subnet.

As new IP addresses are discovered, perhaps from the router's ARP cache, those that happen to have an IP address on the new subnet are placed in *Segment1*. When a new repeater or switch is discovered, it is polled to determine how many interfaces it has, and then the repeater or bridge MIB is read to harvest Ethernet (a.k.a MAC) addresses and the ports they are located on. If any of the devices in *Segment1* have a MAC address found in the switch, a new segment is created, and the device is moved from *Segment1* to the new segment.

As more switches and repeaters are discovered, *ovw* will lay them out as accurately as possible. As long as all the switches, bridges, and repeaters are assigned IP addresses in the same subnet, the layout will be accurate. If the router interface in our example is configured with secondary addresses, and if some of the switches, repeaters, and bridges are assigned IP addresses on all of them, then autolayout will not be able to accurately create the topology map. This is because *ovw* inherently discovers an IP subnet hierarchy. If a switch, bridge, or repeater does not support the repeater or bridge MIBs, then the layer 2 representation inside the subnet won't be accurate. Nonconforming devices will appear to have just one interface. Devices connected to them will remain on *Segment1*. For that reason, it behooves the NNM administrator to pay special attention to *Segment1* in all subnets in search of nonconforming network devices.

Note that if NNM is configured with the incorrect community string for a switch, bridge, or repeater, then there's no indication its network equipment and the icon will be left in *Segment1*.

NNM will poll the interface MIB for devices to obtain the extended interface name to obtain the slot and port numbers of each segment. The user can right-click a connection symbol to display this information.

Third-Party Map Management Tools

Onion Peel Solutions (OPS) produces a comprehensive map management product (Amerigo and Amerigo/L2) that gives a great deal of control over NNM maps, including customizing, saving, and restoring them.

Taking Screenshots of Maps

No book written by this author is complete without the obligatory screenshot section. This is that section.

NNM maps often find their way into reports, manuals, posters, training materials, and documentation. These screenshots result in fairly sizeable files (about one megabyte) because most NNM maps display best full-screen (because larger icon bitmaps can be chosen). For large networks, a minimum screen resolution of 1280x1024 is recommended; 1600x1200 is desirable.

Many find that the NNM menu item for printing a map produces a poor black and white presentation. There are no grey scales and color is lost too. Since a printout can't be included in an electronic report without scanning the paper, you need other methods to capture map images. The methods given in this section can be used to capture any window on the screen, but our focus is on maps.

NNM maps use up to 256 colors because the HP OpenView Windows system uses the classic shared X-Window color palette scheme. This means that other applications concurrently sharing the palette may make less colors available to *ovw*, potentially ruining the color scheme. Start *ovw* and open your map first. This 256-color limit means you can save the final screen shot as a GIF file, let the lossless LZW (Lempel Ziv Welch) compression algorithm reduce the image file to a very manageable size, and retain color fidelity in the process.

Let's discuss screenshots in the UNIX X-Window environment first. Every window on the screen has a window id which can be determined by typing *xwininfo* in a terminal window and clicking the cross hair on the window of interest. An example of a window id is 0x3800011. You don't want the target window to be partially covered by any other window unless you really intend to capture the overlapping portion. So, assuming you want to maximize an *ovw* map window and capture it, proceed as follows:

- get the *ovw* map window id using *xwininfo*

- type *sleep 10 ; xwd -id window_id -frame > mapname.xwd*

- expand the *ovw* map window to fill the screen

- wait up to 10 seconds until you hear the two beeps. The window screenshot is now saved in *mapname.xwd*

The *sleep 10* command gives you 10 seconds to move the target *ovw* window into position. The *xwd* command captures the window and the *-frame* option includes the window borders. You can convert the XWD file format to a more usable format using UNIX graphics utilities such as *display* (part of ImageMagic) or The Gimp. ImageMagic and The Gimp are open source applications. If you use a Macintosh for your publishing, then use GraphicConverter to open XWD files. If you publish on a Windows machine, then use HiJaak Pro 5.0 from Imsisoft to read XWD files.

Next let's consider the case of a Windows machine running an X-Windows emulator such as Hummingbird Exceed. Assume that Exceed is configured to operate in rootless mode. This means each X-Window is displayed as a regular window. Capture the *ovw* map window as follows:

- maximize the ovw map window to fill the screen

- simultaneously press the Alt and PrtSc keys; the image is sent to the clipboard

- switch to your publishing application and paste the graphic

If you want to save the map screenshot in an image file rather than paste the image into your publishing application, perform these steps:

- switch to your favorite graphics application

- choose *Edit:Paste as new image* from the menu

- reduce the number of colors to 256

- save the image in a GIF format

Finally, if you run X-Windows in rootless mode on a Macintosh, then the *ovw* map windows are standard Mac OS windows and the standard key presses will capture the window. Maximize the *ovw* map window and do one of the key presses in Table 5-1 to capture the window.

Table 5-1   Macintosh Screen Capture Key Presses

Key Press Sequence	Method of Capture
command shift capslock 4	capture window to file Picture$n$
command shift 4	capture selection to file Picture$n$
command shift control capslock 4	capture window to the clipboard
command shift control 4	capture selection to clipboard

Special Types of Network Devices

This section is intended to capture in one place various exotic, special, and interesting network devices that affect how maps appear in NNM.

IP routers are special because they have so many different types of IP addresses configured, such as:

- natural loopback address of 127.0.0.1 or similar address on network 127

- a hot standby address that can move between routers on the same LAN segment to provide a stable routing address in the event of a hardware failure. The protocol is called hot standby routing protocol (HSRP)

- a stable primary software loopback address that is fixed and identifies the router even when its interfaces are reconfigured

- an administratively down interface with an IP address also configured for an interface on another router

- an interface with no IP address (unnumbered)

- an interface with one IP address

- an interface with one or more secondary IP addresses

NNM discovers and displays unnumbered links between routers unless prohibited by the *netmon-k discoverLevel2Nets=false* option. The administratively down interface with the duplicate IP address is ignored if the *netmon -I* option is configured. This option is best explained by quoting from *Managing Your Network with HP OpenView Network Node Manager*:

"This option causes netmon to ignore a duplicate IP address if it is in an administratively down state. That is, if an interface with a duplicate IP address is discovered, and the interface is in an administratively down state, it is ignored. If a duplicate IP address interface is discovered which is not in an administratively down state, but the existing interface is in an administratively down state, the existing interface is deleted from the database, and the new interface is added. In both cases, no duplicate IP address event is generated."

Interfaces with one or more secondary IP addresses result in additional subnet icons being created, even though they share the same topology, which results in an inaccurate topology.

A multihomed device that passes the discovery filter will show on the Internet submap if its SNMP agent indicates it does IP forwarding. If the agent is wrong about that, or if the other interfaces are administratively down, or if you don't want the device promoted to the Internet submap as if it were a router, then create an entry for it in the *oid_to_type* file (if necessary) and apply the *M* flag.

Some devices don't have stable IP addresses because they physically move around from one subnet to another, or because they depend on dynamic host configuration protocol (DHCP) and may lose the lease on an IP address and get a different one back. This means the device will seemingly go down, and then up again, or it may appear to have two IP addresses. To deal with DHCP, you need to know the range of IP addresses administered by DHCP and define a corresponding filter in the *filters* file. The rest of the explanation is from the *netmon* man page:

"NNM events which can be issued from external applications, such as a DHCP server, to give NNM notice of DHCP-related activities. They cause netmon to allocate or release, respectively, the IP address related to the interface with the physical address specified in the event. The interface must already exist in the IP network identified by the IP address and subnet mask in the event. The IP address must also pass the DHCP address filter specified in *$OV_CONF/polling* and the DHCP polling options must be enabled."

Port Aggregation Protocol (PAgP) allows up to four fast Ethernet ports to be bonded together under a single IP address to increase performance. The feature works between Cisco routers, switches, and HP9000 systems. The new pseudo interface defined by this arrangement is advertised as another interface by SNMP and even the link speed reflects the aggregate bit rate.

HSSI router interfaces operate up to T3 speeds and may be partitioned into subinterfaces. This is often seen in frame relay networks, where multiple permanent virtual circuits (PVC) terminate on a single high-speed interface. The subinterfaces all appear in the SNMP interface table, and the line speed is manually configured into the SNMP agent to reflect the desired interface speed.

WAN links are generally serial lines between two remote points. When NNM discovers a point-to-point serial link between two routers, it will not draw a subnet icon. For a frame relay WAN circuit, NNM will draw the subnet. Now if all frame relay interfaces are numbered on the same IP subnet, then *ovw* will draw this one subnet. But if this IP subnet is itself subnetted further, then individual PVCs will be shown as distinctly different subnets, mimicking a point-to-point connection through the frame relay cloud.

## CHAPTER 6

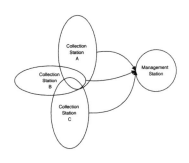

Distributed Network Management

Introduction

Distributed network management is implemented in NNM by defining a relationship between high-level management stations that show a global view of the network, and low-level collection stations that actually discover and poll their patch of the network quilt.

Preparing the collection station requires a properly configured object export filter, a defined *set-community-name*, and a fully discovered management domain.

Determining which devices and objects to export is done at the collection station and it applies to all management stations. Avoid exporting too many objects to avoid overwhelming the management station. For large networks, it is sufficient to export subnets and routers.

Historical SNMP data accumulated by the collection station is not exported to the management station. Therefore, if such data is desired, it will have to be collected in duplicate at the management station, or the user will have to access the collection station directly to display it.

To manage dozens of NNM systems efficiently it is recommended that HP MeasureWare and ITO agents be loaded on them all, and that a central system running ITO and PerfView manage them.

The management station initiates the relationship with the collection stations. It should be configured with the collection station *set-community-name* values or the relationship cannot be established. For large networks you can turn off autodiscovery on the management station and use a *seedfile* to define the collection stations.

Adding a collection station after the management station map has been customized will import additional topology. With careful map management on the management station, the existing customization can be preserved and the additional topology can easily be moved into the proper container.

Occasionally, a collection station database is rebuilt. This causes the managed devices and objects to be removed and imported again. By following a short procedure, the Internet submap at the management station can be restored to its former state with little effort.

The Management Station and Collection Station Relationship

You begin your understanding of distributed network management with a clear definition of the two NNM systems in the hierarchy. Let's emphasize that there are exactly two levels in this hierarchy and that any trickery to attempt to generalize this won't work, at least as of NNM 6.1 or previous versions. The higher level NNM system in the hierarchy is the management station and the lower level NMM system is the collection station. See Figure 6-1.

The collection station performs autodiscovery, status polling, configuration checking, SNMP data collection, receives SNMP traps, and generates events. It maintains a live database and is authoritative for all this information since it directly manages devices within its management domain. Users log onto the collection station and run *ovw* sessions as usual. Large corporate networks may have dozens of collection stations, each representing a patch of the quilt that covers the enterprise.

A collection station does not need to run the *ovrepld* daemon, but it is enabled by default. A filter definition in the *filters* file defines which objects the collection station will pass on requests to a management station via SNMP. This filter is defined using the command line option *-f filter* in the *ovtopmd.lrf* file. This is because *ovrepld* on the management station uses *snmpget* and *snmpset* to communicate with *ovtopmd* on the collection station. Do not confuse this filter with the discovery filter, which is a different filter definition in the *filters* file. Recall that the discovery filter is defined in the *$OV_CONF/polling* file and set in the polling configuration GUI.

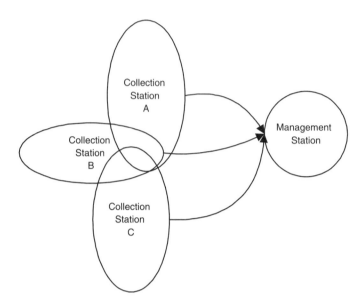

Figure 6-1   Overlapping collection domains.
Three collection stations are shown here with a small amount of
overlap in their collection domains. The management station applies
"the nine rules" to resolve any discrepancies among common objects
imported from two or more collection stations.

Collection stations send status information reliably to management
stations via TCP between their *pmd* daemons. This is in contrast to
topology information which is sent to the management station using
SNMP.

The collection station volunteers no information except when it is
explicitly requested to do so by a management station. The collection
station becomes one when the management station initiates the
relationship. A collection station may be related to more than one
management station. A collection station may be a Windows NT, HP-
UX, or Solaris^{TM} system.

A management station initiates the relationship with its collection stations and uploads the various topology patches into a single end-to-end view of the corporate network. If the collection station management domains are defined correctly, each patch fits together into the quilt with no missing sections. Note that the patches may overlap because the management domains do so.

The management station polls each collection station at five-minute intervals by default. This involves SNMP sets and gets. This may appear to be unusual since NNM normally does very little *snmpset* operations. Network security probes located on the NNM systems and on the network may detect this activity and generate a security alert. Be prepared to work with the security staff to educate them on this subject early in the NNM deployment project.

As the management station uploads objects from the collection station they are placed into the usual NNM databases. The resulting map will contain just these imported devices. The Internet submap will contain hundreds of devices and by default it will resemble wagon wheels within wagon wheels. A map builder will need to customize this map and apply the same care and attention as collection station maps.

A management station need only collect information from collection stations. However, if it is appropriate or necessary, it can also discover and poll some small local management domain. This is fully supported. But given the performance and configuration implications of this approach, the author recommends that autodiscovery be disabled at the management station.

Configuring the Collection Station

The SNMP daemon's read/write community string must be explicitly configured in the */etc/snmpd.conf* file, as shown here:

```
get-community-name:    public
set-community-name:    secret
```

Choose your own community string for the s*et-community-name*, but please—leave the *get-community-name* as *public*. Also, make sure you don't disturb the file permissions (it should be 400 and owned by *root*). You should stop and restart the */usr/sbin/snmpdm* daemon so that it reads the changes you made to the */etc/snmpd.conf* file.

The topology filter, which applies to all database objects exported from the collection station, must be configured. The file *$OV_CONF/ C/filters* should contain an entry which contains:

> NetBackbone "Networks and gateways/routers"
> { Routers || Networks }

Assuming of course that the filters file also defines *Routers* and *Networks*, this filter passes only subnets and routers to the management station. This is a sensible strategy for a large corporate network.

The *$OV_LRF/ovtopmd.lrf* file must be edited to enable the NetBackbone topology filter as follows:

ovtopmd:ovtopmd:
OVs_YES_START:pmd,ovwdb,OVLicenseMgr:-O -f NetBackbone:OVs_WELL_BEHAVED:15:

The parameter *-f NetBackbone* dictates that *ovtopmd* will export only objects that pass this filter to all management stations. If you've just made this change to the LRF file, issue these commands:

> *$OV_BIN/ovstop*
> *$OV_BIN/ovaddobj $OV_LRF/ovtopmd.lrf*
> *$OV_BIN/ovstart -v*

If a large object database (about 20,000 objects) exists, *ovtopmd* will take about 20 minutes to process the filtered database.

Deciding What Devices to Export

In the previous section you saw a collection station export filter that defined only subnets and routers. The result is an Internet submap at the management station showing end-to-end connectivity in the IP sense. Subnets contain only routers and no segments, switches, bridges, or other network infrastructure. Since a large corporate network will contain hundreds of routers with thousands of interfaces and subnets, this is a sizable map. The NNM system performance may degrade if additional network devices are imported from the collection stations.

Regardless, local requirements may dictate that additional devices be visible at the collection station. A prerequisite is that the collection station discovery filter must also pass whatever devices a management station may wish to import. Whenever possible, collection stations should be configured identically to ensure consistency in the export process.

Some strategies for determining what devices to export to the management station are seen in Table 6-1.

Table 6-1   Export Filter Strategies

Object Type	Rationale, Repercussions, and Considerations
routers and subnets	The management station shows all routers on the Internet submap. It's suited for solving end-to-end network problems.
servers, printers, subnets, and segments	Subnets contain server and network printer icons inside their proper segments, and the subnets connectivity isn't visible at all.
routers, switches, bridges, hubs, and subnets	The entire corporate network infrastructure is exported to the management station. The database is potentially huge, so the NNM system must be sized accordingly.

To configure an export filter you have to know a well-defined consistent attribute that uniquely identifies a device. The OID is fairly unique, as is the IP address and device selection name. The vendor name may be too broad. For example, a vendor name of Cisco would pass any product the company manufactures. This would include any workstation or server with an adapter made by Cisco. There are also a large number of standard attributes such as isRouter, isInterface, and isHub. To determine an object's properties (such as sysObjectID), right-click its icon to get the pop-up menu and choose the "Describe/ Modify Object" menu item.

Management Station SNMP Data Collection

The management station does not import the SNMP data collected and stored at the collection stations. Threshold events are propagated from the collection station to the management station. To see the actual data that led to the threshold event, start an *ovw* session on the appropriate collection station, locate the device of interest on the map, and launch the grapher.

There is no technical reason why the management station cannot be configured to collect historical SNMP data itself. This means network devices are polled multiple times per polling cycle (once by the collection station and once per management station). For example, if only routers are exported, then the management station only polls routers.

If the management station also checks performance thresholds, then both the collection station and the management station will generate a threshold event, probably at different times within the five-minute polling cycle, and with different values. This is to be expected since the polling cycles are not synchronized.

Monitoring NNM Systems With ITO and MeasureWare

Managing large networks with many management domains will probably require 15 or so collection stations and two management stations. It is a considerable task to manage that many systems, one that requires automated tools.

If you load and configure HP MeasureWare agents on all NNM systems from a central system you can then use HP PerfView to monitor all critical system resources, some of which include:

- RAM utilization

- virtual memory (VM) utilization

- VM paging rate

- CPU utilization for all CPUs

- disk I/O rate

- queue depth of the disk controllers

- network interface error rate

There is a fair amount of opinion about threshold values for these and other metrics, and there are preset values for them. If these presets generate too many alerts when the NNM system is otherwise working well, then by all means increase the threshold values.

IT Operations (ITO) agents should also be loaded and configured on all NNM systems. The agent may be tailored to monitor specific conditions using customized scripts. During the NNM pilot project (you did do a pilot, right?), abnormal conditions may be discovered manually at first. Write down the commands you used to detect or troubleshoot the problem for later automation. Some examples are:

- monitor load factor rather than CPU utilization

- check management station and collection station communications

- verify that the read/write *ovw* session is active

- check that all NNM daemons are active

- watch log files for well-known error conditions

- monitor processes that use excessive CPU time

- detect hung *ovw* sessions belonging to logged off users

The ITO application can be loaded onto the same monitoring system that PerfView resides. ITO can then detect MeasureWare alarms. You have now created a MOM (manager of managers). Locate this system at the corporate network management center.

Configuring the Management Station

You will recall that configuring a collection station does nothing by itself. Indeed, during a large NNM deployment it is prudent to preconfigure all collection stations so they are ready when the management station is brought online. The actual management station to collection station relationship is initiated at the management station. There may be more than one management station in cases where high availability is required.

Begin the management station configuration process by turning off autodiscovery in the polling menu.

The management station must be configured to include all device community strings, icons, *oid_to_type*, and other such customized files consistent with those on all the collection stations.

A collection station must be present in the management station's object database before the collection-to-management relationship can be established. Manually add them to the management station *ovw* map if you like, but listing the collection stations in a *seedfile* may be preferable to you. Remember the first time you define a *seedfile* in *$OV_LRF/netmon.lrf* you must register the change using *$OV_BIN/ ovaddobj $OV_LRF/netmon.lrf* and stop and start *netmon*. If you edit only the *seedfile,* you need only stop and restart *netmon*.

Note that, by default, *netmon* will attempt to add the NNM system name to the trap destination list for each SNMP agent it communicates with. This means each collection station will have a trap destination entry in the *snmpd.conf* file. If this causes problems at your installation, you can prevent this behavior by including the *-N* flag in the *netmon.lrf* file. Note that starting with the NNM 6.0 release, *netmon* will use the SNMP set community name configured through *xnmsnmpconf* when adding and removing trap destination entries (rather than the mechanism used in previous releases which bypassed normal SNMP authentication measures).

The management station must be configured with the *set-community-names* for the collection stations, as seen in Figure 6-2.

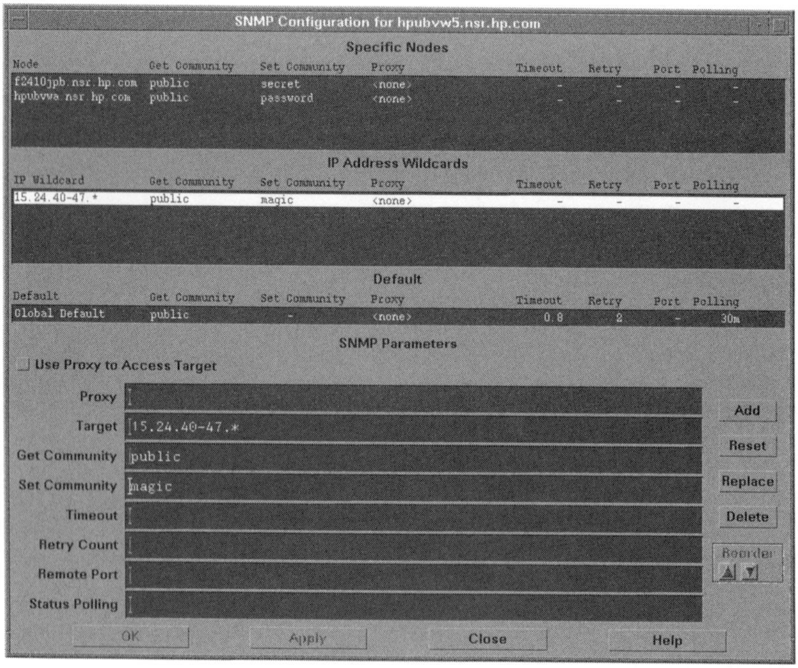

Figure 6-2   Defining collection station community strings.
Enter the community strings manually. Since they are often identical for each collection station, a few minutes of work is all it takes to configure even a few dozen.

Check that all the collection stations are known to the management station by typing this command:

$OV_BIN/ovtopodump -Lr | more

Known collection stations are given at the beginning of the list. This version of *ovtopodump* is very useful because it gives a concise one-line entry per device, including the MAC address.

It's time for the magic. Establish the collection station relationship at the management station by opening a shell window and typing:

$OV_BIN/xnmtopoconf -manage collection_station_name

Repeat this command for every collection station. You can monitor the progress of the devices import process by opening the configuration alarm category and watching imported nodes scroll by in the list. However, be aware that the event correlation system (ECS) may correlate these events so they don't scroll by.

To check the relationship status to a collection station, type:

$OV_BIN/xnmtopoconf -print collection_station_name

After perhaps an hour, all collection stations will have been interrogated and the management station will assemble a composite database of network devices. Some devices known to the management station may be imported from two or more collection stations because of the overlapping patches of their management domains. A primary collection station is designated for such a device. It is possible to set a preferred collection station and to change the overlap using *xnmtopoconf*.

Adding a Collection Station to an Operational Management Station

It would be illogical to assume that all conditions remain stable[1]. Therefore, a time will come when a new collection station must be added to an already fully operational management station. Previous

---

1. Mister Spock once said so.

sections in this chapter apply to first-time installations. Adding a new collection station can be a pleasant experience if some simple precautions are taken.

First, preconfigure the collection station totally, allow it to complete its autodiscovery process, then wait for any manual discovery nudging to follow its course.

Remember to export all map customizations at the management station before adding the collection station.

Configure the management station as indicated above. Now execute *xnmtopoconf -manage new_collection_station* and you should observe new devices appearing in the new object holding area of the Internet submap. Wait until the management station is done importing the additional devices.

In less than ten minutes the new devices can be put into their new "homes."

The procedure is as follows:

- find the *View:Redo Layout* menu and click the *OK* button. This removes all objects from the new object holding area; the map is now a real mess.

- import the map customization that you saved previously. The map looks better—containers are in their correct relative positions.

- create a new container for the new collection station devices

- rubberband and drag all errant icons into the new container

- drag the container close to the cluster of originals

- drag slightly on the window's edge (if it has not been automatically redrawn). *ovw* rescales the map to fit the icons into the available space.

- drag the container to its desired location

- drag slightly on the window's edge (if it has not been automatically redrawn). The map should now be properly customized.

- save the customization

The Impact of Rebuilding a Collection Station

Consider a fully realized management station as one of its collection stations goes down. The status of all the devices normally polled by the collection station remain frozen since no updates are available. Suppose the NNM administrator for the collection station deleted the database and rediscovered the management domain (because of a corrupt unrecoverable database, a hard drive failure, or a major hardware upgrade). While the management station reconnects with the collection station as this discovery begins, the entire previous collection of objects are deleted and a new set of objects are imported.

The result is that the management station container for the collection station topology becomes virtually empty and the objects appear in the new object holding area.

This story has a happy ending if the management station's Internet submap's customization is periodically saved. Then all the devices in the new object holding area should return to their home container when this customization is imported.

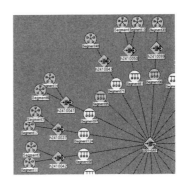

## CHAPTER 7

Configuration Management With NNM

Introduction

The configuration management NNM provides may be broadly divided into five basic areas:

- **discover** IP addressable devices (as well as IPX and layer 2 devices), the network IP structure, routers, switches, bridges, repeaters, and other infrastructure devices

- **collect** and store configuration information about devices and networks in a database

- **check** the configuration information for changes, errors, or inconsistencies

- **present** the network topology and device connectivity using a map hierarchy with IP-centric views, layer 2 views, or physical connectivity views

- **report** the information by providing search capabilities to locate where devices appear in the network relative to the neighboring topology, and by offering text-based reporting tools

It's also instructive to examine the seven-layer OSI model and identify information NNM collects at each layer, as shown in Table 7-1.

Table 7-1   OSI View of NNM Configuration Management

Layer	Description	Information NNM Collects at This OSI Layer
7	Application	HTTP, SNMP, telnet, FTP, and other services (by testing well-known ports).
6	Presentation	n/a
5	Session	n/a

Table 7-1 OSI View of NNM Configuration Management

Layer	Description	Information NNM Collects at This OSI Layer
4	Transport	TCP connections (by reading the TCP section of the standard MIB) and UDP/TCP listeners.
3	Network	IP address, netmask, routing table, and other parameters from the IP section of the standard MIB. IPX information is also available. NNM also identifies layer 3 devices such as routers and assigns devices into subnets according to their IP address and netmask.
2	Link	MAC address, MTU, and other information (using the interfaces section of the standard MIB). NNM also identifies layer 2 devices such as switches and bridges and shows connections between switches and devices on their segments.
1	Physical	Type of interface such as Ethernet, Token Ring, and HSSI (using the interfaces section of the standard MIB).

NNM provides many tools to support configuration management. One of the best ones is the configuration alarms category. Clues about configuration problems on the network abound in this category.

The *ovtopodump* command lets the network manager create lists of information about network devices and objects, both detailed and concise.

The map is NNM's best tool for showing the most important configuration information of all, namely the network topology. It organizes the topology according to network, subnet, segment, and device. Map navigation is easy and device information can be obtained either from the menu bar or via pop-up menus.

NNM displays interface information graphically and offers both a menu bar and pop-up menus to display detailed technical data about each interface.

When the standard NNM menus don't provide the degree of customized data required, the NNM system administrator may create local MIB applications and assign them to any desired position in the menu bar.

Nuggets in the Configuration Alarms Category

NNM examines device configuration information periodically according to the schedule set in the polling configuration GUI. NNM reports any changes, errors, or inconsistencies as a configuration event. It is the author's humble opinion that the configuration alarms category is the most useful NNM feature of all. It's the network manager's friend. Here is a list of common configuration alarms NNM may report:

- a device subnet mask differs from the correct one for that subnet

- the MAC address of a device changed

- a device's route points to a device that's not a router

- the name of a device changed

- a new interface is found in a device

- a new node is discovered or deleted

- a device's sysObjectID changed

Gold in *ovtopodump*

By simply typing:

> *ovtopodump -Lr > report_name*

you can get a very useful one-line summary for each device in the NNM database. On a UNIX system you can pipe the output of the *ovtopodump* command into one or more filters (such as *sort*) to tailor the output for some specific purpose. For example, suppose you want to find out which devices in the management domain don't have DNS entries, simply type:

> *ovtopodump -Lr | sort > report_name*

and examine the entries near the top of the sorted list. The numeric selection names percolate to the top of the list, neatly identifying the devices without DNS entries.

Here is another useful one-liner:

> *ovtopodump -o | grep ".1.3.6.1.4.1"*

This prints a neat report of all discovered SNMP-manageable devices and their corresponding sysObjectID values.

Configuration Information Presented in NNM Maps

The NNM root map displays all the network maps. It usually contains a solitary submap, the Internet submap, but it may contain others such as a layer 2 physical topology map, an IPX map, a storage-attached network (SAN), or a map created by another bolt-on OpenView application.

The Internet submap displays the overall configuration and structure of the IP network. It shows only layer 3 connection devices (such as routers, layer 3 switches, Ethernet switches with a routing module[1], and multihomed hosts) and IP subnets. This map is useful for troubleshooting end-to-end routing problems across the whole network. For example, if you select two routers and pick the *Fault:Locate Route* menu, NNM will graphically display the route a packet would take between them.

Right-clicking over an icon allows you to pick a menu that can provide more information about the device. Note that you can right-click a router interface and obtain configuration information about it. Selecting an icon permits you to use one of the menus to get more information about the device.

Open any subnet submap and you will see connector devices such as switches, bridges, and repeaters joining segments such as Ethernet, FDDI, or Token Ring. Right-click an icon to choose a menu that displays configuration information, or select an icon and use a menu to do so. The look and feel is the same as the Internet submap.

Open any segment submap and you will see the connector devices as well as all the devices attached to the segment. The exact representation depends on the type of medium, which may be a bus (for coaxial Ethernet), a star (for twisted pair Ethernet), or a ring (for FDDI or Token Ring).

Interface Information

Open any device submap and you will see all its interfaces, both physical and logical. A right click brings up the usual configuration menus revealing port, slot, or IP address information. The bitmap

---

1. Only the Cisco router switch module (RSM) shows in layer 3 maps. The switch is a separate symbol for the RSM.

inside the interface icon indicates the type of interface. For example, a bitmap bearing the letter IP means the interface has an IP address configured.

Not all interfaces have IP addresses. It's not uncommon for a point-to-point interface between routers to be unnumbered. This saves a whole IP subnet, an important consideration in situations where subnets are in limited supply. Switch, bridge, and repeater interfaces don't have IP addresses, but the device itself has a pseudo-interface configured with one. This interface is visible when the device submap is opened. Note that if secondary addresses are configured, each will show up as a separate interface symbol.

To view the interface details of a device, use the *Network Configuration:Interface Properties* menu. A table shows the interface index, name, maximum transmission unit (MTU), and status. The menu *Network Configurations:IP Addresses* is also useful.

Creating Custom Menu Items

While the standard NNM menus provide useful information, local requirements often require additional menus to provide access to specialized information. For this reason the MIB Application Builder facility is provided. Three kinds of MIB applications can be constructed entirely by using it.

The *form* MIB application simply retrieves the user-specified MIB values from the selected device and displays them in a simple labeled form. The MIB values can be completely unrelated and come from different parts of the MIB and even from different MIBs.

The *table* MIB application is intended to query an object with multiple instances. For example, you can specify the MTU, interface speed, and input octets MIB values and the table MIB application will query every interface instance of the selected device. The results are displayed in a tabular format. Information in a table must belong to the same MIB group, such as the interface table.

The *graph* MIB application isn't meant for displaying configuration information as are the form and table applications. A numeric MIB value must be the result, and the application polls and graphs (using *xnmgraph*) the data at a configurable time interval which defaults to 10 seconds.

MIB applications can be placed anywhere in the menu structure, but the Configuration Tools menu is the logical choice for interface data. The application can also be assigned to appear on a right-mouse-click by editing its application registration file (ARF). The ARF should be located beneath the directory that *$OV_REGISTRATION/C* points to, or to the directory defined by the *$OVwRegDir* environment variable.

## CHAPTER 8

*Event Management
With NNM*

Introduction

On a good day, the network behaves as intended. All router and switch interfaces are operational, no server is down, printers have a full supply of paper and toner, no configuration errors exist anywhere, no new devices have been detected, every network link is operating well below maximum capacity, and there are zero data errors detected. No events occur. The Internet submap is green as a Northwestern forest. Adrenalin levels at the NOCC are very low. They would be lower except that the NOCC staff knows that bad days follow good ones as surely as rain falls in the Northwest.

To support event management, NNM provides an exhaustive list of preconfigured events. Each event includes a category name, severity code, OID, textual description, help text, and a programmable action.

Devices in NNM's database are either in a managed or unmanaged state. Unmanaged devices aren't polled so NNM generates no events regarding them. Management stations honor this distinction when importing devices from collection stations.

SNMP traps from undiscovered devices may arrive at NNM's event system, as may traps from managed and unmanaged devices. NNM generates internal events regarding the network. All of these events may be configured to cause an automated action.

Routers and other network devices may transmit console log messages to a syslog service that runs on the NNM system. Such logs may be programatically checked for critical conditions that are otherwise not detectable with SNMP and sent into the NNM event system.

NNM predefines six event categories and allows new ones to be defined. For example, it's a good idea to define a special Router Alarms category to receive rerouted syslog messages.

Every event defined in NNM may be modified to suit local practice. Customized actions may also be defined for specific events. These actions may range from executing a repair script to sending an e-mail page.

Event histories are managed using the event database, which may be the old-style *trapd.log* flat file (NNM 5.x and earlier) or the *eventdb* facility introduced with NNM 6.0. Since it's useful to be able to review old events, the size of the database can be increased as needed.

Even a large, well-managed network will cause NNM to generate a steady stream of events, and occasionally, a storm of them. The event correlation service (ECS) is designed to help reduce this flow to a trickle of quality events. ECS may be tuned via user-configurable parameters, and it can be expanded by adding correlation circuits.

On a historical note, for NNM 5.x and before, HP defined event categories and provided an event browser. As of NNM 6.0 the terminology is alarm categories and alarm browser. The rationale is:

> an event is any discernible action
> an alarm is an event important enough to take note of

Managed vs. Unmanaged Devices

NNM subjects a managed object to routine polling for status and configuration, and the *snmpCollect* daemon will collect SNMP data from the managed device. The managed object's icon will reflect its status. An unmanaged device is not polled and no SNMP data is collected for it. Its status isn't known so the icon will not affect the status of its container. The unmanaged object's icon color is wheat.

Network managers frequently unmanage devices or interfaces for various reasons:

- they fall outside the management domain and it's too difficult, bothersome, or inconvenient to prevent them from being discovered otherwise

- the device is being serviced and therefore the map should be green

- the device is experimental, it passes the discovery filter, but it's not part of the mission critical network so you don't want to monitor it

- NNM polling is negatively impacting the managed device and its administrator has politely requested or vehemently demanded that it not be managed anymore

- the interface is always down because it's a backup link used for failover purposes

- this is an extra interface that's configured but not used at all

The terms object and device are purposely used loosely in the preceding discussion. That's because some objects represent actual devices, others represent interfaces and connections, and there are also abstract object containers such as subnets and segments. Therefore, if the network manager selects a router icon and chooses *Edit:Unmanage* from the menu, the router and all its contained interfaces become unmanaged. A router is a real device, as are its interfaces. A single interface can be unmanaged by opening the router icon, selecting the interface, and choosing *Edit:Unmanage* from the menu. But an abstract container icon such as a segment can also be unmanaged, which means all the devices within it become unmanaged.

If you look at a map and see that a device is unmanaged, is that device really unmanaged? In cases where this device belongs in several maps, only if is unmanaged in every map is it truly unmanaged. If just one map contains a managed version of the device, then *netmon* will poll it. Check the actual management status of the device using the *ovtopodump -L device_name* command.

Note that if a device is unmanaged in the management domain of a collection station, and if that device is exported to a management station, then the unmanaged status is also exported. Suppose two or more collection stations either manage or unmanage the device. It can be troublesome if multiple collection stations contain this device because one of them is the designated primary for it, but which one? There are nine rules the management station uses for selecting the primary collection station for an object. The answer to our question is found in rules 3, 5, and 9:

> **rule 3**: If only one of many possible collection stations reporting the object is managed and has non-critical status, then that station has primary ownership of the object.
>
> **rule 5**: If only one collection station has the object in a managed state (either via default or intentional selection), that station is designated as primary for that object.
>
> **rule 9**: The first collection station to report the object is deemed primary by the management station. Ownership of the object is not restricted to that collection station in the event that collection station ceases to monitor the object.

See Chapter 5 of the *HP OpenView Advanced Network Node Manager Student Workbook* for a comprehensive treatment of these rules.

Note that an unmanaged device may still send SNMP traps to the collection station if its SNMP agent has the NNM management system listed in its trap forwarding table. The NNM menus will generally operate on an unmanaged device.

Traps From Expected and Unexpected Sources

SNMP traps are transmitted to UDP port 162 by default. Sources of SNMP traps include NNM and network devices. NNM generates traps internally (often loosely referred to as events) called enterprise-specific traps. NNM may also generate special SNMP traps in response to *ovevent*-programmed actions.

Network devices may have one or more trap destinations configured. Trap destinations are usually the IP addresses of network management stations. These IP addresses may be manually configured, or they may be configured automatically by the device's element manager software running on the NNM system. Multiple trap destinations are desirable when two or more collection stations manage a device because it improves the chances the trap is actually received by one of them. Because SNMP traps are transmitted over user datagram protocol (UDP) packets, they can get lost. UDP offers no detection or retransmission feature, as does TCP. SNMP traps use UDP because it is a lightweight protocol that uses few resources on the agent side.

Note that an undiscovered device may still be configured to send SNMP traps to an NNM system. While they'll be received, it won't be possible to view the device that sent the trap in a map. The MIB for this device must be compiled on the NNM system in order for the trap to be properly decoded. Unfortunately, it may sometimes be difficult to obtain a copy of the current MIB for a device. The MIB describes the SNMP traps, a helpful thing to know.

To obtain the most recent version of a MIB file, check NNM's installation CD, contact the vendor who wrote the MIB file, or search the web (*ftp://ftp.isi.edu/mib/*) for quick access to the MIB file. Make sure the MIB definition loaded into NNM's MIB database matches the version of the MIB in use on the device itself. The NNM installation CD includes hundreds of vendor-specific MIBs for your convenience. Simply load the MIBs that are relevant and useful for your specific network configuration.

Sometimes the receipt of an event is so interesting that the NNM administrator will configure an automated response via the event configuration GUI. For example, if a critical router interface should go down, an appropriate automated response might be to send a short e-mail message to trigger the pager worn by the network manager on duty.

Given the importance of SNMP traps, Table 8-1 provides a short summary of the major categories. The industry standard SNMP general trap numbers are 0-6, and the specific trap numbers apply to general trap number 6.

Table 8-1   Types of SNMP Traps

Trap Number	Description
0	coldStart trap sent when the SNMP agent is first started, which is typically at boot time.
1	warmStart trap sent when the SNMP agent restarts, having been active before. This is often done to force the agent to read its configuration file, which has been changed.
2	linkDown trap is sent when the SNMP agent detects that one of the interfaces has gone down operationally. The trap is sent on an alternate interface if one is available; otherwise, it's lost.
3	linkUp trap is sent when the SNMP agent detects that a previously, operationally down interface is now operational. NNM will change the status of a managed device interface to reflect this.
4	authenticationFailure trap is sent when the SNMP agent receives a request with an incorrect community string. The request is ignored.

Table 8-1   Types of SNMP Traps

Trap Number	Description
5	egpNeighborLoss trap is sent by a router configured with EGP when it loses contact with its neighbor.
6	NCC-1701 specific trap takes a second parameter, the specific trap number, defined by the vendor to indicate a specific problem. For example, a router might generate a "cooling fan failure" trap and a switch might generate a "port 2 segmented" trap.

syslog Streams from Devices and *ovevent*

Network equipment is often configured to log console messages over the network to a host using its *syslog* facility. All UNIX systems have a daemon called *syslogd* that listens on UDP port 514 and logs messages received to a file name indicated in the */etc/syslog.conf* file. See Figure 8-1 for an example.

The actual text logged by *syslogd* will be specific to the device and may even depend on the firmware revision, type of model, and type of interface adapter. The severity of the message is indicated by its text.

How can you monitor this file? Data in the *syslog* files is not monitored by NNM directly and the information in it may not be apparent when viewed through SNMP eyes.

If you're running the ITO daemon, it can be configured to examine this file as it grows, to look for special text strings with special

```
# Log all kernel messages to the console.
# Logging much else clutters up the screen.
#kern.*                    /dev/console


# Log anything (except mail) of level info or higher.
# Don't log private authentication messages!
*.info;mail.none;authpriv.none /var/log/messages


# Router console log messages (Check specific facility of your router)
router                    /var/log/routerlog


# The authpriv file has restricted access.
authpriv.*                /var/log/secure


# Log all the mail messages in one place.
mail.*                    /var/log/maillog


# Everybody gets emergency messages, plus log them on another
# machine.
*.emerg                   *


# Save mail and news errors of level err and higher in a
# special file.
uucp,news.crit            /var/log/spooler
```

Figure 8-1   The *syslog.conf* file.
The UNIX *syslogd* daemon logs incoming UDP messages into one of
the listed log files. For example, routers may be configured to send
their console messages to the NNM system. They will be logged to a
specific file, */var/log/routerlog*.

meaning, and to generate an ITO alarm. Perhaps ITO is not the right
tool since the management application runs elsewhere.

An alternative, and perhaps preferable, solution is to run a small UNIX script in the background to monitor the router *syslog* file. The script can perform the following steps:

- *tail -f /var/log/routerlog* to follow the file and capture new data
- examine each string for specific text
- reformat the string to remove metacharacters
- identify the device that sent the *syslog* message
- assign a severity code (depends on the message content)
- assign an event category (probably a custom category)
- send the message into the NNM event stream with *ovevent*

Predefined and Custom Alarm Categories

The predefined alarm categories and their associated numeric codes are:

```
0 = Ignore
1 = Log only
2 = Error Alarms
3 = Threshold Alarms
4 = Status Alarms
5 = Configuration Alarms
6 = Application Alert Alarms
```

The *xnmevents* GUI displays these and custom-defined categories as shown in Figure 8-2.

The events corresponding to the router console log messages will usually be sent to a custom event category (not shown above). There they can be viewed in the event browser and operated on as usual.

Figure 8-2   The *xnmevents* GUI.
This little window pops up by default when you start an *ovw* session.
Each button color shows the most severe level of the alarms. Pressing
the button brings up an alarms browser that lets you display detailed
information about the alarms in that category. This screenshot shows
the standard categories.

Customizing Event Actions

Each IT organization sets its own standards for severity and remedy.
NNM supports changing event categories, severities, and programmed
actions with a GUI. Figure 8-3 depicts the main event configuration
browser. The *OpenView* enterprise MIB is of interest because all of
NNM's own events are listed here. Many of the default severity and
logging codes may differ from local custom.

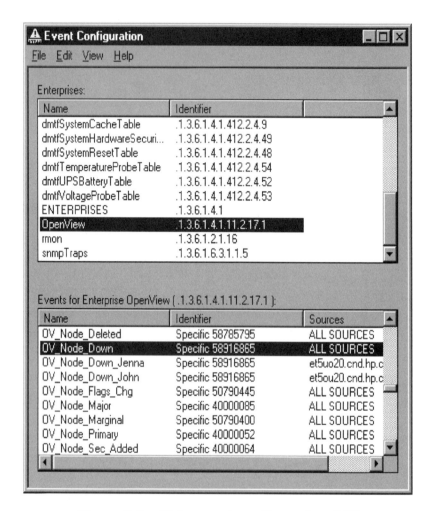

Figure 8-3   Main event configuration GUI.
To locate an NNM event, scroll through the enterprise names and
select OpenView from the list. The lower scrollable area displays all
the NNM events. Note the enterprise-specific trap number in the
middle column. Double-click an event name to bring up the
customization GUI.

Double-click on an event you want to customize and a GUI (see
Figure 8-4) will appear to let you change most parameters, including:

- the alarm category

- the alarm severity

- ignore the event in the browser

- customize the alarm message (add more meaning)

- define an automatic action (send e-mail to a pager)

Figure 8-4   The event configuration customization GUI.
Events may be customized by changing their logging level. Some
events are preferably not seen and may be set to log-only so they don't
appear in the alarm browser. Other events that default to log-only may
be considered important so they can be changed to log and assigned
a category and severity.

The automatic actions available vary from sublime to ridiculous. The
power, which comes from flexibility, is fueled by the NNM

administrator's ingenuity. A list of some obvious examples of automatic actions are as follows:

- send an e-mail to a pager service

- deliver a prerecorded voice mail message

- escalate the event to a manager's voice mail

- synthesize an audible message using the Telemon package

- display a customized window on the screen

- execute a command that actually fixes the problem

- print a trouble ticket

- send control-G characters and beep the console

- flash an icon's color

Managing Event Histories and *trapd.log*

Pre-NNM 6.0 behavior would be to log all events to *$OV_LOG/ trapd.log* and to roll that to *$OV_LOG/trapd.log.old* when the file reached a predefined limit. That limit is set in *$OV_LRF/pmd.lrf* in the form of the parameter -*$OV_EVENT;t;lsize,* where *l* is the letter lowercase L and *size* is the rollover value in megabytes. When *xnmevents* starts, it scans both files. *xnmevents* also retains a separate log of events for each user in a file named *xnmevents.username.* This supports individual user event acknowledgement.

NNM 6.0 behavior differs remarkably from its ancestors. Events are not saved in *trapd.log* by default, but instead are stored in an event database. Fortunately, the logging to *trapd.log* can be reenabled if it's critical to your operation. In *pmd.lrf,* insert the -*SOV_EVENT;t* option, register the file with the *$OV_BIN/obaddobj $OV_LF/pmd.lrf* command, and stop and start *pmd.* If you want to take advantage of the new event database but occasionally rely on *trapd.log*, use *ovdumpevents* to create a file with this data in it.

Post-NNM 6.0 uses the *eventdb* facility and stores traps and events in a database at *$OV_DB/eventdb/*. The default database size is 16 megabytes. Use the *OV_EVENT;bsize* option in *pmd.lrf* to change it (*b* is the letter b and *size* is the database size in megabytes). The event browser interacts with this database and *ov_event* logs to it.

Reducing Event Storms with ECS

NNM 6.0 introduced event correlation services (ECS) to provide the means to intelligently interpret the event stream, reduce its volume, and increase its quality. This solves the problem of servicing events on a large network which can number hundreds per minute. A single outage can generate thousands of events. As it's impractical to react to them all, network managers would resort to one of the following:

- ignore all messages except when a critical device goes down
- reconfigure most messages "log only"
- handle critical alarms only
- use the NNM event browser filter to limit events
- buy a third-party tool for event filtering

The NNM event browser filter lets you configure the following criteria to limit events displayed:

- severity level
- source IP addresses
- wildcard to specify a range of IP addresses or node names
- acknowledged or unacknowledged alarms
- alarm time span
- message string word search
- event type

Simple event filtering is a very crude method for reducing the event stream to a mere trickle. There are nuggets of valuable information buried in the event stream and the right way to find them is to take advantage of ECS. You want the cause of the problem to be identified; you don't want to see all the symptomatic events that result. Study Figure 8-5 for an overview of the event stream within NNM. Note that ECS is active by default. Several correlations are provided bundled with NNM as described in Table 8-2. The exact correlations provided will vary with each version of NNM. Additional correlations may be obtained from third parties, from HP consultants, or by writing your own using the ECS Designer for NNM products.

Table 8-2   Bundled Edition Correlations

Correlation Name	Description
Connector Down	Use the network topology to isolate the root cause of a cascade of device failures to a specific connector. An event storm is avoided and one event is logged to the event browser. The root cause device is shown as a red icon, while effected devices are shown in blue (unknown status).
Scheduled Maintenance	When devices scheduled for maintenance go down, NNM will normally generate alarms. This correlation defines which devices or what range of IP addresses to ignore starting at a given time and for a specific duration.

Table 8-2 Bundled Edition Correlations

Correlation Name	Description
Repeated Event	Allows for the suppression of related events about a particular device. For example, without this correlation, when a device MAC address changes, NNM's check of neighboring device ARP caches will cause NNM to report a mismatch for each one.
Pair Wise	Multiple traps are correlated over a time interval and the parent trap is identified and reported in the alarm browser.
MgXServer Down	New with NNM 6.1, this circuit allows correlation of events between HP OpenView Network Node Manager and HP OpenView ManageX systems.

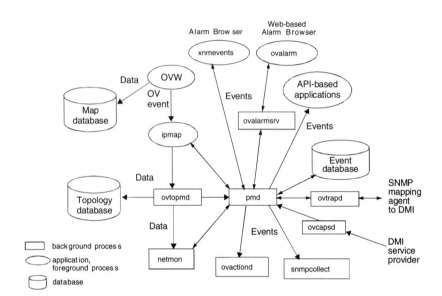

Figure 8-5   Event flows in NNM[a].
This very high-level diagram shows how data flows between the databases and daemons in NNM.

a. Copyright 1999 Hewlett-Packard Company. Reproduced with permission. Hewlett-Packard Company makes no warranty as to the accuracy or completeness of the foregoing material and herby disclaims any responsibility therefor.

## CHAPTER 9

Performance Management with NNM

Introduction

There is an often-heard philosophy out there about performance management in the real world:

> "To do network performance planning properly you have to measure utilization at all points of the network and model the topology in detail. You don't have the resources to measure anything, you don't really know what the network looks like, and it would take forever to simulate it all. Therefore, it's impractical to do capacity planning, and we should continue to provision bandwidth to deal with performance problems."

Regardless of the planning methodology used, it's important to measure network performance in order to manage it. Network troubleshooters need real-time utilization and error data. The help desk needs to view performance data in relation to a user complaint. The network engineering staff needs performance data for capacity planning. The IT group needs data to present at the monthly service level agreement (SLA) meetings.

Providing data for the monthly meetings means configuring NNM to measure agreed-upon performance metrics. Given the difficulty of gathering end-to-end transaction response time data, more robust metrics such as line utilization and active user counts are more practical.

Determining how long to keep NNM performance data online involves a trade-off between performance, convenience, and cost. Troubleshooters need about an hour's worth of real-time data, while capacity planners require up to a year's worth of historical data. Storing more data online can reduce performance and increase system administration overhead unless a more powerful and costly NNM platform is configured.

What is an appropriate SNMP data sample rate? Sampling too quickly may cause some network devices to overload and will certainly increase network management traffic. But long sample intervals miss all the useful variation in the performance metrics. A five-minute sample interval is suggested.

The Heisenberg uncertainty principle of quantum physics can be stretched to explain why excessive SNMP prodding of the network can limit how accurately it can be measured.

How much traffic does an NNM system actually create? You can attempt to quantify this with a simple polling example. Note that configuration checking, status polling, HTTP and Java, X-Windows, ITO, and Measureware contribute traffic as well.

Deciding what SNMP data to collect from the hundreds of possible MIB values is best done using the KISS (keep it simple, stupid) principle. A few system and network utilization and error statistics often suffice. MIB expressions are appropriate because percentages are more useful than raw numeric information.

NNM allows you to configure performance thresholds to generate alarms. Thresholds can be established using baselining, or analytical and rule-of-thumb methods. Set threshold events to low priority unless you have a process for dealing with them.

MIB expressions allow you to configure NNM to sample several SNMP variables, evaluate a formula containing them, and return the result. Typically, you want to calculate a percentage. For example, an error counter is meaningless unless it's normalized by the packet counter and converted to a percentage. NNM provides many predefined MIB expressions which you use out of the box or as a template.

Viewing historical performance data online can be done graphically with *xnmgraph,* or by using the SNMP historical data configuration GUI. Data can be viewed and saved textually using *xnmgraph* or *snmpColDump*.

Presenting data offline means taking a screenshot or exporting textual data to a presentation or spreadsheet tool such as Star Office, Wingz, or one of the Windows or Macintosh equivalents.

SNMPv2C supports 64-bit counters. These are essential for managing links operating at or faster than 100 megabits per second (Mbps). NNM automatically detects devices with SNMPv2C support, and the ifXentry section in the interface portion of MIB2 defines several 64-bit counter variables.

Collecting RMON data is best done with HP NetMetrix. Remote shared-medium Ethernet segments can also be monitored (in a limited way) with NNM directly using the Etherstats group and a few good MIB expressions.

Crossing over to HP NetMetrix means having complete end-to-end traffic flow by application at your fingertips. Network probes or switches and hubs with built-in RMON2 properly situated on the network can collect enterprise-wide performance data that NetMetrix can massage, present, and report.

After you've collected NetMetrix network-wide performance data and a meaningful NNM baseline topology, capacity planning follows. HP Service Simulator can import the performance data and topology. Armed with what-if questions, you can use the simulator to verify that the network can meet performance objectives under various conditions you specify.

Who Needs Performance Data?

Network performance data is an essential component of network management because:

> "you can't manage what you don't measure."

Performance information is needed at every stage in a network's evolution. Those stages include requirements, architecture, design, implementation, routine maintenance, and upgrades. Therefore, it's common to depend on SNMP agents in the network to provide performance data and to use an SNMP-based network management system like NNM to collect it. Consumers of network performance data include troubleshooters, the help desk, network engineering, SLA administrators, financial planners, and system administrators.

Troubleshooters need both real time and historic data to diagnose the root cause of user complaints. They will usually locate the path traffic takes between the user's workstation and the server (see Figure 9-1) and check on media utilization and error percentage rates. If the problem symptoms are active, then a real-time view is necessary. If the problem symptoms have passed, then the historical data at the time the problem occurred is what's needed.

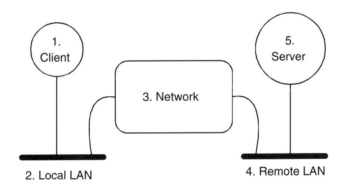

Figure 9-1   Potential performance problem locations.
Troubleshooting network problems between a client system and the corresponding server requires that five locations be instrumented. A performance problem might be caused by a lack of resources, excessive utilization, CRC errors, or packet loss. SNMP agents located at locations 1-5 can help isolate the problem and correct the direction of fingerpointing.

The help desk staff needs to view capacity, error, and packet loss data as they collect basic information about a user complaint. If the user's workstation has a working SNMP agent, it's possible to measure performance data for its LAN adapter; for advanced agents, resource usage such as CPU, RAM, and disk is available. Server systems almost always support SNMP. Client, network, and server systems are all involved in most user performance complaints, so it's important to measure SNMP data at all of them to isolate the true cause. Performance problems are not always caused by the network. For example, it is entirely possible that poor client-server response time is caused by the client having too many applications open, resulting in excessive virtual memory (VM) activity.

The network engineering staff needs operational metrics to validate network changes and bandwidth upgrades. Knowing link utilization is important, but so is knowing the source-destination metrics for various applications. For example, some web traffic will be directed to local servers and the rest may be destined for the Internet via the firewall. The same is true for e-mail. File and print traffic is usually sent to a local file server and a local LAN-attached printer. An understanding of application-specific source-destination pairs provides valuable insight into how a network redesign should be done. While simple link-based utilization data can be used to correct a bandwidth allocation problem, RMON2-based data is needed to collect application-specific source-destination pairs. Display tools such as HP NetMetrix can display this data graphically and create tabular reports as well. This performance data is often input to a more comprehensive network capacity planning process. This validates that a given network design, which clearly provides the necessary connectivity, also provides the necessary performance.

The IT organization needs metrics to comply with service level agreements (SLA) and their user communities. Each user community is a special interest group with specific network needs, and an SLA is an agreement between them and IT about what level of service is expected. The metrics agreed upon must be realizable and measurable. Application response time is very difficult to measure when developers have not instrumented the code. Code that is instrumented using the application resource monitor (ARM) APIs is very easy to monitor with the standard HP PerfView application. Without ARM-enabled application code, simpler SNMP measurable metrics such as utilization are typically the basis for the SLA.

Financial planners use historical performance data to demonstrate to management why money is needed to upgrade the network. A properly presented line chart depicting historical traffic growth plus a credible forecasting technique can ethically and accurately depict the urgency for a network upgrade. See Figure 9-2.

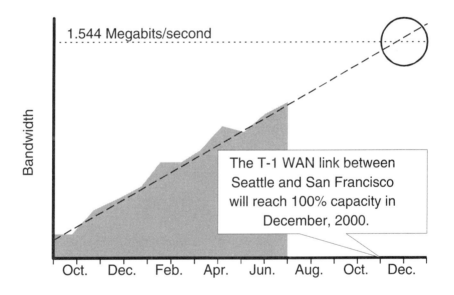

Figure 9-2   Projecting capacity using SNMP data.
NNM can collect historical SNMP utilization data from a router interface. Repurposing the data into a professional presentation gives impact to the message that a network upgrade is critical.

Even system administrators benefit from knowing traffic patterns when they decide where a new server is best placed, much like network designers who benefit from knowing the source-destination traffic a new server will generate.

Providing Data for an SLA

Let's make a list of what users really care about when it comes to their network applications.

What Users Care About:

> response time for interactive transactions
> throughput for file transfers and print jobs
> high availability
> ease of use
> convenience

Now let's make another list of things users don't care about as they use their day-to-day network applications:

What Users Don't Care About:

> network backbone utilization
> percent error rate
> percent packet loss
> ping round trip time

Now isn't that interesting? The very things that network managers routinely measure are of no concern to the users. SNMP provides dozens of performance metrics, none of which relate directly to the user experience. This is because SNMP was designed to manage networks, not applications.

Network managers may take the position that they provide error-free network bandwidth and that application response time is the business of server administrators. Application response time can be measured at the application server if the code is instrumented with ARM. But the transaction response time seen by the user is the sum of client-side response time, server-side response time, and network latency at each network location between client and server. No wonder there is so much fingerpointing when a user complains about performance.

Network and system administrators alike know that capacity headroom is critical for good performance. That's why they measure utilization and that's why an SLA should contain an agreement about this metric. Remember that an SLA is a tool used by the end-user community and their IT service provider to come to an agreement. It is not a monthly excuse to complain, point fingers, exercise political agendas, and take down names.

So you see that an SLA must be "as simple as possible and no simpler"[1] and be based on measurable quantities. For example, it may be agreed upon that the IT department will engineer the connection to the Internet such that utilization is below 50% for 90% of the time as long as there are fewer than 100 active users. Utilization data is easily obtained from the router via SNMP. The number of active users isn't directly measurable with SNMP. Indeed, the measurement is a difficult one to make properly, but it can be harvested from the firewall proxy server log or from the router via its IP accounting feature. Every month at the SLA meeting a simple graph is presented, such as in Figure 9-3.

Determining Performance Data Retention Intervals

The *snmpCollect* daemon will happily save SNMP historical data into its database until the hard drive capacity reaches zero. Unpredictable things happen to mission-critical systems when their disks fill up, so it's necessary that you address how long you want online SNMP data to be available.

---

1. This quote is attributed to Albert Einstein.

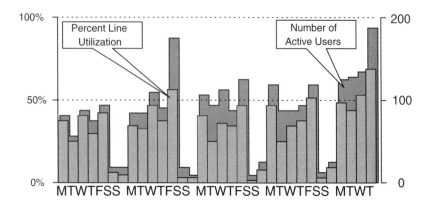

Figure 9-3   A sample chart used in an SLA.
The IT department and the user community have agreed that 90% of
the time the line utilization to the Internet will not exceed 50% as long
as there are less than 100 active users. Just by graphing this data, you
see that Friday is the busiest day of the week and the last day of the
month is also the busiest. Special business days often bring out more
users when they use a different application mix.

If you want to support users performing ad-hoc SNMP data
collections, then you need to provide the necessary disk space for
them. The user is entrusted to behave responsibly. The golden rules of
ad-hoc data collection are:

- massive data collections are generally inappropriate

- very long term data collections should be modest

- delete the data collection when the study is over

- limit rapid polling studies to the session interval

Many NNM systems are configured to collect basic SNMP data on all
devices in the management domain as a general service to the user
community. By default, an out of the box (OOTB) NNM system has
all defined data collections suspended, so no SNMP data is available
without intervention by the NNM system administrator. NNM offers

ovbackup and the data warehouse feature to backup or trim the historical SNMP data.

Trimming the amount of SNMP historical data is necessary because it will eventually fill the disk volume. A bulging database will also slow down the x*nmgraph* data display tool to a crawl as it searches for data to plot. Troubleshooters require only recent SNMP data for their tasks. Long-term performance data used by the network engineering staff can be culled from the NNM backup data just as easily.

To perform SNMP data trimming, HP provides a sample UNIX script in the manpage for the *snmpColDump* application (see Figure 9-4). Most NNM administrators will modify this script to suit their local needs and create a UNIX *cron* job to run it periodically, say, hourly.

```
#To keep only the last 2000 entries in file 1MinLoadAvg

lineno='snmpColDump 1MinLoadAvg | wc -l'
if [ $lineno -gt 2000 ]; then
lineno='expr $lineno - 2001'
else
lineno=1
if
snmpColDump -tTI 1MinLoadAvg | sed -n $lineno',$p' |
awk -F\t '{printf("%d\t%d\t%s\t%lg\n", $4, $5, $6, $3)}' |
snmpColDump -r - 1MinLoadAvg
```

Figure 9-4   A sample SNMP data trimmer script.
This small shell script from the *snmpColDump* manpage trims data in the *1MinLoadAvg* file to 2000 entries. This is a UNIX SNMP variable that measures the average number of processes in the run queue over a one-minute interval. Customize the script by running it against every SNMP data file on the system. Assuming that the NNM system administrator understands the Nyquist Sampling Theorem, the samples in *1MinLoadAvg* are probably taken every 30 seconds. Retaining 2000 data samples corresponds to 1000 minutes (about 16.7 hours) of data.

To speed up the data trimming process on a multiprocessor system, you can launch parallel trimming scripts, with each one assigned to an independent portion of the SNMP database. You'll notice a dramatic speed improvement. An alternative to using *cron* to launch the data trimmer is to configure ITO to monitor the size of the database. ITO can automatically execute the trimmer script when necessary.

Let's review some reasons for retaining SNMP historical data online. Assume the above issues can be mitigated. Perhaps you add more RAID disk stripes, a second SCSI controller, and another CPU to enhance performance. Perhaps you modify the script in Figure 9-4 to resample the data by averaging older five-minute samples into one-hour samples, thus reducing the data volume by a factor of 12. You then benefit from having enough online SNMP historical data that covers the following important periods of any business:

> busiest hour of the day
> busiest day of the week
> busiest day of the month
> busiest day of the quarter
> busiest day of the year
> busiest day of a special event

Troubleshooters can check back to see if the utilization they see now is comparable with that seen at a similar time in the past. For example, historical performance data shows that high network utilization at the end of the month in a sales office is actually normal, as it is at the end of a fiscal quarter.

A final note about long-term SNMP data retention deals with the cost issue of disk drives. At this writing, the cost of an 18-gigabyte internal SCSI disk drive is in the $600 range. Therefore, an 18-gigabyte dual-mirrored triple-striped disk array can be built for $3600 plus change. Obviously, you need to choose a computer platform that can accommodate these disks internally or externally, and this increases the price accordingly. But these figures are not outlandish; in fact, for a mission-critical NNM system they are more than acceptable.

Estimating SNMP Data Sample Rates

When you ask five network managers "what is a sensible sampling rate for SNMP data?" you will get six different answers. There are many conflicting issues responsible for this. Let's review some of them.

NNM itself allows SNMP sampling intervals as small as one second. SNMP agents running on 8-bit hardware as low-priority processes may be unable to respond to an SNMP request for multiple objects in such a short interval. They will often time-out and become unresponsive when pressed too hard. Recall that NNM is configured by default to try an SNMP request three extra times with a 0.8-second exponential time-out (0.8, 1.6, 3.2, and 6.4 seconds for four time-outs totalling 12 seconds). The retries will just serve to overload slow SNMP agents. Therefore, one-second polling intervals are generally avoided because that's smaller than the time-out interval. NNM administrators don't want to spend the extra time to configure specific SNMP timing parameters for specific network devices.

Polling a device on a remote network may incur a one-second round trip latency, especially if there are congested serial links to traverse. The default short SNMP time-outs will just add to the network traffic. For entire subnets it *is* practical to define one set of SNMP timeouts because it involves just one wild card setting in the configuration GUI. Still, one-second polling is too small for this case because the latency will disturb the sampling times by up to several seconds.

High-speed and high-volume SNMP polling can generate considerable network traffic. Given that many NNM systems use a fast Ethernet adapter, it is conceivable that a serial line can be swamped by SNMP traffic to the detriment of mission-critical traffic. A rule of thumb is that network management traffic should not use more than 10% of any link's capacity. Assuming a 200-byte SNMP packet size, you can multiply by the number of devices and divide by the polling interval to calculate the traffic SNMP polling adds to the network. Note that *snmpCollect* attempts to reduce the number of SNMP requests by testing each device's SNMP agent for the number of values it can return in one request. This reduces the overhead of sending multiple, single-valued requests, which is a good thing. It also increases the average packet size well above 200 bytes assumed above. Traffic overhead on the network is another reason for using larger polling intervals.

Short polling intervals on many SNMP objects will cause the *snmpCollect* daemon to consume more CPU time. This can negatively impact a small NNM system. Ideally, you want to keep *snmpCollect* below 10% CPU utilization. On the other hand, if too many concurrent data collections are attempted, *snmpCollect* can fall behind. Help *snmpCollect* keep up by configuring the *-n numberconcurrentsnmp* option in *snmpCollect.lrf*. Monitor the *$OV_LOG/snmpCol.trace* file for problems, because this option can be set too high. Keep this value well below *maxfiles*, the operating system's maximum number of open files parameter. If *maxfiles* is 64, then *-n 35* is found empirically to work well (but check *$OV_LOG/ snmpCol.trace* to verify *snmpCollect's* health). Once again, you have a reason to keep polling intervals on the high side.

We've seen that excessive polling can negatively impact network devices, the network itself, and the NNM system. A one-second polling interval isn't a good idea. But if you poll hourly, all the interesting variations in the network's statistics are averaged into one fairly unrepresentative and virtually useless statistic. Review Figure 9-5 to appreciate how sampling rates effect the quality of the resulting data. When in doubt, choose a five-minute sampling interval. Experience shows this captures enough of the changing statistics of network metrics and yet doesn't stress the network, NNM system, or sensitive network devices.

One-second samples

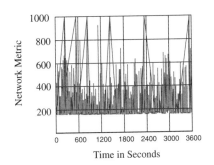

10-second samples

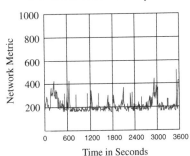

One-minute samples

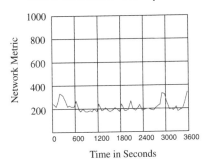

10-minute samples

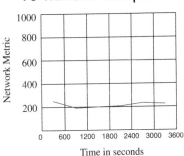

Figure 9-5   How sample rates effect data quality.
High sampling intervals like one second, ten seconds, and one minute
capture all of the interesting variations in the network metric. These
sample rates are too high. The 10-minute samples have removed all
of the interesting information in the data. This is why a common
sampling interval is five minutes.

The Heisenberg Uncertainty Principle of SNMP Polling

Practitioners in the field of quantum mechanics appreciate the famous Heisenberg uncertainty principle which states that it is not possible to determine simultaneously and exactly the position and momentum coordinates of a particle. The product of the two uncertainties is always greater than a minimum value approximately the size of Planck's constant ($6.6256\text{x}10^{-34}$). Quantum physicists know this is because the act of measurement disturbs the process being measured.

Network managers don't have a formal-sounding principle to explain it, but you know that using SNMP management software on a network disturbs it. Polling the network at a rate that lets us measure its real behavior disturbs it so badly that you can use a fairly timid polling interval of five minutes. And your rule of thumb is to limit SNMP traffic to 10% of the line speed. What do you disturb when you use NNM to poll devices? Consider the following list:

- adds to traffic, which only makes high utilization higher
- burdens the network equipment and server systems
- the data itself is subject to jitter due to latencies
- many devices give their SNMP agents low priority

Most of these problems can be avoided. Consider using RMON2 agents to sample network statistics. RMON2 probes don't need to poll the network equipment and HP NetMetrix can upload the statistics periodically with minimal impact on the network.

How Much Traffic Does NNM Create?

A network management system will generate many different kinds of traffic in various amounts. A reasonably complete list of traffic types follows:

- DNS forward and reverse lookups plus zone transfers
- status polling (ICMP echo request and reply)
- SNMP configuration polling by *netmon*
- collection station to management station traffic
- SNMP traps received from the network
- HTTP and Java traffic to remote browser users
- X-Window traffic from remote *ovw* users
- performance data collection by *snmpCollect*
- RMON SNMP traffic collected by NetMetrix
- ITO agent traffic to the ITO manager
- MeasureWare statistic to PerfView

Given the bursty nature of this traffic, a dedicated 100BASE-T full duplex switch port should be used to connect the NMS system to the network. The full duplex feature eliminates the possibility of collisions and the 100-megabit/second line speed ensures high throughput and reduces LAN latency to a minimum. It also allows the remote disk backup process to complete in a timely manner.

Despite the conservative musing above, it's the author's experience that a standard Ethernet connection is generally sufficient. Still, it's preferable to know how much traffic the NNM system is generating. This can be done using one of these methods:

- let the NNM system poll its own LAN interface
- let the NNM system poll the switch port it's connected to
- use the NNM system's MeasureWare agent and PerfView
- use NetMetrix and an RMON probe to monitor NNM traffic
- attach a LAN analyzer to the NNM system Ethernet port

The NNM system is supposed to be situated in the heart of its management domain to minimize the impact of network management traffic by diversifying it. All traffic in and out of the NNM system does not impact just one WAN circuit. Yet if a large number of managed devices and subnets exist at the far end of a relatively slow serial line, you should estimate the impact of NNM traffic to avoid breaking our 10% rule. RMON2 probes with HP NetMetrix can accurately measure the traffic.

Note that the network management staff and the NNM administrators need to work together. It's already problematic that router SNMP agents are assigned the lowest task priorities in Cisco routers. It's less helpful if SNMP traffic is also assigned to a low priority queue by a router's manager, or if the NNM system's IP address is excluded from the router's access control list (ACL). Such antics are symptomatic of dysfunctional teams.

Prior to deploying NNM, the question of NNM's traffic impact can't be answered by measurement, so you need to attempt a quick analysis. Assume that your management domain looks like Figure 9-6. Given the bandwidth of the WAN links and the number of managed devices in each campus area, can you calculate the SNMP traffic impact due to performance polling? (You don't have RMON2 probes or NetMetrix in this discussion). Assume that traffic between sites A and D passes through sites B and C. There is no NNM traffic on the line between sites F and C since both have a direct line to site D. A simple spreadsheet is used to tabulate the data and calculate the results. You

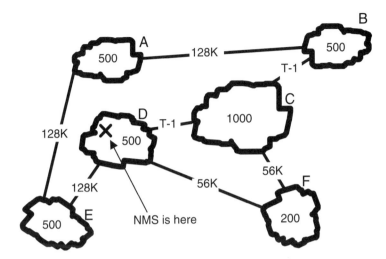

Figure 9-6 Calculating the impact of performance polling.
This network consists of six sites that look like small clouds connected
with WAN links. The number of nodes at each site is given along with
the line speed. You assume in the arithmetic that the line speed equals
the actual data rate available. The arithmetic in Table 9-1 calculates
the line utilization due to the NNM performance polling.

can assume five-minute polling and 200-byte packets. Each device
polled is assumed to have one interface in the sample arithmetic. You
should adjust the arithmetic to reflect your device average interface
count. You calculate that the line between sites E and D suffers a mere
2.1% utilization, the worst of all the lines you calculated. This is well
below your 10% maximum rule of thumb. Table 9-1 organizes the
arithmetic. Polling traffic in bytes-per-second is calculated by
multiplying the packet size in bytes by eight times the number of
nodes and dividing by the polling interval of five minutes times 60
seconds per minute:

$$(\text{packet\_size\_in\_bytes} \times 8 \times \text{Number\_of\_nodes})/(300 \text{ seconds})$$

Now calculate the percent line utilization by dividing the polling traffic in bits-per-second by the line speed in bits-per-second and multiplying by 100:

(polling_traffic/line_speed)×100

Table 9-1   Estimating Line Utilization for SNMP Polling

Link	Traffic From	Nodes Polled	Traffic Bits/sec.	Line Speed Bits/sec.	Line % Utilization
A-B	A	500	2667	128,000	2.1
B-C	A,B	1000	5333	1,544,000	0.3
C-D	A,B,C	2000	10667	1,544,000	0.7
F-D	F	200	1067	56,000	1.9
E-D	E	500	2667	128,000	2.1
C-F	n/a	n/a	n/a	n/a	n/a
A-E	n/a	n/a	n/a	n/a	n/a

SNMP Performance Data in MIB2 and Private MIBs

There are hundreds of useful variables in the industry standard MIB-2. Most are located in the interfaces section, and a few more can be found in the IP section. It is prudent to limit the amount of data you collect to the bare essentials. This avoids overloading SNMP agents, taxing the network, and storing a lot of unnecessary performance data on the hard drive.

Often, a single variable does not tell the whole story by itself. For example, the number of input errors on an interface is meaningless by itself. You have to divide it by the number of received packets and multiply by 100 before it's possible to judge if the error rate is too high.

NNM lets you form mathematical formulas comprised of MIB values. These formulas are called MIB expressions, which are generally much more useful than raw SNMP values. Table 9-2 lists some recommendations plus some threshold settings to get you started.

Table 9-2   Threshold Value Rules of Thumb

NNM MIB Expression	Suggested Threshold Settings	Explanatory Notes
avgBusy5	Alarm 90% for 4 samples. Rearm 50% for 2 samples.	CPU router utilization five-minute average. High router CPU utilization may not be a bad thing.
If%util	Alarm 90% for 4 samples. Rearm 60% for 2 samples.	The interface is treated as a full duplex. High utilization by itself is not a bad thing.
If%inErrors	Alarm 1% for 4 samples. Rearm 0% for 2 samples.	Small but consistent errors are a bad thing.

Table 9-2   Threshold Value Rules of Thumb

NNM MIB Expression	Suggested Threshold Settings	Explanatory Notes
If%outErrors	Alarm 1% at 4 samples. Rearm 0% for 2 samples.	Small but consistent errors are a bad thing.
IP%PacketLoss	Alarm 1% for 4 samples. Rearm 0% for 2 sample.	Packet loss in the router due to buffer overflow and other maladies reduce application performance. For Cisco routers, it counts the number of packets the router could not forward because no ARP reply was received for a hop.

Note that the first entry in this table is not a MIB expression, it is part of the Cisco enterprise MIB. For all table values the recommended sample interval is five minutes. The thresholds given are rules of thumb. The alarm sample duration of four samples ensures the condition is persistent while the two-sample rearm ensures that you detect return to normal situations quickly.

Strategies for Setting Threshold Values

Should you define threshold values for performance polling? What is the staff going to do about a threshold event? What is the local process? The usual answer is that nothing can be done or should be done. After all, if a user is downloading a large file or if a backup is in progress, is it appropriate to hunt down the offending system and shut down the switch port it's connected to? This kind of draconian network policing is certain to cause vehement user reaction.

A threshold event should be classified as a mere warning and not acted upon directly by the staff. There is also an opportunity for an ECS-trained network manager to create a custom circuit that intelligently correlates threshold events into a more useful one. For example, if a significant portion of the network is experiencing threshold events, the custom event correlator should detect this and generate a major event.

Assuming you want to generate threshold events, how should the threshold values be set? Three approaches can be considered.

The easiest answer is to use the published rules of thumb such as those in Table 9-2 and in textbooks on capacity planning[2].

A more difficult approach is to adjust the threshold levels upward until the event rate is acceptably low. This approach is clearly labor-intense since each and every interface has to be monitored and individually tweaked. Another name for this technique is baselining. You monitor the performance metrics for a few weeks for each device and then change the threshold levels accordingly. Note that these threshold levels can be manually added in the *$OV_CONF/snmpCol.conf* file to avoid a lot of tedious work with the SNMP data collector configuration GUI. The format of this file changed at NNM 6.0, so be cautious when you upgrade your NNM system to migrate this file format.

A final approach to setting threshold values is based on analytic considerations. For example, suppose you model a serial circuit as a simple M/M/1 queue. Recall that if this queue is 90% utilized, then the average wait time is 10x the norm. That's a good reason to generate an alarm. For error rates and packet loss, consider the graph

---

2. John Blommers, Prentice Hall, 1996, Practical Planning for Network Growth, ISBN 0-13-206111-2

in Figure 9-7. It shows how the TCP throughput of an application performing a continuous TCP data transfer slows as packet loss increases. Even a one percent packet loss effectively reduces throughput to negligible levels.

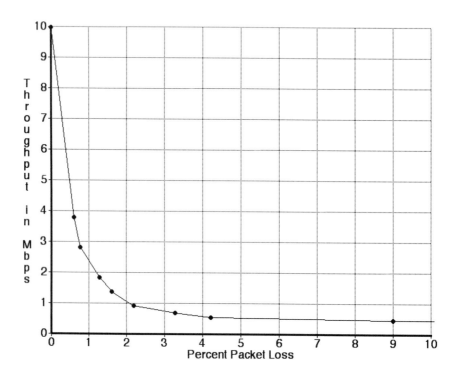

Figure 9-7   TCP throughput vs. packet loss.
An analytic approach to setting error thresholds involves examining empirical data as depicted here. This graph depicts a single streaming TCP data connection between workstations on the same LAN segment which is subject to packet loss. Clearly, the slightest loss percentage effectively negates the streaming advantages of TCP. An error threshold of one percent is justified by this data.

To avoid a random single error burst from generating an alarm, you can take advantage of NNM's clever threshold features. By specifying that a given metric must exceed the threshold value for four consecutive samples, you ensure that only a sustained error condition will generate an alarm. At five-minute samples this means a 20-minute duration is required to trigger an alarm. To ensure the restoration of service is detected promptly, you can set the duration of the rearm interval to only two samples, or 10 minutes. The principles are explained in Figure 9-8.

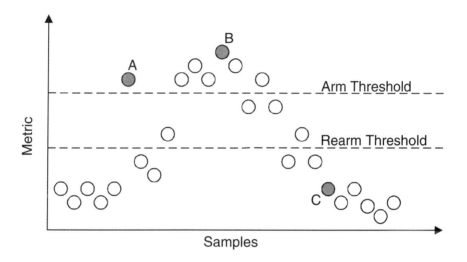

Figure 9-8   NNM threshold parameters.
In the examples in the text you require four consecutive samples to exceed the arm threshold to generate a threshold event. The sample labeled B will generate an event, but sample A will not because only a single consecutive sample has exceeded the arm threshold. Two consecutive samples must be lower than the rearm threshold, so sample C is the only one that qualifies.

How to Create MIB Expressions

Standard MIB2 and enterprise MIBs alike support counter variables for bytes, octets, packets, and errors. Among the really useful metrics you need to manage network performance are percent utilization and percent errors. NNM's historical SNMP data collector predefines quite a few useful MIB expressions. See Chapter 11 of the manual *Managing Your Network with HP OpenView Network Node Manager* for a detailed list of them. A MIB expression is a reverse polish notation (RPN) arithmetic formula made up of standard MIB object identifiers. The expressions are stored in the *$OV_CONF/ mibExpr.conf* file, which you maintain manually using your favorite text editor.

Here is an example of a MIB expression:

```
If%deferred \ "packets deferred/packets transmitted" \
.1.3.6.1.4.1.11.2.4.1.1.1.4. .1.3.6.1.4.1.11.2.4.1.1.1.2. / 100 *
```

The label *If%deferred* in the first field refers to the "interface percent deferred" which is intended to calculate the percent of transmitted packets that experienced a deferral before being transmitted. The backward slash is a field delimiter. The text between quotation marks in the second field is a comment which usually contains information about the MIB expression. In this case, it shows us the formula for calculating percent deferred packets. The third field contains the actual formula in an RPN format (a.k.a postfix format). You see five elements in the example above. The first two are the object identifiers from the HP vendor-specific MIB for packets deferred and packets transmitted; they are placed on the stack. The third element is a forward slash which is the divide operator. This places the quotient on the stack. The fourth element is the integer 100 which is placed on the stack. The fifth element is an asterisk which is the multiply operator, and the result is a percentage left on the stack representing the percent deferred packets.

When the *snmpCollect* daemon encounters this MIB expression in a collection, it requests values for all the objects contained in the expression from the device, evaluates the formula, and stores the result in the database.

Here is an additional example of a MIB expression which measures the packet loss in a router:

```
IP%PacketLoss \ "Percent of packets a router discarded\n\
Computed by:\n\
(100*(ipInDiscards+ipOutDiscards/(ipInDiscards+ipOutDiscards+ipForwDatagrams)\n\
which is a percentage." \
100 \
.1.3.6.1.2.1.4.8.0 \
.1.3.6.1.2.1.4.11.0 \
+ * \
.1.3.6.1.2.1.4.8.0 \
.1.3.6.1.2.1.4.11.0 \
.1.3.6.1.2.1.4.6.0 \
+ + /
```

As a practical matter, Cisco routers include those packets in the *ipOutDiscards* metric that could not be forwarded because no ARP cache entry existed for the target IP address in the dropped packet, despite attempts to find the device's MAC address using ARP. In other words, if a packet cannot be delivered to its destination, the router will increment the counter, even though this has nothing to do with buffer overflow, which is what you are hoping to measure. The lesson here is that despite your best efforts at applying common sense in fabricating a MIB expression, you have to be very clear about what the vendor's SNMP implementation really measures.

See Chapter 11 of the *Managing Your Network with HP OpenView Network Node Manager* manual for detailed information on writing and using MIB expression.

Viewing Performance Data Online

The simplest way to look at historical SNMP data is to select the device you're interested in and choose the *Performance:Display SNMP data:For Selected Nodes* menu. This brings up the *xnmgraph* GUI which displays the device performance data found in the database, if any.

To view live SNMP data from several devices on specific interfaces, you can launch the *xnmgraph* application from a command line. For example, to plot *ifInOctets* and *ifOutOctets* for MIB instances 2-5 for both *node1* and *node2*, use this command:

```
xnmgraph -mib \
"interfaces.ifTable.ifEntry.ifInOctets:In Bytes:[2-5]::::::,\
interfaces.ifTable.ifEntry.ifOutOctets:Out Bytes:[2-5]::::::" \
node1 node2
```

You can use the *snmpColDump* application along with some scripting to print out collected SNMP data. Assume that data has been collected using *snmpCollect* under the label *macDeferred.1*. To print out the average value of *macDeferred.1* for *node1*, use this command:

```
snmpColDump $OV_DB/snmpCollect/macDeferred.1 |
awk -F\t '/node1/{num++; sum+=$3} END{print sum/num}'
```

The file *macDeferred.1* contains the historic SNMP data for all nodes and the *awk* script filters out the data for *node1*, calculates the totals, computes the average value, and displays it.

When troubleshooting a performance problem, suppose that you just received a threshold event in the event browser. Double-click the event, and the offending node is displayed in its parent map. Select the node and use the menus to display the performance data. If the graph is cluttered with other data which isn't related to this collection, you can customize the graph by turning off the other lines.

Users wishing to view SNMP historical data in a web browser may use the contributed Java viewer.

Presenting Performance Data to the Consumer

A network manager spends some of the time making presentations about network performance and isn't always in a position to present the data online. NNM performance data needs to be captured and repurposed for offline meetings.

Assuming that NNM historical performance data is available, a few simple screenshots could suffice. (See "Taking Screenshots of Maps" on page 88.) Note that the standard *xnmgraph* window background is black, which lets the other line colors stand out clearly. The background color is controlled by an X-Window resource located in the *$APP_DEFS/XNmgraph* resource file. The resulting file should be transferred from the UNIX NNM system to the authoring workstation in binary format.

Should textually formatted performance data be preferred, *xnmgraph* may be used to save the displayed data in a text file. While UNIX does not require or recognize file name extensions, it may be appropriate to append the *.txt* extension for the benefit of challenged authoring work-stations that do need them. Transfer the text file in ASCII format from the NNM system to the authoring workstation. The columnar textual data is usually imported into a spreadsheet or word processor to reformat it for presentation purposes.

The *snmpColDump* utility may also be used to save specific SNMP performance data into a text file.

SNMPv2c and 64-bit Counters

The standard integer in SNMP MIB2 is 32 bits long. SNMPv2C MIB defines a new type of integer with the attribute name *unsigned64* that is 64 bits long. Its maximum value is:

18,446,744,073,709,551,615

The reason for specifying such a large counter is found in rfc2233:

```
"As the speed of network media increase, the minimum time
in which a 32 bit counter will wrap decreases. For
example, a 10Mbs stream of back-to-back, full-size
packets causes ifInOctets to wrap in just over 57
minutes; at 100Mbs, the minimum wrap time is 5.7
minutes, and at 1Gbs, the minimum is 34 seconds.
Requiring that interfaces be polled frequently enough
not to miss a counter wrap is increasingly problematic."
```

Note that NNM handles a single counter wrap properly, but if two counter wraps occur between SNMP samples, the result is bad data. Recall that you suggested using a five-minute sample interval for SNMP data collections (See "Estimating SNMP Data Sample Rates" on page 149). Here you see that ordinary fast Ethernet interfaces must be sampled at almost exactly this speed to avoid counter wrap in highly utilized situations. Since it is impossible to know in advance how utilized a circuit is, all of them have to be sampled at five-minute intervals to avoid a wrap. If you use the SNMPv2C 64-bit counters, you can tolerate a larger sample interval for SNMP historical data collections.

The new SNMPv2C 64-bit counters are found in the *IfXEntry* branch in the interfaces section of MIB2, as shown in Figure 9-9. You can find detailed definitions for them in *rfc2233*.

Note that NNM makes a standard configuration check for every SNMP-capable device to determine if it supports SNMPv2C. This

```
IfXEntry ::=
      SEQUENCE {
            ifName                       DisplayString,
            ifInMulticastPkts            Counter32,
            ifInBroadcastPkts            Counter32,
            ifOutMulticastPkts           Counter32,
            ifOutBroadcastPkts           Counter32,
            ifHCInOctets                 Counter64,
            ifHCInUcastPkts              Counter64,
            ifHCInMulticastPkts          Counter64,
            ifHCInBroadcastPkts          Counter64,
            ifHCOutOctets                Counter64,
            ifHCOutUcastPkts             Counter64,
            ifHCOutMulticastPkts         Counter64,
            ifHCOutBroadcastPkts         Counter64,
            ifLinkUpDownTrapEnable       INTEGER,
            ifHighSpeed                  Gauge32,
            ifPromiscuousMode            TruthValue,
            ifConnectorPresent           TruthValue,
            ifAlias DisplayString,
            ifCounterDiscontinuityTime   TimeStamp
      }
```

Figure 9-9   64-bit counters in SNMPv2C.
This is the extended interface section defined by SNMPv2C. Note the Counter64 variables such as *ifHCInOctets* and *ifHCOutOctets* are sufficient such that a 1-terabit/second (1,000 Gbps.) link will cause the counter to wrap in just under five years. The old *ifSpeed* variable is limited to about 2.2Gbps, while the new *ifHighSpeed* variable measures in units of 1,000,000 bits per second.

check can be disabled by specifying the *-2* option in *$OV_CONF/ netmon.lrf*. Some devices and systems may misbehave, log a message, or display a warning when they receive an SNMPv2C request. This *netmon* option avoids the problem. It's better in the long term to update the offending SNMP agents while temporarily unmanaging these devices or putting their IP addresses in *netmon.noDiscover*.

It is not advisable to manage gigabit Ethernet without using 64-bit counters.

Collecting RMON Data

The remote monitoring MIB (RMON) provides very detailed performance data. In this section we'll focus on the Ethernet portion of RMON, which is in the original standard. Extensions for token ring and FDDI won't be covered here. Recall that RMON agents are built into special probe devices, such as the HP LANProbe, which are attached to remote shared-medium Ethernet hubs to monitor them, as shown in Figure 9-10. These agents may be found in network

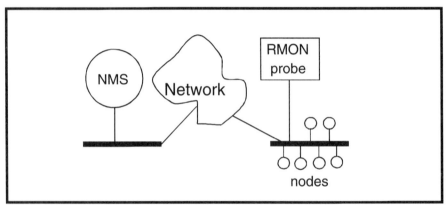

Figure 9-10   A shared medium RMON probe.
The network management station (NMS) uses standard SNMP requests to gather segment statistics from the remote RMON probe. The nodes indicated share the LAN medium and the RMON probe operates in a promiscuous[a] mode to collect statistics such as total bytes, packets, errors, broadcasts, and multicasts. NNM can collect the simpler *Etherstats* group statistics while HP NetMetrix can control the probe to deliver sophisticated, end-to-end performance data across the enterprise network.

a. When it is operating in a promiscuous mode, a LAN adapter is able to capture all LAN frames present on the shared medium, even those not specifically addressed to it. This is a necessary feature for RMON probes and LAN analyzers in general. A LAN adapter is normally able to receive only frames addressed to its MAC address, the all-ones broadcast address, and possibly one or more multicast addresses.

equipment such as switches, where they can monitor all ports. While special software such as HP NetMetrix is best suited to controlling and managing RMON agents, simple Ethernet statistics can be collected using simple SNMP methods.

The Etherstats group of the RMON MIB provides information about the LAN segment the probe is connected to. A shared medium LAN segment behaves exactly as does the traditional Ethernet cable and the Ethernet hub, repeater, or concentrator. All devices share the same medium, so a single RMON probe can monitor all the devices connected to it. A list of the performance variables in the RMON Etherstats group is given in Table 9-3.

Table 9-3   The RMON Etherstats MIB Variables

Variable	Description
etherStatsOctets	The total number of bytes counted.
etherStatsPkts	The total number of packets counted.
etherStatsBroadcastPkts	The number of MAC broadcast packets counted.
etherStatsMulticastPkts	The number of multicast packets counted.
etherstatsCRCAlignErrors	The number of frames with extra bits.
etherstatsUndersizePkts	The number of packets shorter than 64 bytes.
eterstats OversizePkts	The number of packets exceeding 1518 bytes.
etherStatsFragments	The number of collision fragments counted.
etherStatsJabbers	The number of jabber frames (> 8000 bits) seen.
etherStatsCollisions	The total number of collisions counted.
etherStatsPkts64Octets	The number of packets with exactly 64 bytes.

Table 9-3   The RMON Etherstats MIB Variables

Variable	Description
etherStatsPkts65to127Octets	The number of packets between 65 and 127 bytes in size.
etherStatsPkts128to255Octets	The number of packets between 128 and 255 bytes.
etherStatsPkts256to511Octets	The number of packets between 256 and 511 bytes.
etherStatsPkts512to1023Octets	The number of packets between 512 and 1023 bytes.
etherStatsPkts1024to1518Octets	The number of packets between 1024 and 1518 bytes.

Be sure to load the RMON MIB on your NNM system using the *xnmloadmib* GUI before attempting to collect any data from the network. Note that none of these statistics actually measures LAN utilization. A MIB expression is needed that implements the formula:

$$\%\text{utilization} = (\text{etherStatsOctets} \times 800)/\text{ifSpeed}$$

For example, for a standard Ethernet, *ifSpeed* is 10,000,000 bits per second, and let's say you measure 600,000 octets per second. (As a practical matter, *snmpCollect* knows that *etherStatsOctets* is a *Counter32* variable, so it actually differences successive samples and then divides by the number of seconds between samples, returning a rate measured in octets per second.) The formula returns 48% utilization. The variable *etherStatsOctets* is in the *rmon* group under the *mib2* branch, while *ifSpeed* is under the *interfaces* group of *mib2*.

Note that standard RMON statistics measure only MAC layer statistics and are network-layer agnostic. To collect network-layer and application-layer statistics requires RMON2 and an application such as HP NetMetrix that can decode, present, and report the data efficiently. However, for simple shared-medium Ethernet, token ring, and FDDI LANs, standard NNM SNMP data collection suffices for basic segment-level performance management.

Crossing Over into HP NetMetrix

Network Node Manager makes a great launching platform for NetMetrix. NNM discovers all known RMON probes on the network, which NetMetrix can then use. NetMetrix can collect statistics from all these probes in the background. You can then view this historical data. For probes with RMON2 or extended RMON, you can also display traffic between source and destination subnets by application and by system, as shown in Figure 9-11.

Capacity Planning

NNM provides the as-built network topology needed for capacity planning. HP NetMetrix can provide the existing performance metrics. HP Service Simulator can import both topology (see Figure 9-12) and performance data to create a baseline simulation model of your network. What's next, then?

Before you can use the simulator and write a capacity plan, you must have a question to answer. The kinds of questions you might consider are as follows:

- Can the network handle another 1000 users?
- What happens when I consolidate 100 mail hubs into 10?
- What upgrades are needed to support our new ERP application?
- Will adding a second T-1 line meet response time requirements?
- Can the network handle the new print-on-demand technology?

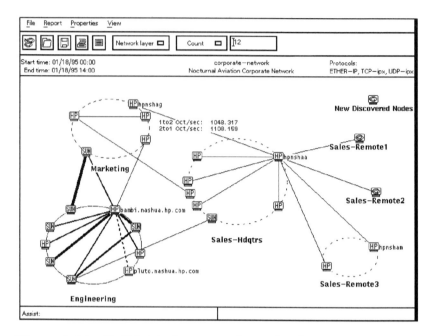

Figure 9-11   NetMetrix Internet view of point-to-point traffic.
Properly located RMON2 probes can see traffic between subnets as
well as local traffic on each subnet. This diagram shows subnets as
ovals. Lines between traffic sources, such as those between the
Marketing and Engineering subnets, show how much total traffic flows
between devices on these subnets. A thick line represents more traffic
than a thin line.

All of these are "what if?" questions. You typically take the baseline
simulation model created with Service Simulator, make changes
postulated in the question, and let the simulator calculate the impact
on response time and circuit utilization (Figure 9-13).

If you are planning to add a new application to the network, you need
data about its traffic requirements. You also need LAN analyzer traces
of the most commonly used transactions. These can be imported into
the simulator. Edit the network topology, move servers around, add
new clients and servers, modify line speeds, and run the simulator to
see what happens. The basic methodology is shown in Figure 9-14.

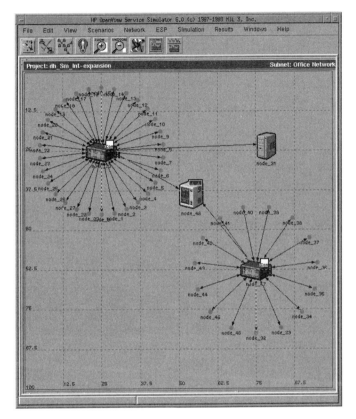

Figure 9-12   A simple network topology in service simulator.
This is one of the tutorials provided with the Service Simulator product. Complex networks are dealt with using hierarchical container objects. In practice, the topology can be imported directly from NNM and then edited to define various what-if scenarios. After traffic profiles are created, the simulation is allowed to run until it reaches a steady state.

Do any circuits operate at capacity? Are transaction response times within acceptable limits? If not, then change some parameters and try again.

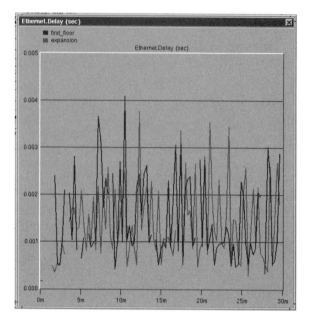

Figure 9-13   Simulation results for Ethernet delay.
One of the outputs of the simulator is the Ethernet delay versus time.
You see that the steady state is reached early in the simulation and
that the worst delay is only about 4 milliseconds.

Conclusion

Having read this chapter, you are now able to decide at which point
between the extremes you want to practice capacity planning. Will
you take the time to follow the full-blown approach in Figure 9-14,
cross your fingers, and simply provision bandwidth to deal with
capacity issues, or will you find a middle ground? Whatever you
decide, may all your capacity plans be successful.

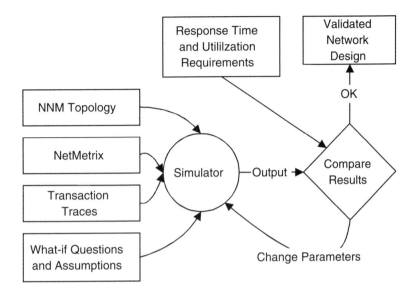

Figure 9-14   Capacity Planning Methodology.
The simulation tool is the core of the capacity planning methodology. A lot of time is saved by importing network topology from NNM, performance data from NetMetrix, and transaction traces from LAN analyzers. Armed with a question, you run the simulator to find out if the network can meet the response time and utilization requirements. If requirements aren't met, go back and move servers around, add bandwidth, change the topology, or reduce the traffic load until they are. When you validate that the network design can deliver the desired performance, you can produce the results to prove it with graphs and charts.

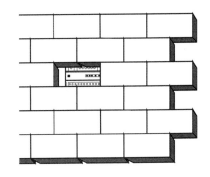

Managing Firewall Environments With NNM

Introduction

The demilitarized zone (DMZ) is a term often used to describe a security island or security perimeter that protects the corporate network from untrusted networks to which it is connected. It's often used to guard Internet connection from intruders (ingress) while governing how much access corporate users have to the Internet (egress).

Working with the corporate security group to implement an NNM solution for managing the DMZ may result in their unexpectedly imposing technical constraints that must be addressed before the solution is acceptable in this special environment.

Special security configurations for UNIX systems in a DMZ environment include limiting available network services and allowing access to specific services like *telnet* to specific users and systems. Avoid denial of service (DOS) attacks by configuring static routes, ARP caches, and DNS data.

Managing a network through a firewall means allowing specific TCP and UDP ports to and from the NNM system through the packet filters (assuming the firewall is based on packet filtering technology). Either the NNM system is outside the DMZ or inside it. The impact on the firewall packet filters is different in each case.

Router access control lists (or *access-lists*) can prevent NNM from discovering and determining their configuration. NNM systems need to be given read-only (RO) access to at least the SNMP daemon (a.k.a. SNMP server).

Packet filtering with a router is a common way to prevent unwanted traffic from an untrusted network to enter the DMZ. The filter typically allows only specific connections to specific servers while simultaneously preventing IP spoofing attacks.

Accessing an NNM system remotely is essential for off-site personnel. Secure solutions range from low-performance dial-up access and medium-performance ISDN and DSL, to high-speed cable modems. Security authentication is available using double passwords, token cards, and VPN.

Disaster recovery is especially important for systems that manage the DMZ (or are located in it). These systems are at greater risk for disaster than normal management systems.

Defining the DMZ Environment

The demilitarized zone (DMZ) is a special network that joins a private corporate network with an untrusted network. That untrusted network might belong to a business partner, a carrier, an Internet service provider (ISP), or other parts of the corporate network. The DMZ supports very specific ingress and egress connectivity between the two networks.

The DMZ contains routers, packet filters, Ethernet switches, DNS servers, web servers, proxy servers, socks servers, and telnet gateways. It's generally a collection of subnets configured for very specific security-minded functionality. Correct operation of the DMZ is critical and it must be managed proactively.

Ingress into the private network is often restricted to SMTP-based services (e-mail). Egress out of the private network is often restricted to web traffic (HTTP), file transfer get operations (FTP), telnet, and SMTP-based e-mail.

How do you manage the DMZ? Since access to the DMZ is restricted, you could situate an NNM system inside it. How would users gain access to the NNM system? You could require users to access NNM physically from within the DMZ. You could also configure a pinhole through the DMZ firewall to pass X-Windows traffic to a golden subnet located on the private network.

Alternatively, you could situate the NNM system on a golden subnet in the corporate network (see Figure 10-1) and configure pinholes that

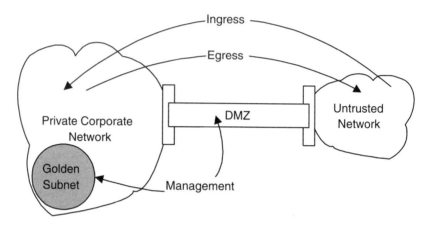

Figure 10-1 Managing the DMZ.
A golden subnet is a specific subnet from within which a specific NNM system is allowed to access managed devices. The golden subnet is located within the corporate network, and network managers access systems located here to manage the DMZ as well as the rest of the corporate network. Routers are usually configured to accept SNMP requests from either any device on this subnet or just specific devices (usually the NNM systems).

allow just this system's network management traffic into the DMZ. Users can access the NNM system from any location since their X-Windows traffic is entirely inside the corporate network.

Working With the Corporate Security Group

The group responsible for network management that provides the NNM tool to the user community rarely finds those users imposing special restraints on the NNM system. They manage the internal network and are trusted by the network managers, troubleshooters, and help desk staff alike. The configuration of the NNM system used to manage a DMZ is very likely to be heavily scrutinized by the security staff.

The security group can benefit greatly by using NNM to monitor the DMZ. What corporate network environment should be managed more closely? By setting thresholds on key metrics, out of the ordinary performance behavior can be spotted quickly. Is there a broadcast storm at the router interface on the untrusted network? Has the error rate gone up? Is utilization well above the norm? Has the connection gone down? Is that a newly discovered node on the DMZ? Why is it there? Why is the CPU utilization of the proxy server suddenly 100%. The inbound SMTP server just went down.

Any equipment located on the DMZ will normally have additional constraints placed on its configuration, administration, and usage. The NNM system administrators should don their UNIX administrator hats and pay special attention to locking down the operating system.

The security group will generally assume that the NNM system is insecure until proven otherwise. They will break out their auditing tools, load them on the system, and tell you what needs to be changed. They may even insist that a security auditing and monitoring daemon run on the NNM system continuously. Access to this NNM system will probably be limited to a few individual accounts only.

Sometimes the politics in the company might appear to give the security group outlandish powers of veto and control, but understand that security-minded professionals are paid to be paranoid. Perhaps the key to successfully working with a domineering security group is to reach a mutual understanding of each other's goals and objectives.

Special Security Configuration for UNIX in the DMZ

Limiting access into the NNM system is where security begins. Shut down all network services first, then turn on just the ones you need. Remove all user accounts and then add back the ones you need. Therefore, the file */etc/hosts.deny* should contain (at least initially) the line:

    ALL: ALL

in order to disable access to all services and all systems. Then you can open up the inbound *telnet* service to some systems by adding a line to the */etc/hosts.allow* file as follows:

```
in.telnetd: john@master1.myco.com, bar@foo.myco.com
```

You may also consider completely disabling *telnet* and use secure shell (*ssh*) for remote access instead. Many UNIX system administrators swear by *ssh*.

You may want to further deter spoofing attempts and configure the *ident* service to require that client hosts cooperate by running *identd*. This service returns the login name of the user requesting a network connection. See the manpages for *hosts.allow, hosts.deny, snmpd.conf,* and *identd* for more detail. Note that *identd* (identification daemon) and *inetd* (internet daemon) are different, yet are easily confused.

Ensure that shadow passwords are enabled. Configure the file */etc/ securetty* to contain only the *console* device entry, so *root* can't log in directly through the network. This forces every user to log in as a normal user first. Disable the *.rhosts* feature. Enable auditing and take advantage of ITO to monitor failed login attempts (or at least write a few simple scripts for this task). NIS and NFS services are consequently disabled to prevent network access to the file system. All daemons that normally run continuously, are started at boot time, and don't provide an essential service, should be disabled.

All non-essential network services controlled by *inetd* are commented out of the *inetd.conf* file. Also consider using "TCP wrappers" to control connections to and from *inetd*. It can allow/disallow connections based on port and/or address. If FTP is important, ensure that */etc/hosts.allow* is used to limit access to this service. On an HP-UX system take advantage of */usr/adm/inetd.sec* to limit access to network services to the golden subnet.

Configure the NNM system to use DNS servers intended for the DMZ, but if the number of managed devices is relatively small, it is safer to use a local */etc/hosts* file instead to ensure configuration control. At the very least, you should take advantage of the BIND version 8 security features.

In general, try to avoid autoconfiguring protocols like ARP and RIP. You should hand-configure the IP and MAC addressees of all devices in the DMZ into the ARP table to avoid spoofing. All routing protocols should be disabled and static routes used instead.

Finally, as a general rule, there should be no world-writable files. Since there are many of these on UNIX systems, and because NNM also creates and uses some, you have to write a script to find them all and modify the permissions. This should be done at installation time, after patches are installed, and then periodically, because the running software may create new world-readable files during normal operation. Where NNM needs to write to certain files generally, the NNM processes should be configured to execute under an additional group to which all these files are members.

Firewalls and NNM Port Usage

There may be situations where the NNM system and the network it is managing are separated by a firewall. This section reviews NNM requirements for various network services in a general way.

There are two main scenarios to consider while reading the rest of this section. In scenario A the managed network and the NNM collection stations are separated by a firewall. NNM must be able to probe through the firewall to reach its management domain. The NNM users have direct access to their NNM system. Scenario B situates the NNM collection station inside its management domain. The users are located on the other side of the firewall and so is the management station. Now both the users and the management station must pass through the firewall to reach the collection station. See Figure 10-2.

To communicate across a firewall you need a complete understanding of the protocols NNM uses. The details are given in the following paragraphs and the data is summarized in Table 10-1.

The *netmon* daemon sends ICMP echo and parameter requests. In general, SNMP get requests on UDP port 161, and the associated replies are necessary for normal operations, including topology updates between a collection station and its management station. SNMP traps may be received on UDP port 162. If there is a collection station on the other side of the firewall, then there will be *pmd* to *pmd* traffic on TCP port 162. HTTP server discovery uses requests on port 80 and 280.

To gain access to the NNM system across a firewall, the *telnet* protocol on TCP port 23 must be passed. To run *ovw* across the firewall, X-Windows traffic on TCP port 6000 must be passed. Alternatively, the web-based NNM console could be used for access. It uses port TCP port 8880.

If there is a name server that must be accessed across the firewall, then UDP port 53 must also pass through.

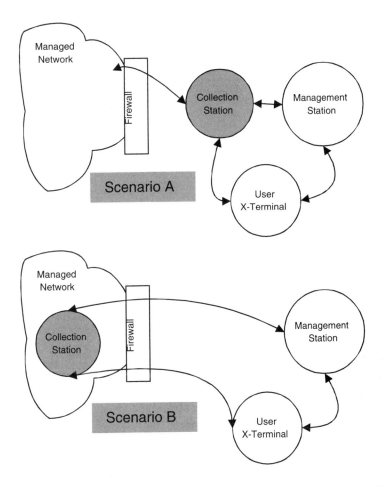

Figure 10-2   Relationship between NNM and the firewall.
Scenario A requires the collection station to manage its network
through a firewall. This relaxes the security requirements of the
collection station and simplifies the pinholes the firewall must endure.
Scenario B places the collection station inside the firewalled network
it is managing, posing additional security requirements upon it. X-
Windows traffic from the users, plus management station traffic, must
be allowed to pass through the firewall, making this a more complex
situation.

Should the convenience of FTP be important, then TCP ports 20 and 21 must also pass the firewall.

Table 10-1   Summary of NNM Port Numbers

Service	Protocol	Source Port	Source	Destination Port	Destination
SNMP	UDP	1024-65535	Mgmt station	161	Managed nodes
SNMP Trap	UDP	1024-65535	Nodes	162	Mgmt station
OV events	TCP	1024-65535	Collection station	162	Mgmt station
ICMP	IP	N/A	Mgmt station	N/A	Managed nodes
HTTP	TCP	1024-65535	Mgmt station	80 or 280	Managed nodes
Telnet	TCP	1024-65535	Mgmt station	23	CS/managed nodes
X-Windows OVW	TCP	1024-65535	Collection station	6000	Mgmt station

NNM uses these TCP and UDP port numbers to communicate with managed devices, management stations, and users. A firewall must be configured to pass these packets for full NNM functionality.

Given the security implications of allowing *telnet* and X-Windows access across the firewall, both the NNM system and the firewall should be configured to pass only traffic to and from well-known systems. Configure the file */etc/snmpd.conf* on the collection station to allow the management station to perform the necessary SNMP set operation on the collection station by configuring this line:

set-community-name: secret[1] VIEW: 1.3.6.1.4.1.11.2.17.4.3.1.1

Router Access Control Lists and NNM

Since routers must operate perfectly at all times, network managers do everything they can to prevent unauthorized access. One feature that's always used is the access control list (ACL), also called simply the

---

1. Of course you should not actually use "secret" as the community string; it is too easy to guess.

access list. This list is a sequence of one-line entries in the router configuration file that can limit access to certain services by certain devices or a range of IP addresses.

Since NNM uses SNMP, it follows that routers should be configured to allow the NNM systems access to the SNMP service on port 161. Access can be further restricted to a certain portion of the MIB (depending on the vendor and the router O/S version). For example, an external access router with a huge routing table will suffer high CPU utilization when NNM queries its routing table. This is very worrisome, since external access routers are monitored closely. By configuring this router to deny access to the routing table, sanity is restored to the minds of the network managers. This does not impact NNM's autodiscovery process since the management domain does not normally extend to the other side of the external access router. A sample access-list is given in Figure 10-3.

```
access-list 2 permit 192.6.173.101
access-list 2 permit 192.6.173.202
snmp-server community public RO 2
```

Figure 10-3   A sample router access list.
These lines in a Cisco router configuration file define *access-list 2* as the IP addresses 192.6.173.101 and 192.6.173.202. The *access-list 2* is applied to the SNMP agent (*snmp-server*) so that only devices in this list can perform an *snmpget* operation (RO). The RO community string is *public*.

Routers in a DMZ environment are configured with restrictive ACLs, and for proper operation of autodiscovery, the NNM system should have access to SNMP. That way, if a new device should appear or if a MAC address or device name should change, NNM can detect this configuration event and generate an alarm.

Packet Filtering With a Router

One of the components of a DMZ (see Figure 10-4 for a contextual diagram) may be a router with packet filters defined in the configuration file. These filters can be configured to defeat IP spoofing attacks, and they can limit external access to specific network servers.

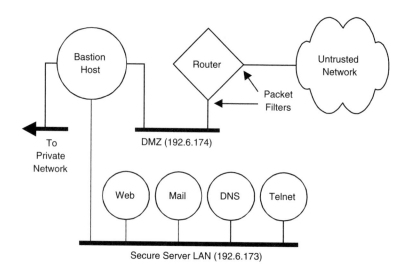

Figure 10-4   The router packet filter.
The router indicated in this illustration is configured with packet filters on its interfaces. The interface connected to the untrusted network passes only packets destined for the web, mail, DNS, and telnet servers. This blocks all direct attacks on the router itself, the bastion host, or devices on the private network, to the left of the bastion host.

IP spoofing occurs when the source IP address of a packet that comes from the untrusted network is forged as if it originated from the corporate network. For example, suppose that the secure server LAN (SSL) is subnet 192.6.173. One router interface is on the DMZ and the other interface is connected to the untrusted network. This interface can be configured to avoid IP spoofing by blocking packets entering from the untrusted network with source IP addresses belonging to subnets 192.6.173 and 192.6.174.

The same external router might be configured to allow packets to enter the DMZ only if they meet the following criteria:

- SMTP (to TCP port 25) sent to the e-mail server
- DNS request (to UDP port 53) sent to the name server
- HTTP replies returning to the proxy web server
- HTTP requests (TCP port 80) connecting to the public web server
- FTP replies returning to the proxy web server
- telnet (from TCP port 23) terminating on the telnet gateway

This prevents *telnet*, FTP, and other clients from entering the DMZ, and allows SMTP, DNS, and HTTP clients on the untrusted network to enter the DMZ.

Accessing NNM Remotely

How can a member of the network support staff who is armed with a laptop computer at a remote location (say, at home or in a hotel room) access one of the corporate NNM systems to work on a problem?

A simple, low-performance solution is to connect a modem port on the NNM system to a prearranged telephone line. The remote staff member dials this number and logs into the UNIX system by supplying their account name, account password, and the dial-up password. A terminal session is initially established, limiting the available toolset to command line applications. However, a point-to-point protocol (PPP) connection can be configured either manually or at login time to allow the laptop to work as a remote network node. The troubleshooter can now run an X-Windows emulator to gain access to the full NNM GUI. Bandwidth limitations of dial-up modem connections will seriously reduce the responsiveness of the X-Windows applications. VNC (virtual network computing) is a good dial-up access solution, as it uses far less bandwidth than X-Windows.

Most corporations provide a more secure and potentially higher performance solution for remote laptop users in the form of dial-up "1-800" access requiring SecureID cards for authentication. The laptop computer becomes a trusted node on the corporate network and the remote network troubleshooter gains access to the NNM system via telnet or X-Windows. Of course, if access to the NNM system is blocked by the network outage, the direct dial-up modem solution is the backup solution.

Remote workers at fixed locations such as their homes are often provided secure access to the corporate network using the speedier 128Kbps ISDN service. ISDN is secure due to automatic number identification (ANI) inherent in the signaling system 7 (SS7) protocol used by ISDN.

Remote users working at home may also enjoy high-speed Internet access in the form of digital subscriber loop (DSL), cable modem, or fiber to the home (FTTH) service. Here, some corporations have opted to use virtual private network (VPN) technology to create a secure, encrypted IP tunnel between their home computer and the corporate network. This provides a workable, high-speed method of accessing the corporation's NNM systems remotely. Again, it's assumed that the network outage does not affect access to the NNM system.

## CHAPTER 11

Periodic
Maintenance Tasks
for NNM

Introduction

Using *crontab* in UNIX is the ideal way to automate periodic NNM maintenance tasks. Many of these tasks are scheduled during the off hours to minimize operational impacts. Any output generated by these automated tasks can be logged or e-mailed to the NNM administrator. Some routine maintenance, such as map customization, remains as a manual task.

The scope of the daily backups can be as simple as running the *ovbackup.ovpl* script, which duplicates data in predefined directories. Entire volumes can also be archived to another system, and site-specific files and directories not in the usual NNM directories should be backed up.

Database repairs should be automated and executed at least weekly. These repairs are disruptive to NNM service and should be done during the off hours. The *ovw -mapcount -ruvDR* and *ovtopofix -cshv* commands can be automated with a *crontab* entry.

Moving newly discovered devices, subnets, and servers to their proper containers is a manual task for the map builder. Their icons appear in the new object holding area of the Internet submap. Map customization is typically done daily.

The NNM map builder backs up the customizations for the Internet submap after changes are made. This is important because the work effort to recreate this map from scratch is both daunting and time-consuming.

Updating MIBs for new devices introduced to the network may be automated, but the process is subject to MIB file syntax errors and should be executed manually to ensure success. New and updated MIBs may be loaded before a new device is installed to ensure that proper autodiscovery occurs.

Deleting unwanted maps is a task that may be automated for off hours execution. Well-run sites allow only properly named maps to exist. Keeping the map count down increases system performance and enhances its reliability.

Reviewing configuration alarms is not an NNM system maintenance task but a network maintenance task. This alarm category reports device configuration errors and represents a highly proactive task that should be executed frequently during the day.

Perusing log files and application alarms may be an automated task. Many of the problems NNM may encounter are logged, while others appear in the application alarm category of the event browser.

A review of MeasureWare data helps identify NNM systems in need of hardware upgrades. This is a task best done weekly using PerfView to examine resource utilization graphs.

Finally, you should peruse the ITO alarms as they occur to address any automated actions. As new automated actions are developed, they should be incorporated into ITO's monitoring routine.

Using *crontab* Entries to Automate Backups

The UNIX *cron* feature is a bulletproof, flexible, easy-to-use, and reliable mechanism to schedule periodic tasks such as backups. Because many of NNM's files are owned by *root*, the backup script should be executed by *root*'s *crontab* entries. The cron feature is so easy to use there are only two variations that need be covered:

> *crontab -l* lists the crontab entries
> *crontab file* creates the crontab entries from *file*

An example *file* might contain the following lines:

```
# run five minutes after midnight, every day
5 0 * * * $HOME/bin/nnm_backup_job >> $HOME/tmp/out 2>&1
```

The first five fields represent time (see Table 11-1) and the rest of the line is the command to be executed when the time matches. This command should invoke *ovbackup.ovpl* (NNM 6.x).

Table 11-1   The First Five Fields in the *crontab* File

Field	Allowed Values
minute	0-59
hour	0-23
day of the month	0-31
month	0-12 (or names like jan, feb, mar, ..., dec)
day of the week	0-7 (0 or 7 is Sunday, or names like sun, mon, ...sat)

Determining the Scope of the Backup

Table 11-2 defines directories which should be backed up. This is a good starting point for the scope of the backup. Note that for NNM

Table 11-2   Directories to Back Up

Directory	Contents
$OV_DB/openview	Map, object, and topology databases
$OV_DB/snmpCollect	Historical SNMP data
$OV_DB/eventdb	Event database
$OV_CONF	Configuration files

Table 11-2   Directories to Back Up

Directory	Contents
$OV_LRF	Local registration files
$OV_REGISTRATION	Application registration files
$OV_DB/analysis	Analytical files
$OV_FIELDS	Field registration files
$OV_SYMBOLS	Icons
/var/opt/OV/tmp	Map customization files
$OV_SNMP_MIBS	Raw and compiled MIB files

6.x you really don't need to deal with all this, since *ovbackup.ovpl* is already coded with this information. This script acquiesces the database writes, backs it up to a known location, and logs the results of the backup in the *$OV_TMP/ovbackup.log* file. See the *ovbackup.ovpl* manpage for more information.

An important question to ask is: "Why back up NNM data at all?" After all, given only the *seedfile* and the map customization file, the network can be rediscovered and the map restored in just a few hours. Assuming the NNM system can be restored from backup in about 10 minutes, the answer to the question is "because it increases the availability of the NNM system." Another answer is "because you want to restore historical information like events and *snmpCollect* data."

Some system administrators adhere to the "keep it simple stupid" (KISS) principle. Rather than back up files in specific directories (and risk missing something), they prefer to back up the entire disk partition (*/opt/OV*), compress the backup file, and transmit it over the network to a backup system. Whichever backup method you decide to use, remember that NNM uses sparse data files that appear to have a huge allocation (in the gigabyte range), but actually use only a few hundred megabytes. The backup tool must handle this type of file.

See Chapter 6 of the *Managing Your Network with HP OpenView Network Node Manager* manual for more information about backups.

Database Repairing

The NNM object, map, and topology databases should be attended to frequently and periodically. This increases the reliability of the tool and improves its performance. During normal operation, NNM will discover, change, and delete objects from the object and topology database even as users create, open, edit, close, and delete maps containing these objects. From time to time there may be operational problems that cause abnormal termination of NNM daemons and *ovw* sessions, leading to inconsistencies in the database. It's important to run the equivalent of "Norton Disk Doctor" on the NNM database at least weekly to prevent database corruption from becoming so bad that it cannot be repaired.

When there are many maps with many authors there will be objects deleted from some maps but still contained in others. Maps that have not been opened and synchronized will contain objects deleted from more actively used maps. The object reference counts should be consistent. This is done by periodically running (as *root*, perhaps using a *crontab* entry) the following command:

    $OV_BIN/ovw -mapcount -ruvDR

Since this command is executed for each map, it is prudent to first delete any maps that aren't needed. No other copies of *ovw* should be running while map counts are being corrected, and the command output should be saved for later analysis.

To repair problems in the database, terminate *netmon* and run the following command:

> *$OV_BIN/ovtopofix -cshv*

These two commands may be executed after the backup script has finished. For large databases these commands may require over an hour to complete.

In a 24x7 environment, periodic maintenance outages requires you to designate backup polling, either by a second collection station or by the management station.

Moving Newly Discovered Devices to Their Proper Container

During a normal day, NNM will discover a few new devices such as servers, Ethernet switches, routers, and subnets. Assuming the Internet submap is customized, it will display a new object holding area at the bottom of the window where new routers and subnets will be placed. In large NNM implementations many collection stations export new devices to the management station where the Internet submap's new object holding area receives all new routers and subnets recently discovered.

Map maintenance involves moving these new devices to their proper container icon. Assuming that the map builder is aware of network changes, the presence of new icons is expected and the proper location is obvious. If not, then some additional information should be collected. Begin by dragging the icon out of the new object holding area into the Internet submap. NNM will draw connections to subnets that contain this device's interfaces. Look at the device name and drag its icon into the proper container. If these clues are not enough, *telnet* to the device and study the login banner for clues. If that isn't helpful, use the MIB browser and query the device's *system* group for the *location* and *contact* fields. Some network administrators have been known to define these fields so others will benefit from it.

A final nugget: "Never customize the *default* map."

Backing Up Map Customizations

Given the daily regimen of finding "homes" for new devices, it follows that the updated map should be backed up. If the map builder experiences "finger trouble," a great deal of work might be lost without this backup.

Map customizations are saved using the *Map:Export* menu. Ensure that the environment variable *$MAP_CUSTOMIZATION* is defined (necessary only for NNM 5.x) or this menu won't be available. The default location for the customization file is */var/opt/OV/tmp/ ipmap.out*. Rather than overwrite this file each day, append the date to it like this:

ipmap.out.mmddyyyy

where *mm* is the month, *dd* is the day of the month, and *yyyy* is the four-digit year. Do not use a two digit year. (Let's not forget the lessons learned from Y2K.)

Note that since map import/export customizations don't save everything, a total backup is better. However, map customizations can be used by another NNM system (such as a redundant backup system), import/export is very fast, and import/export doesn't require a temporary system stop.

Updating MIBs for New Devices

Network hardware vendors frequently enhance the SNMP agents for their equipment, either to support new functionality or to accommodate an erratum. New equipment added to the network may have a corresponding new MIB. It therefore becomes necessary to unload the old MIB and load the new one. This has to be done at each collection station and management station.

In preparation for loading the updated or new MIB, copy the ASCII file into the *$OV_SNMP_MIBS* directory. NNM includes a simple GUI to load and unload MIBs from this location. First unload the old MIB, then load the new one. This has the side effect of deleting old trap definitions and loading the new ones. When this step is done, use the MIB browser to check that the MIB works with the intended device, and that the *snmpCollect* historical SNMP data collection definitions are updated as necessary to reflect the new MIB.

Note that you can load/unload MIBS from the command line with *xnmloadmib*, but it does not process traps by default. You need to explicitly specify this with the *-event* option.

Deleting Unwanted Maps

When users are not discouraged from creating NNM maps at will, they will usually leave them on the system for indefinite periods. To list the maps on an NNM system, use this simple command:

> *ovwls*

This lists the maps and their owners. The consequences of having a lot of maps on an NNM system include:

- larger database

- longer backup time

- out of control users

- longer *ovw -mapcount* duration

- longer *ovtopofix -a* duration

- reduced overall NNM performance

- discovery problems

Obviously, the fewer maps, the better. There is no particular reason to have a map named *default*, although a token map by that name is created for you. You can prevent users from creating their own maps by removing the corresponding registration files. A side effect of this is that each time you update NNM, the registration files will probably change and you have to revisit them to institute your changes. This is a very complex process. Refer to "Controlling Map Access" in Chapter 9 of the *Managing Your Network with HP OpenView Network Node Manager* manual.

Sometimes users unintentionally create a map by incorrectly typing the name of the map they want to open. You can help your users avoid this mistake by creating a system alias for *ovw*, one which you automatically create for them and which is defined in their login environment. For example, if the proper name of the map is "bellevue" then the proper alias command is:

alias ovw /opt/OV/bin/ovw -ro -map bellevue

As long as the user types the *ovw* command they will execute the alias and thus open a read-only copy of the "bellevue" map.

Reviewing Configuration Alarms

The configuration alarm category is teeming with golden nuggets of valuable information about configuration problems in the network. If you must pay attention to a single alarm category, let it be this one. It's one of NNM's most useful features, in the writer's opinion. Configuration management is very important in networks, and it's worthwhile that someone respond to the configuration alarms.

Perhaps the least exciting configuration event is the discovery of a new device or a new device interface. More interesting is the change of a MAC address, but if it occurs over and over again, this may signal a duplicate IP address, which is more exciting.

Another configuration event is the device name change. This suggests a change in the DNS entry for the device, but if the new name is the device IP address or its SNMP name, then DNS has lost the device name. Of course, if the device name changed to its proper name, then the event signals good news.

A very useful configuration event is the "bad subnet mask" alarm. NNM learned the proper subnet mask of each subnet when it discovered it from the local router interface. During configuration checks NNM will test the subnet mask of every device, using SNMP if possible or using the ICMP parameter request if necessary. As long as the subnet mask is wrong, NNM will periodically generate an alarm. Knowing that a subnet mask is incorrect is very useful information because devices suffering from it often have problems communicating with other devices due to bad routing decisions.

Bad subnet masks are usually found in networks that subnet a class B network address into multiple class C subnets. The default subnet mask for a class B network is 255.255.0.0, and this is usually the bad mask's value. If the network is subnetted, the subnet mask is normally 255.255.255.0. Sometimes the subnet mask may be incorrectly set to 255.255.252.0 or 25.252.252.0 or some other permutation that makes one wonder how the device ever worked properly in the first place. Sometimes it's because the local router is configured to support Proxy ARP.

You will find excellent information about subnet masks in Chapter 4, section "Subnet Masks Consistently Configured," and Chapter 5, section "Subnet Mask Issues," in the *Managing Your Network with HP OpenView Network Node Manager* manual.

Another common configuration event detects the incorrect routing table entry. NNM gets the routing table entries for an SNMP-capable device and checks that they in fact point to router interfaces. A common error made when installing network printers is to define the default route to be the print server. Another common configuration error is to define the default route of an X-terminal to be the IP address of its boot server. In both these examples, the device works properly so long as it communicates locally within its own subnet.

NNM will not generate configuration alarms for other, less obvious configuration errors such as:

- no default route defined (detectable using SNMP)

- asymmetric routing

- incorrect fast Ethernet FDX/HDX setting

- incorrect DNS server in resolver configuration

- RIP is not active

These types of configuration errors are not obvious, and they don't have any indicators in SNMP MIBs, though some of them are debatable errors (such as asymmetric routes).

Perusing Log Files and Application Alarms

NNM daemons log information to their log files, some more than others. The directory *$OV_LOG* should be checked for several major log files including *snmpCol.trace*, *netmon.trace*, and *trapd.log*.

The *snmpCollect* daemon logs interesting events in *snmpCol.trace*. If there is some problem collecting SNMP data from a device, *snmpCol.trace* is where the clues will be found. Therefore, check this file periodically. Perhaps the community string has changed and collection has stopped for a device. Perhaps timeouts are limiting data collections.

The *netmon* daemon reports interesting information into the *netmon.trace* file. This file may grow rapidly if aggressive tracing is enabled for *netmon*. Since *netmon* is so important to the proper operation of NNM, check this file for signs of trouble.

The *trapd.log* file (pre-NNM 6.x) may also contain nuggets of information, since many alarms are "log only." Particularly interesting are events that relate to the NNM daemons and applications. Sudden disconnects between NNM applications and daemons may indicate users are having problems without reporting them. These alarms may not reveal themselves in the Application Alarm category if they are "log only."

Rather than manually review these log files, it may be prudent and efficient to create a script that checks these files for known text patterns, execute the script with a *crontab* entry, and e-mail the NNM administrator when interesting text is found.

Reviewing MeasureWare Data

If you run the HP MeasureWare agent on all the NNM systems and use ITO to manage them, you will then receive performance alarms from these systems. Typical resource alarms include:

- swap space utilization
- disk I/O rate
- CPU utilization
- LAN errors
- LAN throughput
- RAM utilization

To balance these alarms against the amount of user activity, it may be prudent to program ITO to monitor the number of *ovw* sessions on each NNM system. Experience suggests that a successful NNM deployment attracts more users than originally anticipated. If resource alarms occur too frequently during the busy hour and the number of active sessions is greater than expected, then some platform tuning in the form of additional CPUs, RAM, or disks may be justified.

Finally, a note about the NNM system's LAN adapter is in order. New, fast Ethernet installations often suffer a phase during which time auto-negotiation between the fast Ethernet adapter and its switch port reverts to half duplex mode at 10 megabits per second. To prevent this, write a simple script to check the NNM system adapter settings and that of the switch port and make it a *crontab* entry.

HP PerfView will also generate charts of these vital statistics. They reveal the daily usage profiles and indicate what time of the day to expect the greatest performance impact on the NNM systems.

Perusing and Updating ITO Alarms

ITO is appropriate for managing a reasonably stable group of, say, a few dozen NNM systems. ITO can be scripted to monitor special NNM problem scenarios. The logs generated by this monitoring should be reviewed operationally. A short list of recommendations for ITO monitoring follows:

- collection station to management station communications

- spinning *ovw* sessions or other X-Windows clients

- *syslogd* should be active

- all NNM daemons should be active (*ovstatus*)

As you gain operational experience and solve NNM problems, additional checks will be found worthy of automation with ITO.

A Day With NNM

Introduction

A typical day with NNM is incomplete without a user approaching you with a special need to gather non-standard SNMP performance data. Often these users can obtain their data with the standard MIB browser and the *xnmgraph* tool. For long-term data collection you may need to add an historical SNMP data collection, since the *xnmgraph* tool does not retain history.

Testing NNM patches may not be a daily event, but a visit to HP's OpenView website should be. Whether your site practices aggressive or conservative patch management, you should always test your patches in the lab before rolling them to all the operational NNM systems.

Verifying correct menu operation for the various user communities should be done after patching, after adding an application, and especially after an NNM upgrade.

Validating a new procedure with NNM is a precursor to documenting it as a best practice. Be sure the procedure's limits are known and also what device, application, and NNM versions it's been tested on.

Testing third-party applications with NNM includes checking configuration files, icons, MIBs, menus, and disk space.

Validating operating system changes is also important. Check kernel tunable parameters, DNS, and performance after patching the O/S or upgrading RAM, disk, or LAN adapters.

Conducting directed discovery may not be a daily event, but occasionally, on a non-production system, you may be asked to create a special map. For example, an end-to-end view between two remote points of the network may be needed to support a capacity planning project.

Creating special purpose maps for operational use may be invaluable to a centralized help desk assisting remote users. Why provide a complex NNM map of the management domain when the help desk needs only several, simpler geography-based views?

Dealing with a router discovery and router interface problems are also common.

Custom Performance Management

While NNM is normally configured to collect SNMP historical performance data, you often need to collect other performance data in an ad-hoc fashion. Often you need to monitor a specific MIB variable for one device for a few hours. The obvious tool is the MIB browser GUI. Select the device icon in the *ovw* map window, bring up the MIB browser from the *Tools:SNMP MIB Browser* menu, navigate to the MIB variable of interest, and press the *Graph* button. The standard *xnmgraph* GUI appears with a 10 second real-time polling of the variable. The polling interval can be adjusted down to an aggressive one-second interval if necessary. You can select the pull-down menu *File:Configure in Data Collector* to easily set it up. Since this live polling does not store data in the *snmpCollect* database, it is not subject to any data trimming activity that may periodically run to limit the amount of historical SNMP data.

Note that it's not strictly necessary to run the MIB browser from the *ovw* GUI. The *xnmbrowser* GUI can run from the command line as follows:

> *$OV_BIN/xnmbrowser -node device_name*

This assumes that the environment variable *$DISPLAY* is already set correctly.

If this particular device is going to be subjected to such daily examination, it may be appropriate to create a simple *ovw* MIB application that can be added to the menu structure. The MIB application created this way will be of type *Graph* and the polling interval and MIB variable can be predefined. Note that creating a MIB application also creates an application registration file (ARF). In environments that customize the menu structure with multiple registration directory trees using *$OVwRegDir*, the default ARF may have to be moved to its proper location to make it available to the appropriate users. For in-depth information see Chapter 9, "Controlling Map Access," in the *Managing Your Network with HP OpenView Network Node Manager* manual.

Long term use of such ad-hoc polling is limited by local administrative practices that may disable many or all of the NNM applications, which may be daily or weekly. Applications launched by *ovw* will be terminated when *ovw* terminates. Launching *xnmbrowser* and *xnmgraph* by hand avoids this behavior.

Any SNMP data collected by *xnmgraph* is discarded when it terminates, so remember to save the textual data with the *File* menu or save the graph with a screenshot.

Diehard command line enthusiasts will point out that SNMP data can be collected directly without graphical utilities using the *snmpget* command as follows:

> *$OV_BIN/snmpget device_name object-id >> /tmp/data_file*

which collects the SNMP variable *object-id* from the device *device_name* and concatenates it to the file */tmp/data_file*. This command is inserted into a shell script that loops and waits in a polling cycle until it is terminated by the user.

To collect historical SNMP performance data you need access to the *xnmcollect* GUI under the menu *Options:Data Collection & Thresholds*. The NNM administrator and other trusted users may add collections here. For more information, refer to Chapter 11, section "Data Collection & Thresholds," in *Managing Your Network with HP*

OpenView Network Node Manager. New collections are added as follows:

- choose a device, mib instance, and sample rate

- activate the collection

- wait awhile for some data to be collected

- view the SNMP data; save it if needed

- suspend the collection until it's needed again.

Note that if the NNM administrator has a *crontab* entry to trim the historical database, then this will also trim the ad-hoc historical data. This can be avoided only if the trimmer script is very specific about which nodes are trimmed, so be cautious about ad-hoc, long-term historical collections.

Testing an NNM Patch

Each day you probably want to schedule a visit to the HP OpenView website at *http://www.openview.hp.com/* to see if any new patches are available for downloading. Hopefully, you don't have to spend time each day to address a new NNM patch.

There are at least two approaches to patch management. The conservative approach delays them for some time interval, perhaps forever:

"If it's not broken don't fix it."

The aggressive approach tests and installs all patches as they become available:

"Fix it before it breaks."

The conservative approach tells you to review each patch for appropriateness to your site. If the patch does not address any problems you and your users experience, then set it aside for later. You may simply choose to wait for a consolidated patch before acting. This philosophy avoids unintended side effects that a patch may introduce. This follows the belief that patches are generally not subject to the same degree of regression testing as a whole product release, even though they are tested thoroughly before being released.

The aggressive approach also tells you to review each patch for appropriateness. Since users may experience problems that patches address, test the patch and install it as soon as possible. By patching more often you may only occasionally get bitten by an unexpected side effect that your testing did not uncover.

Verifying Correct Menu Operation

It's a common practice to customize the NNM menu structure. One goal of menu customization is to prevent certain classes of users from making changes to NNM's configuration. Such users are meant to be operators of the NNM tool. Such users often have the *$OVwRegDir* environment variable defined in their startup shell script to point to a home grown directory tree with registration files, so that when NNM is launched, *ovw* scans this directory structure instead of the standard one at *$OV_REGISTRATION*.

You have to tolerate some potentially tedious regression testing to verify that your custom menus work properly for each user type:

> Is each menu item in the right place?
> Do the selection rules work for each menu item?
> Is the actual code the menu executes loaded and working?

You may have to document the available menus for each type of user. One way is to incorporate *ovw* menu screenshots into the documentation. Why not let *ovw* parse the menus to help you create the documentation? The alternative is to manually draw the menu diagrams.

Validating a New Procedure

Part of the NNM administrator's job is to teach users how to troubleshoot and document problems. Sometimes a keen user will develop a new technique that uses NNM in such a creative way that it reaches the status of a best practice. Before you incorporate the new procedure into the documentation, you should validate it.

Does the new procedure work on all devices or just a subclass of devices? Will these devices always be present on the NNM map? How can these devices be found quickly on the map? Is there a device firmware or operating system revision requirement? Does the procedure depend on a specific version of NNM? Can all users take advantage of the procedure? Can the procedure be enhanced with a new custom menu? Test the procedure yourself. Does the new procedure always work or are there "gotchas"? Does the procedure depend on local conventions such as a device naming strategy?

Testing Third-Party Applications

With over forty HP OpenView products on the market, plus hundreds of third-party applications available, there is a good chance that your NNM systems also host a few of them. They will generally install themselves in such a way as to integrate into NNM more or less seamlessly.

When testing these applications for functionality, also check that:

- the proper icons are loaded
- new device attributes and properties are loaded
- any MIBs are properly installed and loaded
- new *ovw* application menu items appear for the appropriate users
- new daemons can be started and stopped with *ovstart* and *ovstop*
- new ports are documented in */etc/services*
- disk space is still available after the installation
- the application data disk storage requirements are met

Multiple third-party applications may conflict. For example, they may put conflicting entries in *oid_to_sym* and *oid_to_type* for the same component type.

Validating Operating System Changes

The NNM system's underlying operating system (OS) is not a static thing. The OS vendor makes changes to its code base for a variety of reasons, including to:

- maintain a competitive advantage
- comply with Y2K (still)
- avoid obsolescence
- patch coding errors
- add new features
- upgrade subsystems such as DNS or X-Windows

Before plunging ahead with an aggressive upgrade strategy, remember to verify that any OS upgrade is supported by NNM and your third-party applications. Be cautious here. You may find, for example, that a certain third-party application that loads under NNM 5.x refuses to load under NNM 6.x, but will continue to work if NNM 5.x is upgraded to NNM 6.x instead. Here, you are burning the candle at both ends because as time passes you will probably want to load only NNM 6.x or later to shorten system build times. In this example, the third-party application provider will probably not support its product under NNM 6.x, so you are in support purgatory. To avoid such trips into purgatory, check the HP website for compatibility among specific versions of OpenView products.

When making OS upgrades, also make sure that NNM system resources continue to be available after the upgrade. Kernel resources are defined in the text file */etc/system* under Sun Solaris. In HP-UX, the SAM GUI may be used to make kernel parameter changes. The NNM installation document spells out necessary changes to these kernel configurations for proper operation.

Changes or upgrades to subsystems such as DNS should also be validated to ensure that NNM will function properly afterwards. Indeed, NNM is so dependent on DNS working properly that changes made to any component of the corporate DNS should be made with great care, lest there be later cause to don sack cloth and sit in ashes!

Some system changes are made to enhance NNM performance. Adding RAM is a common remedy for excessive disk swapping. Remember to configure sufficient swap space to accommodate the additional RAM. Use PerfView to verify that the extra RAM has reduced VM activity by comparing before and after data.

Likewise, if an additional disk drive is installed and added to an already striped volume, check with GlancePlus that the performance of the disk array has improved.

If an additional CPU is added to the system, verify that its utilization is balanced with the other CPUs. If the OS does not recognize the new CPU, you should be the first to know.

Finally, if the standard Ethernet LAN adapter for the NNM system is replaced with a fast Ethernet adapter, ensure that it negotiates with the attached switch port for a 100Mbps FDX connection. If you decide to add one or more fast Ethernet cards to an HP-UX system to increase LAN performance, consider installing the optional automatic port aggregation (APA) software. It will let you assign one IP address to all cards and will load balance them. Check that the load balancing works properly.

Conducting Directed Discovery

Occasionally, a researcher will visit you and say, "I need an NNM view of the network from A to B showing all the devices between them." The standard maps your NNM shop has do not provide such a network view, perhaps because it spans an area larger than a single management domain, or because the user wants to see devices that are normally not discovered. Therefore, the researcher cannot use a standard NNM system, and you will have to visit your test lab's NNM system and build the map from scratch.

Begin with an empty *seedfile* and disable the discovery filter. Manually add the A and B devices and allow NNM to discover the local topology. Use your understanding of the network topology and carefully manage subnets at each end that will allow discovery of more intermediate topology. Each time a subnet is managed, autodiscovery goes to work and discovers another layer of routers and subnets. Continue to manage single subnets until there is a single path between A and B.

If the path between A and B isn't easy to determine based on personal knowledge of the topology, it may be quicker to attempt a *traceroute* command from A to B to identify all routers between them. NNM's *findroute* command to locate routes using SNMP may also help. You can invoke it from *ovw* by clicking icon A, control-clicking icon B, and going to the pulldown menu *Fault:Locate Route via SNMP*. Then *findroute* draws a white line on the links to graphically depict the route between A and B. Add the list of routers you find into the *seedfile*, stop and start *netmon*, and NNM should soon display the topology between A and B as requested by our friend the researcher.

The usual purpose for such a directed map is to facilitate the study of the operational performance of network components between A and B as part of a capacity planning study.

Suppose you are asked to provide an NNM map showing a backbone view of the corporate network. Only routers and subnets with two or more connections are to be shown in this view. The hard way to do this is to visit the corporate management station and manually edit a copy of the production map to pare out dangling subnets and routers. The elegant way to do this is to have an NNM staff developer write a small OpenView Windows application that creates a submap and populates it with routers and subnets with two or more connections.

Creating a Special Purpose Map

Special maps for operational use may be created using carefully crafted map filters. Administrators of print servers want maps that show only printers and print servers. Assuming the topology database contains the desired devices, you can create a custom map for these administrators with little pain, although you may want them to customize its appearance.

Other user classes may be satisfied with standard maps if only certain devices are hidden from view. You can make them a map by locating all objects with the appropriate attributes, selecting the highlighted icons, and hiding them all at once.

Your local help desk may prefer to have several maps available to them. Suppose your help desk is physically consolidated at one or two sites and gets calls from anywhere in the country. To gather information from a user with a problem in Chicago, only an NNM map of that location is needed. Create such a map by simply hiding the outlying topology for Denver and Detroit even though those areas are in the management domain.

NNM and Routers

A common problem is NNM combining two routers into a single node. This is usually caused by bad DNS data.

HSRP can be tricky, too, unless the correct flags are set in *oid_to_type*. Currently (June 2000), Cisco does not set the flags correctly when they install their element managers. A router running HSRP should be set to "GD". Otherwise, *netmon* will continually add and delete the HSRP address.

Troubleshooting NNM

Introduction

Using the NNM event logs is a first step in troubleshooting NNM. Logs at both management and collection stations should be checked to help isolate the scope of any problems.

Consulting the NNM map is another troubleshooting technique. All NNM systems are on the map, and events and information about devices on the same subnet as the NNM system may provide additional information useful in troubleshooting.

Device names may change unexpectedly in the configuration alarms category. This often points to changes in DNS.

Network topology autolayout errors may be encountered. Sometimes the IP-centric nature of the map hierarchy prevents NNM from laying out network electronics where multiple logical subnets exist on a single broadcast domain. NNM's tendency to retain old but once valid information in the face of new but contradictory information can lead to additional interfaces and connections.

DHCP and WINS (Windows Internet Name Service) may reassign IP addresses once held by network equipment to non-SNMP devices. This prevents NNM from detecting the configuration change, forcing the NNM map builder to manually delete the offending device.

Autodiscovery blues occur when devices refuse to be discovered by NNM despite heroic attempts by the NNM administrator to make it so. Perhaps the shy device is not in the management domain, is not reachable, may be down, is misconfigured, does not communicate with other subnets, or does not provide sufficient information.

Detecting expiring NNM licenses before they expire should be a proactive configuration check automated with ITO. Licenses are not always properly installed, and the temporary courtesy license HP generously provides is good for 60 days.

NNM GUI problems may occur when an X-Windows emulator isn't properly configured to provide resources. Sometimes environment variables become unset, or DNS names do not resolve properly. Color flashing may occur when insufficient color map entries remain for NNM to use. In unpatched NNM systems, sometimes an *ovw* session will become disconnected from its X-Windows display, but the process doesn't quit because it didn't detect the disconnect. The process loops until terminated either by an automated ITO action or by the NNM administrator.

Using Event Logs

If the NNM system itself is misbehaving, the process of troubleshooting requires you to collect data about the problem, and NNM may have clues about itself tucked away in the event logs. This means you should take advantage of the event log browser (for relatively recent events), archived *trapd.log* files (for pre-NNM6.0), or the event database as appropriate. If there's not enough history, increase the size of the event database or *trapd.log*. Also check *netmon.trace* and *snmpCol.trace*.

If the NNM system is a management station, visit some of the collection stations to see if related information is available. If the NNM system is a collection station, visit its management station for related information, and check with other collection stations to see if they are having similar problems. This strategy is a component of the Kepner-Tregoe (K-T) troubleshooting methodology, which teaches you to collect additional information by looking where the problem does or does not exist.

Consulting the Map for Related Objects

One of the benefits of an NNM map is that nearby devices are easy to identify. If there is an NNM problem, nearby devices are perhaps experiencing problems too. Go to the map containing the NNM system and check the event logs for other servers, hubs, printers, switches, and routers for additional clues. There may be *syslog* messages available that may provide even more information.

Device Names Change Unexpectedly

NNM's periodic configuration checking occasionally turns up a device name change. This is a configuration alarm. As such, it represents a nugget of useful information. NNM determines the selection name of an IP addressable device as follows:

- the DNS name corresponding to the lowest IP address, otherwise
- the MIB-2 system name if the device supports SNMP, otherwise
- the IP address if there is one, otherwise
- the device MAC address (assuming layer 2 discovery is on)

A typical device name change often corresponds to a change in the DNS database. The IP address inverse DNS lookup previously returned the original device name, but now it returns some other name. This may be completely legitimate or it may be an administrative error. Another typical device name change is that the name reverts to the IP address of the device. This usually happens when the device entry is removed from the DNS database and the device does not support SNMP. Otherwise, the device name would revert to that specified in the MIB-2 *system* group.

Network Topology Autolayout Errors

NNM will occasionally draw part of a network topology that varies with what you know is correct. This is NNM's way of telling you that it is having some sort of difficulty and is making the best of a bad situation. NNM is very conservative. It tends to make few assumptions and will retain old data that once was accurate over new data that is inconsistent or inconclusive. Usually, this is not a bug with NNM, and by exploring the circumstances surrounding the discovery and layout problems, the reason is almost always found. The remedy may not be as apparent.

Sometimes NNM doesn't lay out part of the network properly because it cannot get the information it needs from a buggy SNMP agent. For example, an Ethernet switch may not properly implement the bridge MIB, so NNM isn't able to correctly identify all of its ports. The discovery problem leads to an autolayout problem.

Since NNM tends to hang on to old configuration information, it may have difficulty when a device configuration radically changes. For example, inserting a new card into an Ethernet switch and restarting it often results in renumbered MIB instances for the ports. At the next configuration check, NNM may add all the new instances in but not delete the old ones. Sometimes the only way to rid the NNM database of this stale data is to delete the device and then ping it from the NNM system to force a rediscovery. Note that since maps won't be affected by this until they are opened, the map count for this deleted object will be inconsistent.

NNM's IP-centric design will create a subnet container for every subnet it discovers. If a router interface has one primary address and three secondary addresses, then NNM will show the router as having four subnets attached. This is completely true from an IP viewpoint. Suppose that the additional subnets are needed to support an increasing number of devices. Each device discovered is situated into its proper subnet container. Now suppose that the switches are assigned IP address at random from the available four subnets. NNM will draw the physical topology in each subnet incorrectly, as shown in Figure 13-1. The fix is to readdress the switches to the same subnet. In this subnet, NNM will be able to correctly draw the physical topology. If some of the switches are addressed within the same

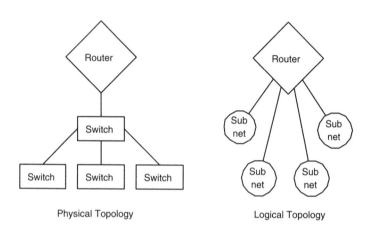

Physical Topology   Logical Topology

Figure 13-1   NNM autolayout and secondary subnets.
Consider a router interface with a primary IP address and three secondary addresses. This interface has four subnets. Suppose that there are four Ethernet switches connected to this interface and that each switch is configured on a different subnet. NNM's logical IP view will insert each switch inside its subnet icon. This means that the expected physical connections between the switches can't be correctly drawn. The fix is to assign all four Ethernet switches an IP address on one of the subnets.

subnet, they will be connected properly, but their peers will be lodged within the other subnet icons, ruining NNM's ability to lay out the correct topology.

DHCP Reassigns an IP address

Suppose you remove an Ethernet switch from service and return its IP address manually to the DHCP lease pool. As NNM performs a status poll every five minutes, this switch will appear to go down. Meanwhile, you install a replacement switch with a different legitimate IP address. You manually ping it and NNM discovers it, adds it to the map, and shows the new network connections. Suddenly, a non-SNMP capable device comes online, issues a DHCP request, and receives the recycled switch's IP address. NNM's next five minute status poll succeeds and the old switch (seemingly) goes back up! But NNM is no longer able to communicate with the old switch SNMP agent, and leaves the switch icon and its connection on the map, even while the new switch is also shown with very similar connections. Given NNM's tendency to trust old data, the old switch will not be removed from the database. The only solution is to manually delete the old switch from the map. Of course, one might argue that network equipment IP addressees should always be leased permanently, but the problems do not stop there.

A variation of this problem is that the new switch is given the same IP address as the old one. On the next configuration check, new interfaces appear and NNM discovers them, but the old interfaces are not deleted and simply go down. Again, the fix is to delete the switch and rediscover it. Now you can't blame it on DHCP.

Let's suppose that you have an existing workstation that is in the NNM database but doesn't support SNMP. The workstation gets its IP address from DHCP and the lease is for five days. Now the workstation is shut down and moved to a new subnet, where it is promptly is assigned a new IP address and again is discovered by NNM. Now NNM considers it to have two interfaces, one up and one down. Since it has no SNMP agent, NNM cannot determine if the workstation is truly a router or not, but since there are two interfaces, NNM promotes it to the Internet submap, just like it would a router.

While NNM will delete a node that is down for seven days by default, it will not remove an interface that is down for seven days. Again, the fix is to delete the workstation and allow it to be rediscovered.

At this point it is clear that the NNM 6.1 DHCP-supported features can be brought to bear on such problems. First, in the *$OV_CONF/C/ filters* file, define a filter that matches the range of IP addresses subject to DHCP assignment. Visit the *Options:Network Polling Configuration* menu and enable this DHCP filter. The DHCP server must be configured to transmit the SNMP traps *OV_DHCP_Alloc* and *OV_DHCP_Release* to the NNM system, where *netmon* will receive them. The result is a reduction in configuration alarms regarding DHCP devices. NNM will delete the IP addresses for devices with IP addresses that match the DHCP filter after they have stayed down for a specified time. This time interval can be controlled by typing:

> *xnmpolling -delDhcpAddrTime interval-spec*

and it is enabled by typing:

> *xnmpolling -delDhcpAddrsOn*

This is subject to the option *-dhcpFiltName filter-name.* All these features can be enabled or disabled using the command:

> *xnmpolling -dhcpHandlingOn*

The *xnmpolling* GUI saves its configuration data in the *$OV_CONF/ polling* file. See Figure 13-2 for a sample screenshot of a DHCP configuration with the *xnmpolling* command.

Autodiscovery Blues

NNM's ability to autodiscover network devices is legendary, but once in a while an NNM administrator will despair over some device that NNM just won't discover.

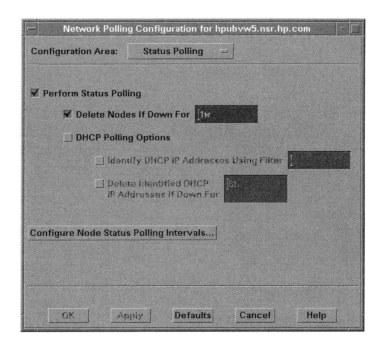

Figure 13-2   DHCP configuration parameters.
This GUI lets you provide NNM with special knowledge about devices
whose IP addresses are under DHCP control. After checking the
DHCP Polling Options box, you must specify the name of the DHCP
matching filter in the *$OV_CONF/C/filters* file and optionally allow
NNM to delete a DHCP-assigned IP address that's been down too
long.

Recall that *netmon* is responsible for the autodiscovery process. It is
guided by the optional *seedfile* parameter in the *$OV_LRF/netmon.lrf*
which it reads every time it starts up. The *seedfile* is often used to
define the initial management domain at the time of first discovery.
Entries can be added to the *seedfile* later to expand the management
domain. The NNM map builder or administrator can also interactively
expand the management domain. Autodiscovery only occurs within
the management domain, that is, on the managed subnets. The
netmon.noDiscover file contains IP addresses which *netmon* will
ignore when it encounters them.

A common discovery problem is that despite pinging an undiscovered device and demand polling the nearby switches and routers, a device is not discovered, and the reason is that there is not a managed subnet within which it resides. The solution is to manage that subnet if it exists or to manually create it if it doesn't. Then a single manual ping of the device from the NNM system should result in discovery. This works because *netmon* monitors ICMP traffic with a raw ICMP socket and looks for new IP addresses in the traffic stream.

If a device is down or unreachable at the time its IP address is discovered (perhaps from an entry in some ARP cache), then *netmon* can't confirm its existence and the device is not discovered.

Sometimes a device seems to remain undiscovered when it has actually been discovered. Its icon is hidden deep inside a segment container because *netmon* can't communicate with the device SNMP agent. This prevents *netmon* from discovering the device is really a switch or a router so it can't be displayed in the subnet or Internet submap views. The solution is to ensure that the device SNMP agent is enabled, that NNM is configured with the proper community string, that the device access list permits the NNM system to communicate with the SNMP service, and that the flags in *oid_to_type* are correct and complete for this component (e.g., a hub should have the "H" flag).

Finger trouble (also known as operator error) may be responsible. It is possible that the undiscovered device icon has been hidden by an operator. To test if a device has been discovered, use the *ovtopodump - RISC device_name* command.

After a device is manually deleted from a map it is common to then rediscover it with a *ping*. But if other closed maps contain the object, then its reference count won't reach zero and rediscovery will not take place. Here is a good reason for adopting a single-map strategy. The solution is to leave all maps open in read/write mode, or to execute the *ovw -mapcount -ruvDR* command as *root* with no maps open.

Other reasons for discovery problems include:

- the IP address is not in an ARP cache on an SNMP-capable node

- the IP address has aged out of the ARP cache

- packet loss prevents *netmon* from verifying the device

- the device cannot communicate outside its subnet

- the device is turned off

- the device has been down seven days and is deleted

- the remote side of a serial link can't be found if -R is specified

- the device has a temporary IP stack that is now unloaded

- the device does not use IP

- a switch or bridge filters out the MAC address of the device

- an incorrect SNMP ACL on the device is blocking access

- an unknown community string is configured on the device

- you have reached the 250 node limit on a 250-node license

Detecting an Impending License Expiration

An installation problem will occasionally manifest itself sixty days later when the NNM license expires. You should always monitor an NNM system using the command:

$OV_BIN/xnmtopoconf -test station_name

where *station_name* is the name of an NNM system. The output of this command is very informative and includes the expiration date of the license. It may be prudent to configure this test command into ITO to detect license problems automatically.

NNM GUI Problems on UNIX Systems

The X-Window system on the user's UNIX workstation must be properly configured for pain-free operation. A common complaint is that a GUI, usually *ovw*, cannot connect to the display. This may be caused by an incorrect or unset *$DISPLAY* variable, insufficient permissions to connect to the display (*xhost* + fixes this), the name of the display cannot be resolved using the local DNS resolver, or there is no IP route between the NNM system and the workstation running the X-Windows emulator.

An active *ovw* session may be abruptly terminated because the user's workstation locked up, the user exited the X-Windows environment ungracefully, or the X-Windows emulator locked up. Sometimes this type of failure is not communicated to the *ovw* session, which continues to attempt I/O to its display. On unpatched NNM systems this may result in a spinning *ovw* session which may consume an entire CPU. The spinning process must be terminated manually, either by its owner or by *root*. ITO can be programmed to monitor for this behavior and to execute the termination command (a *kill -9 ovw_pid*).

If the physical size of the monitor is too small, then some of the taller GUIs cannot display in their entirety. This may result in missing buttons at the bottom of the window. It's recommended that a 1280x1024 monitor be used, or at least a virtual screen of that size should be available that can be panned when the physical dimensions of the monitor are less than recommended.

Font problems sometimes occur because the X-Windows emulator installation does not include the necessary fonts. A possible fix is to perform a full install of the software, or to upgrade to the most recent version. A second fix is to configure an X-Windows font server on the network and configure the X-Windows emulator to use it. A work-around is to examine the application defaults file for the application, look for font resources, identify available substitute fonts, create an X-Windows application *resource_file* in the user's home directory configuring these new fonts, and use the *xrdb resource_file* command to activate the resources. The application will use the substitute fonts next time it is invoked and cease issuing font warning messages.

Color problems may occur when *ovw* executes on a display whose public color map has insufficient free colors. This seems to happen often when a web browser is already running when *ovw* is launched. The fix is to exit the browser and any other applications that use a lot of color before executing *ovw*.

Finally, there may be performance problems with the NNM GUI. This may stem from a lack of available resources on the workstation, starving the X-Windows emulator of needed RAM, CPU cycles, or TCP sockets. Try quitting some applications to free up RAM and CPU cycles, and configure the X-Windows emulator to use more TCP sockets (the default limit may only be 16, which is generally inadequate for NNM use).

CHAPTER 1 4

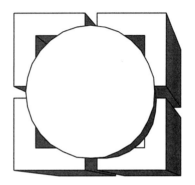

Cross-Platform
Issues With NNM

Introduction

NNM is used in multivendor heterogeneous network environments.
The X-Windows or web browser GUIs tend to exhibit differences
depending on the particular client-side computer, operating system,
browser, and X-Windows emulator. This chapter brings together these
issues, some of which are mentioned briefly in other sections of the
book.

X-Windows compensates for differences in the underlying operating
system, windowing system, graphical display properties, user
workstation performance, and network capacity.

Java version and performance issues require that both Solaris and HP-
UX are properly patched and that Netscape 4.6 and later be the cross-
platform browser of choice.

Bandwidth requirements for X-Windows are actually quite modest
unless actual bitmap background images must be sent. A 56Kbps
WAN link offers marginally acceptable performance (when few
bitmaps are displayed across it), and serial line compression at the
router can reduce latency. VNC over 56Kbps dial-up links performs
better than X-Windows.

Printing with NNM across multiple operating systems, X-Windows,
and web interfaces prompts us to return to "Taking Screenshots of
Maps" on page 88.

X-Windows Differences

The X-Windows model allows the application to operate on a different
computer than the display. The application is called the X-client and
the display is called the X-server. The two communicate with *xlib*
calls transmitted over TCP/IP. When an X-client executes on a UNIX
workstation with a built-in X-server, the highly efficient local

loopback driver replaces the physical network connection between the application and the display. It is not unusual for a UNIX-based NNM system to run a local *ovw* session while ten or more additional concurrent remote users are executing additional *ovw* sessions. Each remote user may be using a different type of computer and software for X-Windows emulation.The X-Windows standard allows for and supports these differences.

The X-Windows standard operates at the network, transport, session, and presentation layers. This makes it operating-system agnostic. An X-Windows emulator works the same regardless of the underlying operating system, which might be Windows, Mac OS, Linux, UNIX, or BeOS.

The X-server deals with differences in the graphical display. The screen dimensions may be 640x480 and hopefully at least 1280x1024. The X-server may even provide a logical panned window that exceeds the physical dimensions of the display.

In the rooted mode, the X-Windows emulator creates the entire X-server in a single, sizable native window. This normally requires the application server to be running a window display manager such as *xwm*, *vuewm*, or *dtwm*. X-terminals may provide a built-in window manager. In the rootless mode, each X-Window is displayed a native window and is subject to the local windows manager.

The X-server also deals with the color depth of the display. Early displays supported only monochrome or 256-color displays, while modern displays support millions of colors at 24-bit depth. Thus, one user may be operating a 256-color display while another may be using a 24-bit display concurrently. The X-client application is made aware of the color availability and adjusts itself accordingly.

The X-server makes fonts available to the X-client, and will inform an application if a font is not available so another can be substituted. The X-server is responsible for all font rendering just as it is responsible for rendering low-level *xlib* graphics commands for drawing geometric shapes and colors.

Communication between the X-server and the X-client uses TCP which adapts to differences in LAN or WAN speeds. The user experience with a congested or low-speed WAN connection isn't as good as with a LAN connection. Likewise, a user with a low-end workstation doesn't enjoy the same graphical performance as a user with a high-end workstation.

Java Issues

NNM 6.x provides good support for read-only web access to NNM maps and utilities (including some configurations such as reporting, ECS, and the alarm browser), though not all NNM features are available. Ideally, any web browser would work, but in reality only a few browsers are supported and the version of Java must be checked and patched. Check the installation section of the NNM manual for the most current versions data. See Table 14-1 for a list of supported Java-enabled browsers at the time of this writing.

Table 14-1   NNM-Supported Browsers

Platform	Browser and Java Version Needed
Solaris 2.6	Thread patches for Java runtime, 105181-11 (or later), 105284-20 (or later), and 105490-7 (or later) for setuid. Patch 105210-02 (or later) for error code exit status. Netscape Navigator web browser version 4.6 or later.
HP-UX 11.X	iconv() patches PHCO_17317 or later for English and Japanese systems, iconv() patches PHCO_14775 or later for Japanese systems, Java Runtime Environment (JRE) application patches PHKL_14750, PHKL_17935, PHKL_18141, PHCO_17556, PHSS_18013, PHCO_18103, PHSS_15853, PHSS_17535, PHSS_17419 (or later). Netscape Navigator web browser version 4.6 or later.
Windows NT	Microsoft Internet Explorer 5.0 or greater.
All systems	Netscape 4.6 or greater.

The performance of the Java client is strongly dependent on the speed of the client platform processor and display subsystem. Note that third-party and homegrown Java applications may impose additional configuration and version constraints on the client system.

Also note that web access to NNM requires an open write-enabled map to be running in an X-Windows *ovw* client. To limit access to authorized users, require a password. This is enabled by editing the file */etc/opt/OV/share/www/conf/session.conf* to ensure the line *UserLogin: on* exists. Enter user IDs with the *ovhtpasswd username* command and the passwords are stored in the */etc/opt/OV/share/www/*

etc/htpasswd file. Finally, note that file *$OV_CONF/ovw.auth* allows any user from any host access by default.

Bandwidth and X-Windows

Several myths surround the X-Windows system and one of them concerns the bandwidth requirements. The transmission of bitmaps, mouse movements, and lack of compression are often cited.

X-Windows does not generally transmit bitmap graphics unless the application specifically requires it. For example, the small bitmaps inside device icons must be sent across the network regardless, and a background bitmap image must likewise be transmitted over the network. These intrinsic data types have nothing to do with X-Windows and everything to do with the *ovw* application requirements. All other objects drawn on an X-display are rendered locally as *xlib* instructions describing them are received. A green 100x100 rectangle is not transmitted as a bitmap, but as a concise, tiny graphical *xlib* instruction between X-client and X-server. For efficiency, these instructions are buffered.

Tracking cursor motion is also cited as a bandwidth consumer, but the cursor is tracked locally at the X-display and not transmitted to the X-client (unless it happens to be a drawing application and the user is actually drawing a freehand curve). The X-display sends an event to the X-client when a button is pressed or the mouse passes over a hot spot. Even these tiny packets are buffered for efficiency.

X-Windows works admirably across WAN links. For slower WAN links it's often standard practice to enable serial line compression on the routers. At least 56Kbps is needed for an X-Windows session, but latency is more an issue than bandwidth.

Compression solutions for X-Windows include Serial XPress from Tektronics, XRemote from NCD, and Low Bandwidth X (LBX). LBX is part of the X11R6.3 spec, and it's implemented in Hummingbird's

Broadway product. Note that VNC is a low-bandwidth alternative to X-Windows.

On a final note, enabling the X-terminal backing store can improve performance. When an obscured window is raised to the front, the X-Windows terminal will redraw the window from the backing store. This means the remote X-client need not redraw the window.

Printing With NNM

NNM may be operated from an X-Windows emulator or from a web client on any operating system that supports X-Windows and Netscape 4.6 or later. Given the rich variety of platforms, there is no consistent way to print information presented by NNM. See "Taking Screenshots of Maps" on page 88 for a cross-platform discussion.

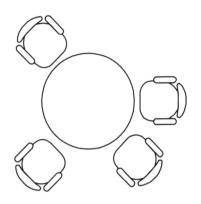

Staffing Issues for NNM

Introduction

Deploying NNM is often seen as a technical exercise that benefits from a project management approach because of the scale and complexity involved. In addition, there are staffing issues (not problems) with an NNM deployment.

Who exactly are the NNM users? Many users only need read-only map access, such as the help desk staff and network troubleshooters who use NNM to collect information about problems on the network. Map permissions give the NNM administrator control over who has read/write map access.

Who then will build and maintain these read-only maps? This user or group will own the operational maps and have read/write access to them. You should suggest that *root* not be the map builder.

Who troubleshoots the NNM application itself? A support hierarchy for the user community probably begins with the local site NNM champion, followed by the IT staff's NNM administrator, the UNIX system administrator, or an NNM consultant. A support contract with HP's Response Center is needed to deal with NNM product problem resolution.

Who resolves DNS problems? NNM depends on proper and correct operation of name services. But name servers are distributed and their host masters obtain their information from other system and network administrators, and client systems may use a variety of naming services. Add dynamic DNS, WINS, and DHCP servers to the mix, and you begin to see how many different people it might take to resolve a DNS problem.

Who resolves NNM product problems? Usually, you expect the IT group to do this in their test lab. Problems can be duplicated and called into the vendor for resolution if necessary.

Who performs system administration? The NNM application administrator may wear both the NNM and the UNIX administrator hats at smaller sites. Larger companies may have separate NNM application administrators and UNIX system administrators.

Who develops custom applications? This is typically a programmer, developer, or analyst trained in C/C++, Perl, Java, and in the HP OpenView API. However, any user can take advantage of NNM's MIB Application Builder.

Determining Users for the Read-Only Map

Let's review how a map is opened in read-only mode. First, NNM maps become read-only when the user specifies the following *ovw* command line option:

> *ovw -ro -map map_name*

Second, if map permissions (use *ovwls* to view permissions and *ovwperms* to change them) prevent a user from obtaining read/write access, the map is also opened in read-only mode. Third, once a map is opened in read/write mode, additional copies of the map can only be opened in read-only mode. Fourth, a map opened with the web browser interface is always read-only. See Chapter 9 of the *Managing Your Network with HP OpenView Network Node Manager* manual for detailed information.

What possible benefit is there to opening an NNM map in read-only mode? The user isn't able to move icons around the map, add or delete icons, or customize the map in any way. Only map builders need to do this on operational NNM systems. The user can navigate the map, activate menus and applications, look at events and performance graphs, and generally view information. This is appropriate for the help desk staff, troubleshooters, and network technical staff who use the tool rather than administer it.

Who Are the Keepers of the Maps?

NNM maps are a set of files that are collectively assigned consistent file system permissions that correspond to map permissions. This means that maps have independent read and write permissions plus owner and group names associated with them. The owner of the map is the keeper of the map and has read/write permissions for it. Production maps are intended for general read-only use so the map owner is the designated map builder. For large networks, keeping maps customized is a major responsibility, and it's usually assigned to a dedicated map builder. Not that *root* isn't capable of editing any NNM map, but it isn't a good idea to make root the map's owner. The absolute power of the *root* account is not needed simply to edit maps. Therefore, it's best if the map builders are members of a UNIX *group* who collectively have write access to the production maps.

Who Creates MIB Applications?

NNM provides a feature that uses a simple GUI to create new custom MIB applications. The user specifies if the application displays data as a form, table, or graph, and which MIB variables will be retrieved. The form application is suited for displaying any combination of scalar MIB values, one per line. The table application is suited for displaying structured tabular information, such as a list of network interfaces. The graph application is suited for displaying time-varying scalar values, such as performance data.

The IT group supplying the NNM tool for general use will prefer to supply their own MIB applications since they impact the menu structure via the application registration files. Therefore, the NNM menu for the MIB application builder may be removed from the production NNM systems for general users. Only the NNM tool support staff has this menu. The MIB application builder registration file is therefore missing from the application registration directory for general users, but not for the NNM support users. Recall that menu customization is controlled through the *$OVwRegDir* environment variable. The business of customizing menus is a complex affair, so be sure to take advantage of the information in Chapter 9, "Using ARF Files to Control Menu Choices" of the *Managing Your Network with HP OpenView Network Node Manager* manual.

Ad hoc creation of MIB applications is best supported for a different group of users that share a different application registration directory from regular users. The duration of a troubleshooting scenario can be shortened if the user is able to create spur-of-the-moment MIB applications.

Who Troubleshoots NNM Itself?

Years of experience have convinced this writer that until users develop confidence in NNM they will tend to blame the tool for any difficulties they encounter. It is also the writer's experience that most of the time NNM is working correctly. By looking under the hood you can usually explain the symptoms in terms of a real problem in the network. Occasionally, of course, there is an "errata" in NNM. (Readers familiar with the chip manufacturing industry will recognize this politically correct term.)

When a user experiences difficulties with NNM, they should call their IT support desk telephone number, send them an e-mail, or post a question on the NNM list server they provide. Large companies may have an NNM site focal who acts as a point of first contact for the site user community.

The NNM system administrator is familiar with how the application and the operating system is configured, and is often the individual who can troubleshoot, reproduce, validate, isolate, work around, and often fix a problem.

Companies may also choose to retain the services of an NNM consultant on a periodic or ongoing basis, especially in the first year or two after NNM is deployed. The consultant can work with the users directly to deal with problems.

The OV Forum is an independent organization with a website at *http:/ /www.ovforum.org*. This site has a search engine and an e-mail service for the OpenView discussion list. It is a valuable resource to the NNM community. You should become a member of the OpenView Forum to realize the full benefits it can offer.

Last but not least is HP's support services. HP's OpenView website is at *http://www.openview.hp.com,* where product news can be read and from which patches may be downloaded. Customers with a support agreement can also search the problem resolution database and make telephone calls to the Response Center.

Who Resolves DNS Problems?

Domain name servers are organized in a distributed hierarchy. Authority for the information they serve is delegated to authoritative sites, so it isn't unusual to have many host masters. Any or all of them may be able to take credit when a problem raises its head. Typical DNS problems include:

- a name server is lame
- a record is deleted
- reverse lookups fail
- old data is returned
- a lookup times out
- the wrong name server is authoritative
- some router interface IP addresses are not returned
- forward and reverse translations don't match

The host masters get their information from system administrators. If a router administrator doesn't supply all the IP addresses in a router to the host master, then credit belongs to the router administrator. If a reverse lookup fails and the forward lookup succeeds, it may be because the host master has not configured the inverse records properly. When a system administrator decommissions a server and asks the host master to delete the corresponding DNS records, then a failed name lookup is expected and the error is with the user.

Occasionally, a DNS problem is not caused by a name server but by the resolver routine at the client:

- the wrong name server is used by a resolver
- the SEARCH path scans the wrong domain
- the default domain name is incorrect
- the resolver can't handle a large number of addresses

Credit for resolver problems isn't due to the host masters, but lies with the administrators of the end user systems, who might be the users themselves. They may configure their resolvers to take advantage of multiple name resolution mechanisms. The order in which these mechanisms are accessed is platform-dependent. In UNIX, the order they are searched is specified in the */etc/nsswitch.conf* file. These mechanisms include:

- domain name service
- WINS
- /etc/hosts
- LMHOSTS
- NIS
- NetBIOS name request (a broadcast mechanism)

Tools for troubleshooting DNS problems include:

- examine the resolver configuration files

- *nslookup* command

- *ping* command (**p**acket **int**ernet **g**roper)

- *dig* command (**d**omain **i**nformation **g**roper)

Finally, the coupling between DHCP servers and the dynamic updates they (are supposed to) send to DNS servers may be at fault, suggesting the DCHP administrators might also share credit when a DNS-related problem surfaces.

Who Resolves NNM Problems?

We've seen how problems apparently with NNM may be related to DNS, DHCP, routers, client-side resolvers, and user inexperience. With so much fingerpointing, who corrects the direction of the finger-pointing? That would be the whole team of experts discussed above. Real NNM product problems are handled by the local NNM champions and by the IT department's NNM experts. These people have the full NNM training under their belts.

The NNM product champion(s) also has a lab with a test NNM system used for testing patches, verifying configurations, conducting regression tests, and replicating problems. This person also has access to the HP Response Center to discuss problems, gather information, collaborate on workarounds, and submit bug reports.

Who Performs System Administration?

The operating system on which NNM runs is either Solaris, HP-UX, or Windows NT. The client systems may be any system running X-

Windows emulation or a Java-capable web browser. All these systems require system administration. Large companies may have an organization dedicated to providing client and server system administration for the rest of the company. In smaller companies, the NNM application administrator wears the hat of the system administrator as well.

UNIX system administrators may have a special issue with the *root* account. They would like to limit access to *root* but this can seriously limit how much the NNM application administrator can do. Therefore, a close relationship based on trust and mutual respect must be developed to avoid problems.

Who Develops Custom Applications?

A staff developer can write, document, test, maintain, and support homegrown NNM applications. Developers understand the UNIX applications development environment, including source control, the windowing system, the NNM developer kit, and languages (C, C++, Perl, Java, TCL, Tk, and shell scripting). The kinds of applications that might be written locally will integrate into the NNM menu system via application registration files, at a minimum. Some applications may run in the background, such as a historical SNMP data trimmer, a specialized SNMP configuration, or a performance data collector. Other applications may be integrated tightly into the OpenView Windows environment, such as a tool for aligning icons vertically and horizontally and a tool for creating a special submap of the network backbone.

Best Practices for NNM

Introduction

This chapter is a summary of the best practices introduced throughout the book.

Platform sizing must be done before deployment. The platform must be scalable to avoid a poor user experience and prevent costly downtime during a box swap. Information for platform sizing can be obtained during NNM product evaluation. Table 16-1 on page 254 will aid you in system sizing.

ITO is a great tool for managing the managers. It lets you automate a lot of system monitoring tasks to increase your efficiency. It also reduces downtime by detecting problems before they can affect the user community.

Menu management is important because it increases the stability of the NNM system while ensuring that various user types have all necessary functionality.

Project management is a necessary skill that helps keep a project on track by detecting when critical path activities are placing the entire schedule at risk.

A dedicated system administrator is an essential team member to handle the sheer amount of work and provide the strong technical expertise needed to support a large NNM rollout.

Platform Sizing

A first estimate can be made using HP's publication, *Network Node Manager Performance and Configuration Guide*. This document provides a methodology for sizing a system based on the following considerations:

- number of objects
- number of nodes
- collection station overhead
- management console overhead
- number of *ovw* sessions
- number of web-based sessions
- amount of SNMP data being collected
- alarm rate
- backups
- polling rate
- database overhead
- on-demand maps

This guide easily becomes dated as new versions of NNM and new patches are released. A conservative approach is to make a first estimate with the guide, double the results, and allow for growth. Remember that a computer system gets its performance from resource headroom. It's good to underutilize a system to ensure it performs as snappily as possible.

Some of the inputs to the above methodology require detailed knowledge about the number of managed objects. How are you supposed to estimate that? By taking advantage of HP's free 60-day evaluation period, loading it on an available computer, and developing a baseline object count for your own network. See Table 16-1 for a summary of field data for sizing an NNM system.

Table 16-1   NNM System Sizing Examples[*]

System	Networks	Segments	Nodes	Interfaces	Routers	RAM Meg	CPU	Database Meg	Disk Stripes	Users
1	393	1846	1450	61344	111	3328	4	263	4	9
2	340	805	803	27399	92	2560	3	94	2	10
3	619	1149	782	16033	125	1024	2	81	2	8
4	390	1260	1324	45006	66	1792	3	212	3	11
5	400	1666	1351	20643	127	1024	2	105	2	8
6	146	774	663	19469	29	1024	2	73	2	8
7	131	180	179	5111	35	1024	2	20	2	3
Mgt stn	2492	11	643	8570	634	1024	2	80	3	8

[*]These examples are from an actual NNM deployment. The first seven systems are collection stations. Eight others are not shown. A total of 15 collection stations export routers and subnets to the management station. Note that while the flat file database is not unreasonably large, the number of CPUs and the number of users require at least two disk stripes for acceptable performance on the smaller systems.

Once NNM is deployed and you've discovered your network, the user community becomes active and the demands on the systems increase. As time passes, the NNM administrators apply patches and upgrades that repair defects or add functionality. The growth in resource consumption requires that you anticipate the need to upgrade resources such as:

- the number of processors
- the amount of RAM
- the LAN adapter speed
- the amount of disk space
- the amount of disk striping

It would be a mistake to deploy an NNM system that could not be upgraded quickly in the field. It behooves you to monitor the NNM system resources with the MeasureWare agent and assess the data weekly with PerfView Analyzer. This allows you to proactively schedule field upgrades before the user community begins to grumble about poor response time.

ITO Manages the NNM Systems

Do you manage the distributed NNM systems from a central location? Then an automated system management tool such as HP IT Operations (ITO) can improve your productivity, reduce your problem time-to-resolution, and increase the uptime of your systems. You can add NNM systems to ITO and view all NNM systems in a single window, as shown in Figure 16-1.

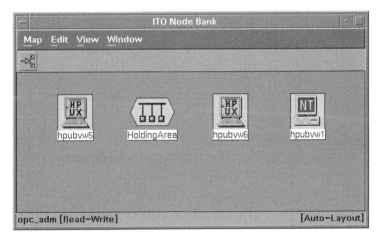

Figure 16-1   The ITO window of NNM systems,
This example shows three NNM systems being managed by ITO. The icon color indicates the status of the monitored components in each system.

You can take advantage of the customized ITO monitoring to perform the following checks:

- that the read/write map is open and running properly
- the */var/adm/messages,* a *syslog* file for known problem signs
- detect and terminate spinning processes, especially for X-clients

Since ITO also monitors MeasureWare alarms, you probably want to examine the preset threshold settings and change them so they reflect your own experience. Otherwise, you are going to receive a lot of unwanted alarms for conditions that you know from experience are not degrading the user's response time.

Menu Management

To protect the NNM system from the ravages caused by users and yet ensure that users are able to do their jobs, it is important to customize the NNM menus. Begin by doing a thorough requirements analysis of the user needs. Use large sheets of paper and represent the menu layout to which you want each user type to have access. These sheets represent the gathered requirements. Validate them with the users. If your company has a steering committee or other such organization that represents the user community, this formal body can validate the requirements. Each menu has to be identified with a corresponding requirement. For example, if a given user type has to be able to perform ad hoc SNMP data collections, then the menu items to create data collectors and to display the collected data must be provided.

The heavy lifting that follows is the process of finding the standard NNM application registration files (ARF) located in the *$OV_REGISTRATION* directory for each menu item, creating additional directory structures for each user type (pointed to by *$OVwRegDir*), and editing the ARFs accordingly. Note that homegrown menu items must also be considered, as must any additional applications that you provide, such as HP NetMetrix and

CiscoView, since these too add menus to NNM. This short summary by itself is dangerous, so please refer to Chapter 9, "Using ARF Files to Control Menu Choices," in the *Managing Your Network with HP OpenView Network Node Manager* manual.

Note that the application of NNM patches or the installation of NNM updates can change the default menu structure. Always be prepared to have the menu structure tested for functionality after any software changes occur.

Define user groups based on the role or task to be performed. Uses with the same role should be in the same group and should be presented with a common menu format. This makes training easier.

Project Management

For large NNM installations you need to take advantage of a project manager, the keeper of the schedule. See Figure 16-2 for a sample PERT chart. The project manager (PM) need not be in direct control of the NNM implementation. At a minimum, the PM monitors the schedule, compares it to actual progress, and raises a red flag when an event on the critical path doesn't complete on time. The PM meets frequently to gather information from team members, developers, installers, the user community, and management. Deliverables such as technical requirements, installation manuals, and training materials are also monitored by the PM.

Project management is both a position and a role. On large NNM implementations, the work can consume most of an individual's time, so a full-time PM position is needed. On smaller implementations, the NNM project lead can assume the role.

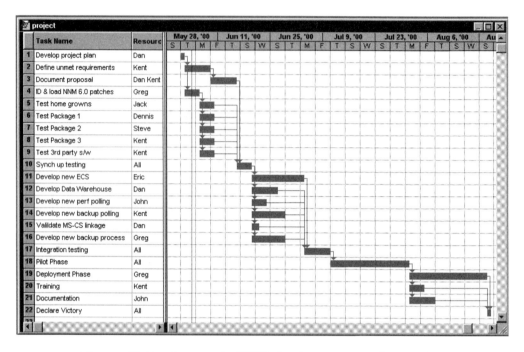

Figure 16-2   A sample NNM deployment project schedule.

Dedicated System Administrator

The system administrator performs a great variety of technical tasks to support an NNM deployment project. They are as follows:

- install the latest operating system on the platform
- configure the networking subsystems
- add users and account management
- system tuning
- disk striping
- upgrade hardware
- develop backup and restore scripts
- manage the system to which backups are done
- write installation scripts for homegrown code
- interface with developers
- troubleshoot installations
- download, apply, and test NNM and OS patches
- install ITO agents and develop custom monitoring scripts
- solve problems with user accounts and X-Windows
- customize the graphical environment

After the NNM deployment, the same system administrator continues to provide a valuable support function.

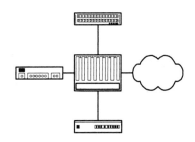

NNM Case Studies

Introduction

Let's wrap up the book by reviewing several NNM installation case studies. We begin with a large global manufacturing company, review a natural resource company, a bioengineering company, a vehicle manufacturer, a community college, a national consulting company, a small engineering firm, and a worldwide computer company.

A Global Manufacturing Company

The large manufacturing company depends upon its mission-critical IP backbone to communicate between hundreds of sites located all over the world. To deploy an NNM system at each physical site wouldn't be cost effective so you select 30 sites with local network support staff instead. Each site will receive a collection station and two sites will receive a management station. Most of the NNM user community accesses their NNM systems using an X-Windows emulator running on their Windows systems. A few users prefer Macintosh computers running MacX, or Linux systems running their built-in X-Windows software. The system administrators use the built-in X-Windows software in their UNIX workstations to access remote NNM systems.

The NNM systems are staged at the corporate IT department and shipped to their destinations according to a schedule. Each system is loaded with the current version of the OS, the appropriate OS patches, NNM and its current patches, and third-party bolt-on applications with their current patches. Since these are UNIX systems, they are configured as NIS+ replicas that contain all user account information. It is intended that each site be able to access another's NNM system for support and backup purposes.

When the NNM system is physically installed at the destination site, its network configuration is preconfigured and the system immediately sends an e-mail message to the system administrator when it boots for the first time. At this point there is no *seedfile* configured. NNM's initial management domain is the local subnet only. All that remains is for the central IT staff to work with the local map builders to refine the management domain for the site and build up the *seedfile* accordingly. Usually, the site's discovery filter is modified to allow discovery of site-specific equipment, such as mission-critical servers, but the standard corporate discovery filter only allows for network equipment such as routers, switches, and hubs.

The local network support staff frequently wants to make small changes to their NNM system that would require *root* access to the *seedfile* and *filters* file. Since *root* access is strictly limited to system administrators, and since the UNIX skills possessed by the staff varies, a small GUI is written for them that allows viewing and modifying the data without requiring direct access to the files. This is a good example of how an NNM-trained developer can help implement additional functionality.

The central IT system administrator can manage all remote NNM systems using the standard X-Windows interface. If WAN performance issues limit using X-Windows, a simple low-overhead *telnet* session can be used. Should the UNIX system suffer a hard crash, a terminal server is cabled to a serial port to allow direct access to the diagnostic port. The system is shipped with a bootable CD-ROM in the CD tray as an alternate boot device.

Each NNM system executes a VNC (virtual network computing) session and maintains a read/write *ovw* session with the map. The system and NNM administrators can attach to this VNC session for map maintenance purposes.

Each collection station is configured to export subnets and routers to each of the two management stations. For such a large IP network, it is neither practical nor cost-effective to export more of the site topology. Each management station operates independently, although the

Internet submaps are kept identical so that each station can act as a backup for the other.

Each NNM system performs its own scheduled backup and transmits the backup file to a central repository at the corporate IT site. The backup script automatically e-mails the backup log to the system administrator.

A Natural Resource Company

The natural resource company has sites across North America. You choose to manage the entire network centrally with a single, large NNM system located in the corporate data center. This UNIX system is intended to support 30 concurrent users, so you install the maximum number of CPUs and the maximum amount of RAM supported. You install a second, small backup NNM system at another location.

Rather than depend on *snmpCollect*-style SNMP polling for performance management, you install RMON probes at all critical LAN and WAN points. HP NetMetrix manages the probes and downloads the performance data. The probes also generate threshold alarms. This removes the performance overhead of collecting performance data from the NNM system and offers better control over the data collected.

The IT staff took all the formal HP OpenView training and hired a consultant for two full weeks to install NNM, direct the discovery of the network, set up SNMP data collection, train the staff, buy lunches, and document the entire network management strategy and implementation.

No discovery filter is used. Instead, you manually guide the NNM discovery process by managing subnets as they are discovered until all of the network is on the map. Here, you depend on a map builder who knows the corporate network topology and can partition the Internet submap intelligently. As each subnet is managed and discovery in it takes place, you observe what devices are found and then unmanage and hide those you don't want to manage. This usually means hiding workstations and non-SNMP devices and managing network infrastructure, printers, and servers.

A Bioengineering Company

The small bioengineering company has one main data center. Low-speed, point-to-point WAN links radiate outwards from a single router to 30 small remote sites. These sites are located throughout the farm belt. Since low-bandwidth lines are expensive and not redundant, you want to know at once if a link goes down. You can reduce the NNM polling interval accordingly.

A single, small, non-dedicated UNIX workstation is capable of managing all the devices located on this network, including data center switches, routers and servers, plus all the remote routers, printers, and workstations. The Internet submap requires only minimal customization. The entire process of installation, configuration, discovery, and customization took less than a day.

Performance management of the main router is simply a matter of collecting interface statistics on all ports. This keeps performance polling traffic off the WAN links.

A Local Vehicle Manufacturer

The local vehicle manufacturer is located within one state and has six manufacturing plants, one data center, and a corporate office. NNM is used to manage the network infrastructure and critical servers at each site. You configure a DNS server on the single NNM system, a small UNIX workstation.

The IT group and the help desk use the system, so only two maps are needed. The help desk uses a read-only map. NNM polls the mission-critical servers and core routers every minute, instead of the five-minute default.

You provide on-site training for the users and IT staff, covering networking, DNS, and NNM fundamentals. Users really benefit from taking their training on their own network using their own NNM system. The training materials include a thick student workbook.

Because the IT department embraced DNS throughout the company, there was an impact to the application developers working there. Their applications stopped working because they were still using */etc/hosts*-style names, rather than fully qualified domain names in their code. Some education was needed so they understood that the user might be located on one subdomain, while the target server is located in a different one.

A Community College

This community college has several campuses. To manage its network you purchased NNM to run on an existing UNIX workstation. Since the college used all HP equipment, NNM was able to autolayout each subnet with perfect accuracy by taking advantage of the HP enterprise-specific MIB. This was before the days of the industry standard repeater and bridge MIBs.

In addition to monitoring the network infrastructure, the NNM system also managed HP3000 and HP9000 server systems on all the campuses. Performance polling of the network equipment that provides Internet access was set up to detect when a line speed upgrade was needed.

A National Consulting Company

The consulting company has a network of a dozen sites using Cisco site routers and HP hubs for the site LAN. You install NNM on an existing HP-UX workstation, configure the necessary router community strings, and prepare to manually direct NNM to discover the network. Unfortunately, the workstation's subnet mask is not set correctly. NNM assumed that the entire class B network was flat and prepared to discover the entire network. NNM depicted the single subnet as a dense wheel of icons. After correcting the NNM system's subnet mask, autodiscovery proceeds normally.

The network administrator quickly partitions the map by site and consults with his peers to verify that some specific topology information was consistent with NNM's discovery and autolayout. While all the routers were configured with the proper subnet masks, the corporate standard appeared to allow computer systems to default their subnet mask to 255.255.0.0. As a result, NNM generated a torrent of configuration alarms, complaining that many devices had an incorrect subnet mask. There wasn't anything to be done about it from an NNM point of view.

Curiously, the network behaved correctly despite the fact that many devices had no routing table entries. It turns out that the Cisco routers had proxy ARP enabled by default. This kept things working.

You configure NNM to monitor the performance and status of the WAN links of the routers and unmanage any systems you had no control over. This has the pleasant side effect of reducing the configuration alarms relating to bad subnet masks.

A Small Engineering Firm

This small firm has a single two-story building. A single LAN provides every engineering workstation access to several file and print servers. The print servers drive LaserJet printers for standard documentation and large-format plotters for engineering drawings. Each server handles about a dozen workstations.

You install NNM on an existing UNIX workstation and discover every networked system on the lone subnet without any effort. The */etc/hosts* file provides name-to-address resolution.

NNM monitors only a few dozen systems and you set the polling interval to one second without fear of overloading anything. This small firm depends on the LAN for its livelihood and wants instant notification of any outages to reduce the Mean Time to Repair (MTTR). The LAN administrator uses X-Windows to access NNM and is able to start working on a problem before users can call to complain.

A Worldwide Computer Company

The IT department of this computer company is responsible for managing the corporate WAN. Other organizations provide site LAN management. Consequently, IT does not want NNM to discover any infrastructure and turns off autodiscovery. The backbone routers have a non-standard get community string to prevent site-based NNM systems from discovering beyond their management domain by accident.

A *seedfile* lists every router with a WAN connection and, at startup, NNM promptly begins drawing all the connections between these routers. There are hundreds of routers, and the Internet submap becomes quite dense. A map builder leverages his knowledge of the network to partition the map into geographies.

NNM is configured to poll the WAN links for capacity management purposes. Since each link is full duplex (FDX), only inbound port statistics are sampled at the routers. This halves the amount of data harvested.

Many of the larger manufacturing sites deploy their own copy of NNM for site management. There, too, the Internet submap is quite dense and requires partitioning to be useful. RMON probes are deployed on shared media segments for performance management.

Since the LAN is subject to frequent moves, adds, and changes, a *crontab* entry forces a nightly demand poll (with *xnmpolling*) of the hubs and switches to speed up the convergence of the topology discovery and autolayout.

Glossary

AARP   AppleTalk address resolution protocol. When a Macintosh doesn't know what network numbers are valid at start-up time, it broadcasts an AARP probe packet to find a valid node address in the start-up network number range.

ABR   Available bit rate. In ATM LANs, this is the lowest quality of service that a device may request. No bandwidth guarantee is made by the ATM switch, and the device may suffer cell loss when the ATM LAN has to guarantee delivery for higher QOS devices.

AC   Alternating current. AC usually refers to the type of power used by network and computer equipment. It may be 115 volts single phase or 220 volts three phase. Uninterruptable power supplies provide conditioned AC for mission-critical systems such as computers running the NNM application and network equipment.

Access List   In routers, this is a list of allowed clients and the local services they can access. This is a security feature vastly superior to SNMP community strings. For DNS servers running BIND 8 or later, the access list defines which name servers are allowed to perform a zone transfer. The access list is also a general-purpose method to filter traffic passing through a router.

ACL   Access control list. This mechanism is used to extend the simple owner/group/world read/write/execute permissions of the standard UNIX file system to increase the flexibility of file access. For example, a file may be given an ACL that gives only certain users in various groups write permission. Routers also employ access lists to limit access to certain services by a list of devices.

ADSP   AppleTalk Data Stream Protocol. AppleTalk applications may use this byte-oriented service to transmit streams of data reliably.

AFP   AppleTalk file protocol. The remote file access protocol used between Macintosh clients and file servers.

AM   Amplitude modulation. A carrier's amplitude is varied in proportion to the amplitude of the data signal, as in AM radio. Quadrature amplitude modulation is a modem modulation scheme that varies both the carrier signal's amplitude and phase.

ANI   Automatic number identification. This is part of the SS7 protocol. ANI is offered commercially to telephone customers as caller ID, whereby the caller phone number and name are displayed at the receiver.

ANSI   American National Standards Institute. The United States member body of the International Standards Organization is ANSI.

APA   Automatic Port Aggregation is an HP-UX feature that bundles similar LAN adapters into a single high-speed, highly-available load-balancing single LAN adapter. It works in conjunction with Port Aggregation Protocol.

API   Application programming interface. A documented set of function calls that programmers use to perform useful tasks. For example, the Berkeley socket library is a set of APIs to let programmers write code to move data between networked applications using TCP/IP standards.

ARF   Application Registration File. This file defines how an NNM application integrates into the NNM menu structure, including the location of its menus and the selection rules. An ARF may also define a button or a pop-up menu.

ARM   Application response measurement. A set of APIs to instrument an application for automated performance data collection during operational use.

ARP   Address resolution protocol. A broadcast mechanism used on local area networks to determine the MAC address corresponding to the LAN adapter of a local system with the requested IP address. The MAC address is stored in an ARP cache for reuse. NNM harvests ARP caches to discover IP addresses.

ASCII   American standard code for information interchange. A seven-bit standard way to represent characters.

ASIC   Application-specific integrated circuit. An integrated circuit built for a specific purpose, as opposed to a general purpose.

ASN.1   Abstract syntax notation one. A standard used to describe the way SNMP MIBs are written. ASN.1 is a general-purpose standard for specifying data used by a communications protocol.

ATM   Asynchronous transfer mode. A high-speed switching technology based on 53-byte cells.

AUI   Attachment unit interface. The Ethernet/802.3 physical 15-pin D-connector standard for connecting transceivers to network devices.

Automagically   Refers to a feature or process that occurs automatically, as if by magic.

AV   Audio-visual. An environment that takes advantage of visual and audible elements. A video conferencing connection is an AV application. AV is an older term that has been supplanted by the general-purpose term, multimedia.

AVI   Audio video interleave. A simple file format for video on Windows platforms.

BASE   Baseband refers to the modulation technique used in the IEEE twisted pair standards such as 10-BASE-5, 10-BASE-2, 10-BASE-T, and 100-BASE-T.

Base64   A method for converting binary files to ASCII form suitable for e-mailing using SMTP. UUENCODE and BinHex are similar methods.

BER   Basic encoding rules. This is a method of encoding ASN.1 types as a string of octets.

BER Bit error rate. The rate at which bits are transmitted in error on a communications circuit. Errors are often caused by electrical or magnetic interference at the physical layer of the OSI model. A bit error rate tester (BERT) is an instrument that measures bit error rate.

BGP Border gateway protocol. A routing protocol frequently used between multihomed autonomous systems (AS) that connect to the Internet.

BIND Berkeley Internet Name server Daemon implements the domain name service (DNS). BIND version 8 brings a new database file syntax and improved features such as security, synchronization, and dynamic updates.

BinHex Binary to hexadecimal. A conversion method that allows one or more binary and ASCII files to be converted into ASCII form for transmission by SMTP. It is popular on Macintosh computers.

BLS B-level security. A standard set of features for defining security levels.

BNC Baby N-connector. The small coaxial connector used by the 10-BASE-2 thin-LAN standard.

BRI Basic rate interface. The 64 Kbps channel of an ISDN circuit.

BSD Berkeley software distribution. A term generally referring to the Berkeley variant of UNIX.

Caching-only name server This is the simplest configuration for a DNS name server that takes advantage of the caching feature for increased performance. This type of name server is authoritative for no domains, and refers to root name servers for all information. On an NNM system, this cache fills quickly so most requests are satisfied locally, reducing network traffic and lookup latency.

CACI   A software company specializing in network and system simulation products used in capacity planning.

CAD   Computer-aided design typically refers to a high-end drafting package used to document architectural building plans and network topologies.

CATV   Cable television, an analog method for distributing television channels with 6 MHz channel allocations using 75-ohm transmission facilities that terminate in RG-59 coaxial cable at the end user drop.

CBR   Constant bit rate. An ATM service that guarantees delivery of fixed-bit-rate data such as audio and video data.

CCNA   Cisco certified networking associate. A person that passed a test blessed by the Cisco company, a well-respected manufacturer of network electronics such as routers and switches.

CCR   Current cell rate. In ATM switches, this is the rate at which 53-byte cells are being switched.

CD   Compact disk. A plastic disk that stores digital data used to represent audio tracks or a file system. It holds about 650 Mbytes. The DVD standard holds about 4.7 Gbytes in the same form factor.

CDE   Common desktop environment. A standard look and feel for UNIX X-Windows graphical workstations developed by HP, SUN, and IBM. It sports a trash can, a file manager, a desktop, and multiple work spaces.

CDPD   Cellular digital packet data. A method to transmit IP data from portable computer equipment such as laptop computers and digital personal assistants.

CER   Cell error ratio. The ratio of ATM cells with errors to the total cell count.

CERT Computer emergency response team. An organization that supports computer users, especially in the area of security breaches.

CGI Common gateway interface. A programmatic interface between hypertext on a web page and the UNIX environment. For example, form data can be processed using a CGI script written in Perl and added to a mailing list program.

CHAP Challenge handshake authentication protocol. Used to pass the user account name and password to authenticate a dial-up PPP connection. The name and password are not sent in the clear.

CIDR Classless interdomain routing. A routing protocol that takes advantage of the allocation of contiguous blocks of class C IP addresses to simplify routing information. Its invention avoided problems associated with large routing tables on the Internet.

CIR Committed information rate. A guaranteed minimum bit rate on a frame relay permanent virtual circuit for which the customer is charged a service fee and at which the service provider guarantees delivery.

CISC Complex instruction set computer. A computer that has large, complex, variable-length instructions stored as ROM microprograms, which require multiple clock cycles to decode and execute, and which requires a large number of transistors, resulting in a very hot chip that is often cooled by a fan. Performance is gained by massive parallelism and pipelining. Examples include the Intel line of X86 chips and the Motorola 68xxx line.

CLEC Competitive local exchange carrier.

CMS Color management system. Ensures that color images seen on a display, printed on paper, input by a scanner, and stored in a file maintain their integrity when moved to another computer with a different display, scanner, or printer. CMS is an essential element in the publishing industry.

Collection Station   An NNM system configured to poll and discover over its collection domain and report filtered management information to a management station. Typically, the topology filter defines which managed objects are reported to the management station. Exported information includes device configuration data and events.

Community   SNMP version 1 defines a simple, unencrypted community string for get/read/access and another for set/write operations. The correct community string must accompany any SNMP request for it to be honored, otherwise it's completely ignored, and an authentication trap will be sent to all configured trap destinations.

COTS   Commercial-off-the-shelf. Refers to products, typically software, that can be purchased in the marketplace as a final, polished supported product that will perform all the required functions without any modifications whatsoever, using only standard and supported configurations and installation options.

CPU   Central processor unit. An integrated circuit with the basic intelligence behind all computer equipment. Examples include the Intel X86 line, the Apple/Motorola Power PC, HP's HPPA, and the HP-Intel Merced chip.

CRC   Cyclic redundancy check is an additional 16- or 32-bit check field calculated by the network adapter from the encapsulated data to protect the integrity of the transmission. The receiving adapter recalculates the CRC field from the received data, checks it against the transmitted value, and either discards the frame (as Ethernet adapters do) or requests a retransmission (as HDLC links do).

cron   A UNIX facility for automatically time scheduling command scripts such as backups and historical SNMP trimmers. The crontab command is used to manage entries in *cron*.

CRT   Cathode ray tube. A term often used to refer to a computer monitor screen. In televisions, it is called the picture tube.

CS Collection station. An HP OpenView network management station responsible for discovering, managing devices in its management domain, and maintaining a configuration database. The CS polls these devices periodically. A collection station may forward event and topology information to an OpenView management station.

CTD Cell transfer delay. The amount of time it takes an ATM cell to traverse the switched network. This will include the "wire time," multiple hops, and queuing delays at congestion points.

CTI Computer telephony integration. A set of tools and products for integrating telephone technology with computers. Applications include automated calling units that allow a bank to automatically call customers and, if they answer, to transfer the customer to a live agent within a second.

DAS Dual attach station. A device that connects to both of the FDDI rings and therefore has a very reliable LAN connection.

DCE Distributed communications environment. A set of standards that emerged from the Open Software Foundation for doing multiplatform client–server networking in an open, standards-based manner not controlled by vendor; or,

DCE Data communications equipment. Typically, an ASCII terminal connected to a modem, a router connected to a DSU/CSU, or a computer connected to a hub or switch. The modem, DSU/CSU, and hub/switch are referred to as the data communications equipment, and the ASCII terminal, router, and computer are the data terminal equipment.

DDP Datagram delivery protocol. A protocol for delivery of datagrams without connection-oriented services such as multiplexing, buffering, retransmission, or reliability. DDP is part of AppleTalk.

DEC Digital Equipment Corporation. A company founded by Ken Olsen. DEC blazed the minicomputer frontier with its PDP and

VAX systems. It is now a wholly owned subsidiary of Compaq, a PC clone maker.

DEL   The delete or backspace character varies from system to system. It may be the Del key itself, the Backspace key, or control-H. It is a plague at the presentation layer of the OSI model.

DEN   Directory enabled networks support directory services such as Novell Directory Services (NDS) or lightweight directory access protocol (DLAP).

DES   Data encryption standard. An internationally accepted standard for encrypting data using symmetric, private, 56-bit keys intended to make business transactions safe but interoperable.

DFS   Distributed File System. A derivative of the Open Software Foundations Andrew File System, which provides an open standard for remote file access across networks.

DHCP   Dynamic host configuration protocol. A standard to allow a device to determine its IP configuration from a DHCP server instead of a local configuration file. This method considerably simplifies the administration of an IP network in the presence of frequent moves, adds, and changes. DNS and NNM can be configured to intelligently handle information provided by DHCP servers about newly assigned names and IP addresses.

DLT   Digital linear tape. A quarter-inch-wide tape used for high-capacity backups. A DLT array holds many such tapes and cycles them in and out of the drive mechanism automatically under control of the backup software.

DMZ   Demilitarized zone. The LAN segment between the bastion host and the ISP's router. It is vulnerable to attack from the Internet because it is directly connected to it.

DNS   Domain name system. A hierarchical, scalable, distributed standard for host name-to-IP address resolution. It allows sites responsible for their own IP address and system names to build an authoritative name server, and it allows other name servers to find them transparently to the end users. NNM depends on a fast accurate DNS for proper operation of its configuration management functions. The NNM system should run a local caching-only name server for maximum performance.

DSAP Destination service access point. A 1-byte field in the IEEE 802.2 frame format that identifies the upper-layer protocol contained in the frame.

DSL Digital subscriber line. A copper circuit between the central office and the customer premises operated digitally.

DTE Data terminal equipment. In the RS-232 world, the data terminal equipment is the terminal, printer, plotter, or computer serial port. The modem is the data communications equipment. In the Ethernet world, the data terminal equipment is the networked X-terminal, printer, scanner, or computer, and the hub or switch is the data communications equipment.

DTP Distributed transaction processing occurs when a client passes a user query to an upper-tier application server, which in turn may process it and make another query to its upper tier, perhaps a database server.

DVD Digital video disk. A standard file format for a CD-ROM with much higher capacity than the earlier 640-megabyte technology. Movies stored on DVD disks are meant to be played back by stand-alone DVD players driving a standard television or by movie playback programs on desktop computers (which may require hardware support to decode the movie's MPEG-2 encoded frames). DVD may also mean digital versatile disk.

EAROM Electrically alterable read-only-memory is an integrated circuit that contains instructions and data.

EC Electronic commerce. A catch-all phrase depicting the migration of point-of-sale transactions to Internet-based transactions. This includes advertising, accepting orders from customers in a secure way, allowing customers to check on the status of their order, and so on. These systems must be up on a 24×7×365 basis. Customers span the globe and speak many languages.

ECS   Event Correlation System. Attempts to reduce high-volume symptomatic event activity into a low-volume causal one. ECS is a standard component as of NNM 6.0.

EDI   Electronic data interchange. The transmission of documents by electronic means using standards.

EIA   Electrical Industries Association. A group that defines electrical transmission standards, such as the familiar EAI RS-232-C.

ELM   Electronic mail. A standard UNIX mail reader.

EMC   A vendor of large-capacity, high-availability disk arrays.

EMI   Electromagnetic interference. Any electrical or magnetic waves emanating from unshielded conductors may induce voltages in sensitive equipment and disrupt its operation. This may happen to computer equipment, generally causing the operating system to crash and data to be lost. It also happens to radio, television, wireless, and audio equipment.

EMP   Electromagnetic pulse. Usually of very high amplitude, generated when a nuclear weapon explodes, it can destroy sensitive electronic equipment, especially semiconductors.

EPS   Enterprise parallel server. A cluster of HP9000 HP-UX computers capable of handling very large applications with very high performance.

ESP   Extrasensory perception. A sixth sense possessed by some gifted people that endows them with information not available to ordinary people.

Extranet   When a private corporate network must also service customers and business partners over the Internet, the special network arrangement has this new 1990s term associated with it.

FAT   File allocation table. A simple means of allocating blocks of data on a disk using a 16-bit integer to represent the allocation block number. This method is inefficient for large disk volumes, since many small files are allocated the full allocation block. The FAT-32 file system addresses this inefficiency. The FAT file system is found mainly on Windows computers.

FAX   Facsimile. A method for scanning paper documents, transmitting them over standard telephone lines, and printing them at the receiving end. A Fax machine, typically with a built-in dialer, is used at each end. Fax technology uses CCITT group 3 compression to improve throughput.

FCA   Fibre Channel Association. An organization intended to promote the fibre channel technology. Note that this spelling differs from the word *fiber.*

FC-AL   Fibre channel arbitrated loop. An implementation of fibre channel that daisy-chains up to 127 devices on a single loop.

FCS   Frame check sequence. An additional field attached to the frame by the link layer protocol, which is calculated from the payload data. The receiver checks the FCS field against the data field as an integrity check. The term FCS is sometimes used in place of the term cyclic redundancy check (CRC).

FDDI   Fiber distributed data interface. A time-tested fiber-optic LAN and MAN technology operating at 100 megabits/second. It features a dual counterrotation architecture that is self-healing, providing high availability.

FDX   Full duplex. Refers to a data communications channel that can simultaneously send and receive data. Fast Ethernet, gigabit Ethernet, ATM, and fibre channel are examples of technologies with full duplex capability.

FIF   Fractal image format. Employs a pattern-based compression method that finds variations of similar patterns in an image that differ only in position, orientation, scaling, and stretching. A nice illustration is an image of a field of ferns, which has a single shape that is found almost everywhere in it, and which can therefore be highly compressed. Decompression is much faster than compression.

Firewall   Network equipment installed between the Internet and a private intranet for the purpose of providing network security. The firewall equipment is often a combination of multihomed computer systems and routers that run packet filters, proxy servers, circuit gateways software such as *socks,* and monitoring software. The area in which the firewall operates is sometimes called a DMZ.

FLDB   File location data base. The centerpiece of the Distributed File System, which provides a global name space for clients to access their files. The file location database is usually replicated to ensure high availability of the file system.

FM   Frequency modulation. Imparts information to a fixed frequency carrier signal by varying its frequency linearly with the applied signal. This makes the signal relatively immune to interference and fading.

FPS   Frames per second. Refers to the video frame rate of a digital video stream. A frame rate of 30 frames/second is considered high quality. The bandwidth required to transmit a digital video signal increases in direct proportion to the frame rate. Compression techniques are necessary to reduce this data rate to a reasonable level.

FPX   FlashPix. Another file format that contains multiple file resolutions in multiples of two. In conjunction with a proper image web server, this allows a remote web user to indicate a position on a low-resolution image, whereupon the server transmits a higher-resolution subimage. The user sees this as zooming in to get new detail. FPX format is popular with digital cameras.

FTP   File transfer protocol. The classic Internet protocol that allows a user to log into a remote machine using either a personal or an anonymous account, navigate and view the remote file system, upload and download ASCII and binary files, and even create and delete directories. It is embedded in all popular web browsers.

GEO   Geosynchronous Earth orbit (22,300 miles above Earth). Positions an object in a fixed position over the equator because its period of rotation matches that of Earth. This is useful for fixed-antenna Earth stations such as communications satellites and direct TV broadcasting satellites.

GID   Group ID. Users on UNIX systems are assigned a group name that maps to a numeric group ID used to govern file and directory access. The command *id* returns the user and group ID.

GIF   Graphics interchange format. An image file format popular on the Internet. It supports a 256-color palette, LZW lossless compression, interlacing, and multiple images per file (used to make animated GIFs).

GIS   Geographical information systems. Computers with an application for the storing, cataloging, accessing, and printing of geographical features such as property lines, easements, gas lines, communications circuits, land elevations and cover, rivers, streams, dams, buildings, roads, and highways.

GUI   Graphical user interface. UNIX systems provide an X-Windows-based common desktop environment (CDE), a set of tool bars and utilities to support common activities like reading mail, web browsing, application launching, and file management. Applications running in the X-Windows environment must present a window with buttons, scroll bars, text, and graphic viewing areas, plus tools for manipulating information. This graphical user interface is accompanied by a standard set of window manipulation features for positioning, scaling, iconifying, and closing the window. Each window is obliged to offer a menu bar or button bar to let the user open and close files and perform other tasks related to the functioning of the program. For example, Adobe Frame Maker on UNIX has a graphical user interface to allow the author to write books.

HDLC   High-level data link control. A layer 2 protocol often used on router serial circuits to reliably transmit data. It can detect errored frames and request retransmission, making it a connection-oriented protocol.

HDX   Half-duplex. Describes a data communications channel that can only communicate in either the forward or the reverse direction at one time. An example of a half duplex LAN technology is standard Ethernet.

HIPPI   High-performance parallel interface. A copper twisted pair, point-to-point, simplex, serial standard running at 100 or 200 megabytes/second. Variable-length IEEE802.2 encapsulated frames support multiple network layer protocols such as the venerable TCP/IP.

hosts   */etc/hosts* is a text file used by UNIX systems for name-to-address resolution. Lookups are resolved locally by the resolver routine. This file must contain at least the name and IP address of the system itself. */etc/hosts* is a fallback position to take when DNS cannot be depended on for consistent, complete, and accurate service. The old name for this file is HOSTS.TXT.

HPPA   Hewlett–Packard precision architecture. The marketing term for HP's RISC-based computer systems, such as the HP3000 and HP9000. The term PA-RISC is also used.

HP-PB   Hewlett–Packard precision bus. An early generation of HP's I/O subsystem used in the HP9000 family.

HSC   High-speed controller. The name of HP's fast I/O bus technology.

HSRP   Hot swap routing protocol. A Cisco feature that allows a standby router on a LAN to take on the local default router IP address when the designated primary router fails. Local devices on the LAN continue to use the same default router IP address during router fail-over. There is no requirement that local devices know how to discover routes. See the manpage for *oid_to_type* to configure NNM to handle this protocol.

HSSI   High-speed serial interface. An example is the 45 Mbps serial WAN line of a router T3 circuit.

HTML   Hypertext markup language. A text-based language for laying out web pages. Web browsers render HTML by displaying text, images, buttons, forms, and other objects such as sound clips and streaming videos. Any piece of text or graphics can possess a link to another location on the Internet, which the user simply single-clicks to navigate there.

HTTP   Hypertext transport protocol. The protocol used between web browsers and web servers to transmit pages of HTML, images, sound clips, or movies.

IBM   International Business Machines. A major computer vendor known for its proprietary MVS operating system, SNA networking, and the EBCDIC character set.

ICMP   Internet control message protocol. Defined in RFC 792 to support IP functions such as remote loopback testing (*ping*), ICMP redirects for dynamic end-station routing table updates, and parameter requests for network management. *netmon* listens on a raw ICMP socket for discovery and status information.

IEEE   Institute of Electrical and Electronics Engineers. A global standards body that drafted the famous IEEE 802.3 10-Mbps LAN standard.

IETF   Internet Engineering Task Force. A volunteer organization that provides technical support for the development of networking standards that directly affect the functioning of the Internet. The members write, moderate, approve, and publish requests for comment (RFC) documents, which may be found at *http://www.internic.net/rfc* and other mirror sites.

IMAP   Internet message access protocol.

IMSP   Internet message support protocol.

Internet   An IP network consisting of multiple high-speed private backbone networks connected at network access points. The public gains access to it via Internet service providers.

Internet submap   This is the default name of the NNM map showing routers and subnets, and it's usually the home map for most users. This map shows the IP structure of the network. The map builder will usually partition this map when there are more than 100 routers and subnet icons.

Intranet   A private corporate network suddenly becomes an intranet when web-based services run on it. There is no other difference.

IOPS   Input–output operations per second. A standardized performance metric for the network file system measured with the Laddis benchmark. An IOP represents about 4 kilobytes of data transferred between the client and server systems.

IP   Internet protocol. Defined in RFC 791, it is a standard for an OSI layer 3 network protocol that provides 32-bit classful addressing.

IPC   Interprocess communication. A mechanism that allows several processes to exchange messages reliably. The applications typically make use of a standard set of APIs to facilitate communications.

IPX   Internet packet exchange. A proprietary network protocol invented by Novell and used in their Netware products.

IR   Infrared. A range of frequencies just below that of the visible light spectrum and used for wireless line-of-sight communications and in fiber optics.

ISDN   Integrated services digital network. Provides data and voice transmission services to businesses and homes over 64-kbps basic rate channels. Two basic rate channels may be bonded together to create a 128-kbps data channel. ISDN supports a packetized data service and a dedicated virtual circuit service suited to voice and digital video.

ISO   International Standards Organization.

ISP   Internet service provider. Offers individual subscribers and businesses access to the Internet. The ISP offers dial-up PPP, frame relay, ISDN, or dedicated access, maintains a domain name server (DNS), and in turn connects to regional or national service providers which form the backbone of the Internet.

IT   Information technology. An all-encompassing term used to describe a collection of technologies that provide access to information, including LAN, WAN, computers, and software.

IT/O   IT Operations. An HP product that provides the tools, methodologies, and processes needed to manage a network of computers.

ITU   International Telecommunications Union. An international standards body.

JDK   Java developer kit. A collection of software, tools, applications, and documentation to support an application developer in writing Java applets and programs.

JFS   Journal file system. An implementation that provides fast recovery of the file system after a UNIX system crashes. Normally, the UNIX buffered file system is checked using the standard utility *fsck*, but this is very time consuming and isn't guaranteed to recover all the data.

JPEG   Joint pictures expert group. Defines a standard for compressing bitmapped millions-of-colors images with user-defined levels of lossiness. These pictures often look better than GIF images and are usually much smaller, making JPG files popular in web pages.

JVM   Java virtual machine. The Java byte code interpreter.

L2TP Layer 2 tunneling protocol. Encapsulates one link layer protocol inside another.

LAN Local-area network. A collection of cable segments interconnected using hubs, switches, bridges, and routers that extends over a relatively small area, such as a building. Distances are limited to a few kilometers, and even those distances require fiber-optic cables and repeaters. Examples of LAN physical media are Ethernet and FDDI.

LANE LAN emulation. Required to fool IP into thinking that an ATM LAN adapter accepts reasonable (1500-byte) frames as the maximum transmission unit (MTU), as opposed to the 53-byte cell of native ATM.

LANIC LAN interface card. An input–output adapter in a computer or router, which usually implements layer 1 and 2 of the OSI model. The adapter has buffer memory to hold frames, a microprocessor, and ROM. The adapter computes the frame check sequence, recognizes special MAC addresses, and implements all the function associated with the particular LAN standard.

LAT Local area transport. A link layer protocol developed by Digital Equipment Corporation (DEC) to allow terminal servers to communicate with the DEC VAX computer.

LATA Local access transport area.

LDAP Lightweight directory access protocol. A standard for looking up information such as e-mail addresses and the location of networked resources.

LEC Local exchange carrier.

LED Light-emitting diode. A two-terminal semiconductor that emits light when an electrical current flows through it. LEDs are used for equipment indicators and for driving fiber-optic cables.

LEO Low Earth orbit. An orbit that is 500 to 1000 miles above Earth.

LFS   Local file system. The distributed file system server's physical logging system that can restore the server quickly after a crash.

LLC   Link layer control. A layer 2 protocol that identifies the nature of the payload carried within a frame.

LVM   Logical volume manager. An HP-UX tool for partitioning and managing a group of physical disk drives into one or more logical volumes, each containing a file system.

LZW   Lempel Ziv Welch. A lossless compression technique used to compress image files, typically in the GIF format. It is patented by Unisys, which licenses it to developers of graphics programs.

MAC   Media access. A functional layer defined by all LAN standards for giving link layer access to the physical layer for transmission of a frame. It is also a term used to describe the link layer, Ethernet, a layer two address of FDDI, and Token Ring LAN adapters. The Apple Macintosh computer is called a Mac.

MAE   Macintosh application environment. A mature product from Apple Computer that emulates the complete Macintosh Operating System (Mac OS) on a UNIX system (HP-UX and SUN computers) within an X-Windows environment. Users can load, run Mac applications, and share UNIX resources.

MAN   Metropolitan area network. A network that spans the geography of a metropolitan-sized area such as a city or campus. Fiber-optic cables are typically used to support such distances.

Management Domain   The set of managed subnets is the management domain on which NNM will perform polling and autodiscovery. The initial management domain may be defined in the *netmon seedfile*; it defaults to NNM's local subnet. For a collection station this same domain is called a collection domain.

Management Station   An NNM system that is configured to upload topology and event data from NNM collection stations and integrate this into a single data base. The management station need not poll any network devices, but may be configured to do so.

This architecture allows for a highly scalable distributed network management solution.

MAPI   Mail API. A standard for integrating electronic mail with applications.

MAU   Media attachment unit. The IEEE's name for the Ethernet transceiver that implements the physical, electrical, and mechanical layers of the OSI model. The MAU connects the network device to the LAN cable; or

MAU   Media access unit. The IBM term for their token ring interconnect hardware.

Mb   Megabits. Usually means millions of bits (1,000,000) in data communications circles. Sometimes it means 1,048,576 bits, the square of 1024.

MB   Megabytes. Usually means millions of bytes (1,000,000) in data communications. Sometimes it means 1,048,576 bytes, the square of 1024.

MEO   Medium Earth orbit. An orbit about 8000 miles above Earth.

MIB   Management information base. A description of the data about which an SNMP-managed device is able to return information. This includes configuration information (such as the type of LAN adapter) and performance data (such as the number of bytes sent on a LAN adapter).

MIC   Media interface connector. Used to connect FDDI cable. It is rectangular, keyed, and connects two fibers.

MII   Media-independent interface. The 100-BASE-T connection standard between the transceiver and the network device.

Mil3   Produces network simulation tools that integrate with HP OpenView and NetMetrix. Mil3 is now called OpNet Technologies Inc.

MIME Multipurpose Internet mail extensions. A method for transmitting non-ASCII files as SMTP messages. SMTP only supports single-part, 7-bit ASCII text, and MIME headers identify the attachments using headers that SMTP ignores. It is up to the user's e-mail program to parse the e-mail message MIME headers and reconstruct the attachment files.

MIPS Millions of instructions per second. A simple performance metric for CPU chips. It's also been called "meaningless indicator of performance" because MIPS is such a simple metric.

MIT Massachusetts Institute of Technology. An institute of higher learning and the developer of the X-Windows standard.

MOM Manager of managers. A network management station that in turn manages information from a lower tier of network management stations. The lower tier will filter information and pass only high-level data to the MOM.

MOSS MIME object security services.

MPOA Multiprotocol over ATM. A standard for transmitting multiple network protocols over an ATM network.

MPEG Moving pictures expert group. A video compression standard capable of both temporal and spatial compression. MPEG-2 requires hardware decompression. That is why a DVD CD-ROM player needs an MPEG-2 card in order to view videos on a desktop computer.

MPP Massively parallel processing. An architecture for interconnecting upward of hundreds of CPU chips to create a high-performance supercomputing device.

MS Management station. An HP OpenView system that accepts event and topology information from lower-tier collection stations (CS). The MS has a high-level view of the network, while the collection stations have a detailed view of a limited subset of the network.

MSS   Multiprotocol switched services.

MTA   Message transport agent. That part of an e-mail system responsible for moving messages from the originating user e-mail agent (UA) to the destination UA.

MTBF   Mean time before failure. The average amount of time a device remains operational before experiencing a failure. This value is usually the mean of a Poisson distribution.

MTTR   Mean time to repair. The average time it takes to detect a failure, replace the device, and restore service. The repair time can be reduced by stocking a hot, preconfigured spare on site.

MTU   Maximum transmission unit. The largest number of bytes a LAN adapter can accept from the upper layers. The LAN adapter will then wrap a frame around these data for transmission. Ethernet's MTU is 1500 bytes, and the framing adds 18 bytes for a maximum frame size of 1518 bytes.

MUA   Mail user agent. An e-mail program such as *elm*, *pine*, or Netscape Mail.

Multihomed   A system with more than one network adapter is said to be multihomed. This allows the system to be directly connected to multiple subnets.

MX   Mail exchange. A special record provided by the domain name system (DNS) that allows an SMTP mail system to determine the correct system to forward e-mail to. For example, e-mail sent to *user@system.company.com* should not be sent directly to *system.company.com*'s IP address when it's behind a firewall. Rather, it should be sent to *mail.company.com*, which is what the DNS would return when a DNS request for its MX record is made.

NAP   Network access point. A location where network service providers (NSP) interconnect their networks. These are located in San Francisco, Chicago, New York, and Washington, D.C.

NC   Network computer. Typically, a diskless computer that boots from a server and gets all its applications and files from it. This reduces administration and hardware costs.

NCPM   Network connection policy manager. A DNS-based, load-balancing product from Hewlett–Packard.

NCS   Network compute system. A set of programming standards that allows an application to distribute its functions across a TCP/IP network of like-equipped systems to increase performance and reliability.

NDIS   Network Driver Interface Specification. A standard for supporting multiple network protocols such as IP, IPX, and NetBUIE over a single LAN adapter on a Windows computer.

NetPC   Networked personal computer.

NFS   Network file system. An industry standard for file and print sharing supported by UNIX, Windows, and Macintosh vendors. NFS™ is a component of Sun's ONC architecture.

NHRP   Next hop routing protocol. A method for performing layer 3 switching.

NIC   Network interface card. Another word for a network adapter or LANIC.

NIS   Network information service. The part of the network file system that provides a consistent domain view of user and group IDs, host files, service files, and other maps as appropriate.

NLS   Native language support. A set of utilities to allow application developers to isolate the language-dependent strings in their code to make it easy to use that code in other countries that don't use English.

NMA   Network management architecture. A way of structuring how networks are managed by a product. An example is HP Open-View Network Node Manager.

NMS   Network management station. A computer executing network management applications, such as HP OpenView Network Node Manager.

NNM   Network node manager. An SNMP-based hierarchical network management product. It's what this book is all about. It provides configuration, event, and performance management.

NNMGR   Network node manager. Another way to refer to this.

NOCC   Network Operations and Control Center. Contains staff and equipment for monitoring the network, handling user calls, and reacting to problem situations such as line outages and equipment failures. One of the tools a NOCC uses is a large display of the network, such as that provided by NNM.

NSP   Network service provider. A company with a national backbone that connects to the four network access points (NAP) in San Francisco, Chicago, New York, and Washington, D.C.

NT   A Windows proprietary operating system.

NTSC   National Television Standards Committee. A standard format for video used in the United States describing the number of scan lines, the horizontal and vertical scan rates, and the encoding of timing, intensity, and color information.

OAM   Operations and management.

Object   An abstraction used in NNM to deal with items being managed. Objects have attributes such as selection name and isNode that are determined at discovery time. Interfaces are objects with attributes such as IP addresses and MAC addresses. Nodes are objects that contain interfaces.

OC3   Optical carrier 3. A standard for transmitting data at 155 megabits/second over fiber-optic cable, typically used in ATM and synchronous optical networks (SONET).

ODI   Open Data Link Interface. An alternative standard to NDIS on Windows platforms for supporting multiple networking protocols on one LAN adapter.

OID   Object ID (system object ID) (sysObjectID). These are all used interchangeably in this book. This SNMP variable, unique to each vendor's equipment, allows NNM to assign a unique icon to it. Defined in the *system* part of the MIB, this system object ID may also be used in the discovery filter to indicate which device types should be discovered.

OLTP   Online transaction processing. A system for executing user units of work, called transactions, while the user waits for the results.

OS   Operating system. A comprehensive collection of programs for coordinating the execution of applications by providing services such as file and peripheral I/O, authentication, memory management, multitasking, multithreading, preemption, and security.

OSI   Open systems interconnect. A model from the International Standards Organization that defines the functionality of networked applications in a seven-layer model. The OSI also defines broad categories of network management such as configuration, event, performance, security, and accounting.

OSPF   Open shortest path first. A standard routing protocol that considers the number of hops and the bandwidth of each hop in the routing metric. It also updates routing tables using link state changes and supports the notion of areas across which routing information flows in a controlled manner.

OSS   Operations and support systems.

PAgP   Port aggregation protocol. A Cisco Systems protocol that can aggregate multiple fast Ethernet ports on a switch to create a virtual higher-speed link. This can be used to provide higher-speed links into a switched subnet from a router. It can also be used to increase the link speed into a file server from an Ethernet switch.

HP's Automatic Port Aggregation (APA) software supports this protocol. The SNMP agent presents this aggregate as a new interface with an appropriate interface speed.

PBX   Private branch exchange. A small telephone exchange owned and operated by private companies for supporting the internal telephones as well as providing access to outside lines. A PBX is located on the customer premises.

PCI   Peripheral component interconnect. A standard I/O specification used in desktop and UNIX systems alike. PCI has wide industry support, and high-performance adapters for SCSI disks and video adapters are commonplace.

PCL   Printer control language. A complete page description language developed by Hewlett–Packard for its printers.

PCR   Peak cell rate.

PDF   Portable document format. A file format invented by Adobe Systems for the cross-platform distribution of documents. The major advantage is that the end user of the spreadsheet, presentation, report, mathematical scratchpad, or other, need not own a copy of the authoring software to use that document. The Acrobat Reader is all that the end user needs, and it's free; or

PDF   Product description file. An HP-UX product file that describes the properties of all files contained in a specific product. This lets the system administrator verify that no online product files have been tampered with.

PEM   Privacy enhanced mail. E-mail that supports privacy features such as encryption.

PGP   Pretty good privacy. Public-domain message encryption software generally used to protect e-mail from being intercepted by unwanted third parties.

PINE   Pine is not *elm*, another e-mail program with more features than *elm*.

PNG Portable network graphics. A new image format for storage and compression of millions-of-colors images. It combines the benefits of GIF and JPG without the uncertainty of the Unisys patent on LZW compression used in GIF file formats.

POP Point of presence. A place where a network service is available. For example, an Internet service provider may offer a dial-up service by making available a local telephone number.

POP3 Post Office Protocol version 3. Allows dial-up users to securely access their electronic mail boxes and copy messages to their desktop computer for offline reading and replying.

POTS Plain old telephone system. A cutesy term referring to the analog telephone system's front end, the last mile, or the local loop, which is generally an analog communications system. Beyond the central office (CO), the telephone network is digital.

PPC Power PC. A RISC CPU chip developed by Apple, IBM, and Motorola (AIM) that powers the Apple Macintosh computers.

PPP Point-to-point protocol. A standard means for routers from multiple vendors to exchange packets containing multiple network protocols. However, it is commonly used between desktop computers and Internet service providers to support automatic dialing (of alternative numbers), login, authentication, negotiation of PPP parameters, exchange of IP addresses, and optionally, the exchange of name-server IP addresses.

PPTP Point-to-point tunneling protocol. Provides a secure path through an insecure network (such as the Internet) between two networks that are otherwise separate. It may also be used to provide secure access to a corporate network from a desktop computer connected to the Internet.

PRI Primary rate interface. A 1.544 megabit/second ISDN line.

PS PostScript. A page description language developed by Adobe Systems. PostScript includes font technology, screening, color separation, and color management. PostScript is interpreted by a raster image processor (RIP) to create a high-resolution color bit-map for output to laser printers, ink jet printers, and image set-ters. PostScript is the industry standard for printing.

PVC   Permanent virtual circuit. A logical connection that's perma-nently established and requires no setup or tear down. An exam-ple is a point-to-point leased line. A frame relay network provides a PVC between two routers defined by the two end-point data link channel identifiers (DLCI). A frame relay PVC appears as a subinterface on a Cisco router.

QOS   Quality of service. A metric that includes throughput, latency, timing jitter, and cell loss. QOS is supported by ATM networks to allow concurrent transmission of time-sensitive data, such as streaming digital video, and non-time-sensitive data, such as file transfers and e-mail.

RAID   Redundant array of independent disks. A technology that combines multiple independent disk mechanisms into a single logical unit in order to provide increased performance, greater flexibility, and high availability. The technology includes mirror-ing (RAID 1), parity (RAID 5), redundancy, and striping (RAID 0) mechanisms.

RAM   Random access memory. The semiconductor chip storage medium from which the central processing unit receives instruc-tions and data.

RAS   Remote access server. A computer or special communications equipment equipped with modems designed to accept connec-tions from remote desktop computers in a secure, reliable, albeit low-performance manner.

RBOC   Regional Bell operating company.

Resolver   A small piece of code that client systems call to resolve network names to IP addresses, or resolve IP addresses to names.

RF   Radio frequency. Electromagnetic signals between approxi-mately 1 and 1000 megahertz.

RFC   A request for comment. An Internet engineering task force document, which may define a standard, report a technical result, or make a recommendation.

RFP   Request for proposal. A document distributed by one party to multiple vendors to solicit a formal proposal for services.

RIP   Routing information protocol. A standard, simple, low-overhead protocol for the exchange of routing tables between routers and participating end systems.

RISC   Reduced instruction set computer. A design paradigm that simplifies the instruction set of a CPU to reduce the complexity of the chip design. The resulting chip runs faster and cooler than its complex computer instruction set (CISC) counterpart. Examples of RISC chips include the IBM/Apple/Motorola PowerPC (PPC), Hewlett–Packard Precision Architecture (HP-PA), Digital's Alpha, and Sun's Scalable Processor Architecture (SPARC).

RMON   Remote monitor. An industry standard for remotely monitoring a shared media LAN segment, with a promiscuous probe supporting the RMON management information base (MIB). Ethernet statistics, traffic source–destination pairs, automatic thresholds, and packet capture are available. The RMON-2 standard extends the information available from layer 2 to layer 7 of the OSI model. NNM is capable of directly accessing the relatively simple *EtherStats* portion of the MIB while NetMetrix supports all nine RMON groups.

RMP   Reliable multicast protocol.

ROM   Read-only memory. Semiconductor memory that stores a fixed program to allow a computer to find a boot device and start up from the code stored there. The HP-UX systems can search for boot devices and allow the user to select one.

RPC   Remote procedure call. An application programming interface (API) that allows a program located on one computer to issue a function call whose parameters are wrapped in a request packet and sent across the network to a server process where the actual function code resides and executes. Results of the remote function execution are returned in a reply packet.

RSP   Regional service provider. A level 3 provider of Internet services, located between level 4, the Internet service provider, and level 2, the national backbone provider. RSPs often provide DNS services.

RSVP   Reservation protocol. A standard intended to support time-sensitive multimedia traffic in the presence of data over routed IP networks.

RTMP   Reliable multicast transport protocol; or

RTMP   Routing table maintenance protocol. A protocol in the AppleTalk suite responsible for keeping the routing tables current in an AppleTalk network.

SAAL   Signaling ATM adaptation layer.

SAM   System administration manager. An HP-UX system administration front end that greatly simplifies common tasks.

SAN   Storage Attached Network. Consists of one or more file servers which typically use fibre channel technology to provided large amounts of fast disk storage to networked clients.

SAP   Systems, Applications, and Products in Data Processing. A comprehensive suite of business applications from the German company SAP AG; or

SAP   Service advertisement protocol. A broadcast or multicast service that file servers (especially Netware) use to advertise available resources such as printers and disks.

SAR   Segmentation and reassembly. A function of the Internet protocol (IP) that fragments packets larger than the underlying LAN media maximum transmission unit (MTU) for transmission and reassembles them at the destination system. The reassembly process deals with fragment reordering, but cannot recover lost fragments.

SAS Single attach station. A device that connects to only one of the two FDDI rings.

SATAN Security administration tool for analyzing networks. A UNIX-oriented set of utilities that probes networked systems for well-known weaknesses as an aid to improving their security configurations.

SCR Sustained cell rate. A metric used in ATM.

SCSI Small computer systems interface. A parallel daisy-chained interface that allows a computer to access hard disk drives, CD-ROMs, tapes drives, scanners, and such. A single SCSI bus can accommodate any mixture of these uniquely addressed devices consistent with the operating system's ability to support them.

Seedfile A file used by *netmon* to define the initial management domain. It usually lists the routers connected to the subnets to be managed.

SDK Software development kit. A product containing manuals, libraries of code, and tools to support the rapid creation of new applications by programmers.

SET Secure electronic transaction.

SGI Silicon Graphics Incorporated. A manufacturer of high-performance UNIX systems used in graphics, 3D rendering, and video arts.

SLA Service-level agreement. A contract between a service provider, such as an IT department responsible for managing networks and computers, and the end users. Metrics may include uptime, response time, throughput, and reliability of service. These metrics are typically collected over a one-month period and reviewed with the user representatives.

SLIP   Serial Line IP. A standard for encapsulating IP packets over an RS-232 circuit. SLIP is a predecessor to PPP.

SMB   Server message block. The basic protocol used by LAN Manager, Samba, LM/X, and AdvancedServer/9000 to provide file and print services for Windows client computers.

SMP   Symmetrical multiprocessing. An operating system feature that allows it to use multiple processors efficiently using load-balancing mechanisms that don't favor one processor to execute kernel code.

SMTP   Simple mail transport protocol. An Internet standard for transmitting and forwarding single-part 7-bit ASCII messages.

SNA   Systems network architecture. IBM's former name for its data communications products.

SNMP   Simple network management protocol. An RFC-compliant protocol. Version one provides only the *get*, *getnext*, *set*, and *trap* operators between a management station and a managed device agent. Later versions v2 and v3 provide additional operators such as *get-bulk* and *inform.*

Socks   A secure circuit relay protocol through which client systems inside a private network obtain a secure connection to Internet-based servers.

SONET   Synchronous optical network. The fundamental fiber-optic technology and signaling techniques used by the telephone companies, which is used for ATM networks.

SPARC   Scalable processor architecture. The SUN Microsystems RISC CPU chip.

SQL   Structured query language. A standard means to request information from a database.

SRM   Scalable reliable multicast.

SS7 Signaling system 7. The standard used by the digital telephone network to establish, reroute, manage, and control voice and data calls.

SSL Secure sockets layer. An API developed by Netscape Communications to support the secure exchange of sensitive customer information between the web browser and its server. This is a necessary feature of secure Internet commerce.

SSN Secure server network. A LAN segment connected to a bastion host in a firewall configuration, access to which is governed by the bastion. This LAN is more secure than the DMZ LAN facing the Internet.

STP Shielded twisted pair. A LAN wiring standard that adds shielding around pairs of twisted insulated wires to improve its transmission properties. Shielding reduces electromagnetic interference and susceptibility.

STS Synchronous transport signal. The fundamental 51.84-megabit/ second clock speed for SONET and ATM.

SVC Switched virtual circuit. A logical connection across a network that is established prior to data transmission, maintained for the session, then torn down at termination. ISDN supports this.

TAXI Transparent asynchronous transmit and receive interface. An FDDI-like interface definition for ATM.

TCO Total cost of ownership. An estimate of the annual cost of supplying a service to a user. For example, the TOC for a networked Windows computer includes the cost of the hardware, software, installation, help desk support, service, downtime, formal training, informal training, and "futzing."

TCP Transmission control protocol. A transport layer standard defined in RFC 793 used to provide reliable, flow-controlled, multiplexed connections between communicating systems.

TFTP   Trivial file transfer protocol. A very simple protocol typically used to upload and download network electronic device configuration. X-terminals, routers, hubs, switches, and bridges often support it.

TIF   Tagged image format. A cross-platform image file format capable of holding color space conversion data, multiple layers, and alpha channels.

Trap   An SNMP trap is a single UDP PDU sent by an agent to a trap destination to signify some event of interest. Traps carry a community string, a generic trap number (0-6), a 32-bit specific trap number (if the generic trap number is 6), plus additional parameters as defined by the trap. NNM stores trap definitions obtained from MIB compilation in the *trapd.conf* file.

TTL   Time to live. An 8-bit field in the IP header defined by the sender and reduced at least by one by each intervening router. If there is a routing loop, the last router decrements the TTL to zero, discards the packet, and notifies the sender with a "TTL exceeded" ICMP message.

TTRT   Target token rotation timer. A value agreed on by all members of a FDDI ring for the time it takes for the token to circulate around the ring.

TV   Television.

UA   User agent. Typically, in the e-mail sense, this is the user's e-mail program. Examples include *mailx*, *elm*, *pine*, *advmail*, Netscape Mail, cc:Mail, and Zmail.

UBR   Unspecified bit rate. A quality of service (QoS) in ATM networks for which the connection will accept any bit rate available. This service is suited for data transmissions.

UDP   User datagram protocol. A transport protocol above IP that does not provide and therefore does not have the overhead associated with reliable transmission and multiplexing. UDP is used by applications such as SNMP, DNS, and NFS.

UID   User ID. A numeric and alphabetic identifier unique for each UNIX user.

UPS   Uninterruptable power supply. A device that filters public power, stores it in a battery, and delivers clean continuous AC power even during failure of the public power grid. The UPS may be SNMP managed. Servers often collect data from their UPS via an RS-232 cable so that an orderly shutdown may be performed when the UPS battery runs low.

URL   Uniform resource locator. A way to address a web page or service on the Internet. For example, *http://www.hp.com/openview* is a URL that specifies a hypertext document on system *www.hp.com* in folder *openview.*

UTP   Unshielded twisted pair. A cabling system used in LAN technologies such as the IEEE 10-BASE-T and 100VG-AnyLAN. The cable pairs are twisted to reduce radio-frequency interference and reception of electrical and magnetic noise.

UUCP   UNIX to UNIX copy. A standard protocol between UNIX systems to copy files. It was used historically to move e-mail over dial links among a loosely knit but vast community of UNIX systems.

UUENCODE   UNIX to UNIX encode. A technique that transforms binary files into 7-bit ASCII format suitable for transmission by SMTP. UUENCODE is also the name of the program that does this, as well as the inverse operation, UUDECODE.

VAN   Value-added network.

VAR   Value-added reseller.

VBR   Variable bit rate. A quality of service in ATM networks characterized by a fluctuating data rate.

VC   Virtual circuit. A logical connection through a switched network that moves data along it between two end systems.

VCC   Virtual channel connection. A connection via a virtual circuit.

VLAN Virtual LAN. A way to create multiple LANs within a group of Ethernet or ATM switches to which devices may be assigned based on their MAC address, switch port number, network protocol, or application. This avoids a major configuration management issue with flat switched networks, that is, broadcast control.

VM Virtual memory. Refers to the practice of providing a linear memory model for applications that can exceed the amount of physical memory by incorporating disk-based swap space to store relatively infrequently-used memory pages. Excessive VM pressure can result in high disk I/O and reduced application performance, so disk drives are often striped to increase performance.

VM Virtual Memory. Operating systems use a special disk swap file or disk swap partition to extend the memory available to application beyond that which is physically installed. For example, a system with 128 megabytes of physical memory may use swap space to make 256 megabytes of memory available to applications. Since disks are much slower than real memory, the VM subsystem attempts to make real memory available to active applications while swapping the memory of relatively inactive ones.

VNC Virtual Network Computing. Cross-platform software permitting an authorized user to connect to a full X-Windows console at will. The VNC does not depend on a video adapter or physical CRT for its operation. The VNC is a convenient place to display the read/write NNM map.

VOD Video on demand. A service by which a customer specifies that he or she wants to see a movie at a specific time. A digital video server at the service provider's facility is then primed to deliver the analog video stream on a predefined scrambled channel.

VPN Virtual private network. A means to use the Internet to create a secure tunnel between multiple private networks.

VSAT   Very small aperture terminal. Usually a small satellite dish antenna.

VUE   Visual user environment. A desktop paradigm for UNIX systems built on the X-Windows system. It includes a task bar, a trash can, and automated tasks. Most of VUE's elements were contributed to the CDE standard.

WABI   Windows application binary interface. A product from Sun that emulates the Windows windowing system to allow users to run their favorite Windows applications without owning a PC.

WAN   Wide-area network. A network such as T1, T3, ATM, OC3, SONET, frame relay, and ISDN characterized by its ability to cover global distances well beyond the reach of LAN technology. The fiber and cable infrastructure is owned by carriers.

WINS   Windows Internet Name Service. A NetBIOS global naming service for Windows TCP/IP systems.

WRQ   Walker Richer Quinn. A Seattle, Washington, company famous for its terminal emulation programs and, more recently, for its X-Windows emulator, Reflection/X.

WWW   Worldwide web. A term used to describe a collection of hyperlinked web servers accessed from desktop computers running web browsers for the purpose of disseminating and sharing information of all kinds.

XDMCP   X-Windows display manager control protocol. Used to give X-Windows users the means to log in to a UNIX system. A daemon process such as *xdm* listens for XDMCP requests from X-terminals and provides a login window for user authentication and access.

XDR   External data representation. Used by the network file system (NFS) to deal with differences in file system semantics between clients and servers running on different platforms, such as PCs, Macintosh, and UNIX systems.

ZIP   Zone information protocol. Used by AppleTalk to propagate, manage, and access zone information across an AppleTalk network.

Index

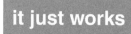